OVERCOMING ANXIETY

ARCHIBALD D. HART, PH.D.

OVERCOMING ANXIETY

WORD PUBLISHING
Dallas · London · Sydney · Singapore

OVERCOMING ANXIETY

Scripture quotations in this book are from the following versions:

The King James or Authorized Version (KJV); The New King James Version (NKJV), copyright © 1979, 1980, 1982, Thomas Nelson, Inc., Publisher; The New American Standard Bible (NASB), © The Lockman Foundation 1960, 1962, 1963, 1968, 1971, 1972, 1973, 1975, 1977; *The Living Bible* (LB), copyright 1971 by Tyndale House Publishers, Wheaton, IL, used by permission; The Holy Bible, New International Version (NIV), copyright © 1973, 1978, 1984 International Bible Society, used by permission of Zondervan Bible Publishers.

The following trademarks are used in this book and owned by the corporation listed:

Anafranil®, a product of the CIBA-GEIGY Corporation, Atarax®, a product of Roerig Division, Pfizer Incorporated; Ativan®, Serax®, Inderal®, products of Wyeth-Ayerst Laboratories, division of American Home Products Corporation; BuSpar®, a product of Mead Johnson Pharmaceuticals, division of Mead Johnson Laboratories, a Bristol-Myers Company; Centrax®, a product of Parke-Davis, division of Warner-Lambert Company; Librium®, Valium®, Dalmane®, products of Roche Products, Inc., Manati, PR 00701; Klonopin™, a product of Roche Laboratories, division of Hoffman-La Roche Inc., Nutley, NJ 07110; Paxipam®, a product of Schering Corporation; Restoril®, a product of Sandoz Pharmaceuticals Corporation, Sandoz Division; Tofranil®, Tegretol®, products of GEIGY Pharmaceuticals, Inc., division of CIBA-GEIGY Corporation; Tranxene®, a product of Abbott Laboratories, Pharmaceutical Products Division; Vistaril®, a product of Pfizer Laboratories Division, Pfizer Incorporated; Xanax®, a product of The Upjohn Corporation.

Library of Congress Cataloging-in-Publication Data:

Hart, Archibald D.
    Overcoming anxiety / Archibald D. Hart.
      p. cm.
    Includes bibliographical references.
    ISBN 0-8499-0686-5 : $12.99
    1. Anxiety—Religious aspects—Christianity. 2. Peace of mind—Religious aspects—Christianity. I. Title.
    BV4908.5.H37 1989
    152.4'6—dc20
                                        89-28477
                                          CIP

Printed in the United States of America

9 8 0 1 2 3 9 BKC 9 8 7 6 5 4 3 2 1

To Sylvia Joy

A daughter full of grace and beauty, who is greatly loved
Her heart is always full of song,
and this brings joy to all our lives.
As she embarks on the adventure of motherhood
may she be the source of yet greater joy.

CONTENTS

Figures, Tables, and Personal Inventories ix
Preface xi
Acknowledgments xv

PART 1: UNDERSTANDING ANXIETY 1

1. Anxiety—Central Problem of our Age   3
2. Worry and the Christian   17
3. Understanding Your Anxiety   32
4. Anxiety, Guilt, and Depression   46
5. Prisoners of Panic   56
6. Fears and Phobias   74
7. Anxiety in Childhood   94
8. Unhealthy Ways of Coping with Anxiety   108

PART 2: POSITIVE HELP FOR ANXIETY 119

9. Pinpointing the Source of Anxiety   121
10. Controlling Anxiety through Correct Thinking   138
11. Taking Control of Panic   156
12. Nap Your Way to a Tranquil Life   170
13. Understanding Antianxiety Medications   186
14. Preventing Anxiety in Childhood   199

Epilogue: A Balanced Life 218
For Further Reading 221
Index 223

FIGURES, TABLES, AND PERSONAL INVENTORIES

FIGURES

1.	Forms of Anxiety	11
2.	Constructive versus Destructive Anxiety	13
3.	Understanding Guilt	50
4.	The Origin of Phobias	76
5.	How Threats Develop into Anxiety	96
6.	Building Blocks for a Defense against Anxiety	122

TABLES

1.	Symptoms of Anxiety	33
2.	Symptoms of Generalized Anxiety Disorder	43
3.	Similarities between Panic Disorder and Agoraphobia	84
4.	Differences between Good and Poor Sleepers	183
5.	Duration of Effectiveness of Tranquilizers	193
6.	Steps to Be Followed in the Treatment of Anxiety	195

PERSONAL INVENTORIES

1.	Test Yourself: How Anxious Are You?	8
2.	General Anxiety Questionnaire	35
3.	Pinpointing Your Type of Anxiety	37
4.	Are You Experiencing a Panic Attack?	57
5.	Assessing Your Fears	80
6.	Anxiety and Self-Esteem: Thoughts for Reflection	90
7.	Is Your Child Overly Anxious?	102
8.	Are You Hard on Your Child?	106
9.	Record of Panic Attack	163

Blessed is the man [and woman] who trusts in the Lord
And whose trust is the Lord.
For he [or she] will be like a tree planted by the water, . . .
And it will not be anxious in a year of drought
Nor cease to yield fruit (Jer. 17:7–8, NASB).

"Don't worry—be happy." This was the title and theme of a song that swept the pop charts in 1988. Why was it so popular? I suspect it is because that phrase expresses one of the deepest yearnings of the human heart.

Wouldn't it be wonderful to be free of all worry? We could really be happy if there were no cares to eat away at us and nothing to threaten our tranquillity. But twenty years in the therapist's chair has taught me one important lesson: Anxiety is intricately interwoven with the essence of living. You cannot live and be free of anxiety.

"Don't be anxious; anxiety is the exact *opposite of faith.*" So reads a tract written by a popular preacher. "Don't be anxious at *any* time for *any* reason," writes another Christian leader.

But how is this possible? And why *should* we be free of anxiety? Is it because God doesn't like anxious people, or because anxiety is synonymous with sin? Is it because anxiety serves no useful function in the human psyche? These are puzzling questions. Anxiety is an enigma to many, and while we can effectively treat its symptoms, we still do not fully understand its function in human experience.

Anxiety's very presence in human experience, however, seems to point to some useful purpose. Like pain, anxiety appears to be an important "warning system" that alerts us to danger. Just as pain is necessary to warn us of a potential threat to our physical well-being— to tell us, for example, that we are standing on a thorn or burning our fingers, so anxiety serves to send us important messages of impending threat or danger to our emotional well-being.

Yes, we must have some anxiety. Without it, we would become the emotional equivalent of leprosy victims, who often suffer irreparable physical damage because they don't feel pain and therefore don't seek treatment for cuts, burns, and infections.

But do we have to suffer from so much anxiety? Do we have to continue to feel relentless worry even after we've recognized threats and taken steps to avoid the danger? These are the questions to which this book is addressed.

Despite our high level of sophistication and technological expertise, anxiety and its related manifestations remain a major psychological and medical challenge. Intuitively we know that prescribing massive doses of tranquilizers is not a satisfactory solution. We also know that the incidence of severe anxiety disorders is on the increase. Distress, restlessness, nervousness, fear, and panic, far from being alleviated by modern living, are on the increase. Competitiveness, crowded living conditions, and too much stress are making things worse, not better. The stress of twentieth-century living affects everyone, and part of the price we pay for it is increased anxiety.

Scores of people in every neighborhood already suffer from persistent anxiety-related problems: difficulty in sleeping, stomach problems, and generalized pain—always pain! They worry themselves into an early grave or fret away their precious life seeking peace in meaningless rituals.

And what will the twenty-first century bring? Better tranquilizers? Perhaps! Certainly not less anxiety. With problems such as polluted air, contaminated food, the "greenhouse effect," space warfare, and nuclear waste (to name just a very few) already staring us in the face, a person would have to be awfully naïve not to be at least a little anxious about the future.

But even in our present time, millions of Americans are experiencing incapacitating anxiety that lasts long enough, is severe enough, and causes sufficient dysfunction to disturb their everyday living and require psychological therapy and/or medical treatment. Just how many suffer from some sort of anxiety problem? No one really knows. One estimate puts it as high as forty million (15 percent of the population). According to a recent news report,[1] thirty-five million Americans suffer from periodic panic attacks alone, and this is only one form of anxiety disorder.

Clearly, anxiety is a neighbor on your street, if not a resident in your own home. It is a pervasive problem that profoundly affects every one of us. And while we now know a lot about how to treat the more severe anxiety disorders, there is still much confusion about the best form of treatment.

Many other emotional problems have their roots in anxiety. One study, conducted in England several years ago, found that one-third of

---

[1] *Pasadena Star News,* 30 January 1989.

those who suffer from depression also have severe anxiety symptoms. Clinically, of course, the close connection between anxiety and depression has been known for many years. Often a problem originally diagnosed as depression later turns out to be anxiety, and vice versa. The situation is further complicated by the fact that some of the medications used to treat anxiety will worsen depression and some antidepressants will aggravate an anxiety problem. This can be perplexing, even to professionals, and can make treatment very much a hit-and-miss exercise for the inexperienced.

This book, therefore, is dedicated to providing a better and more complete understanding of the very painful and debilitating malady that is anxiety. Much of what has been previously written is now either out of date or does not address the topic of anxiety in *all* of its forms. And if there is one thing that must be understood about anxiety, it is that anxiety is "multifaceted." It can take on *many* forms, and the more you know about *all* of them, the better you will be able to help yourself.

And you *can* help yourself if you suffer from anxiety. This is a word of encouragement I want to offer to the reader who might at first feel overwhelmed with the complexity of the problem. Unlike many other emotional problems, most anxiety disorders respond well to a "self-help" approach. There is much one can do for oneself to both prevent and cure an anxiety problem. All forms of medical help are only temporary. Medications that calm the nerves or relax the muscles are helpful, but are only useful if they buy the time needed to bring your life under control—to master your fears and reduce your susceptibility to anxiety. In the end, the problem will be back in your own lap again, so you might as well learn to handle it yourself at the outset.

The tremendous response I have had to my book, *The Hidden Link between Adrenalin & Stress,* [2] encourages me to believe this book will be helpful also. Since much anxiety (especially of the acute panic variety) is the consequence of over-stress and an increased sensitivity to the stress hormones, this book is a natural follow-up. Most of the letters I have received from readers have described confusing symptoms and misguided treatment of what appears to be stress-related *anxiety.* It has become clear to me that as many, if not more, readers need help in overcoming anxiety problems as they do in coping with stress.

The help I offer in this book is practical and simple—as far as one can be "simple" in discussing such a complex problem. Your success at

---

[2] Archibald Hart, *The Hidden Link between Adrenalin & Stress* (Waco, TX: Word, 1986).

mastering your anxiety will, of course, depend on the seriousness with which you follow the advice I give. If you find you cannot implement the advice I give or that the exercises are too difficult for you, then I urge you to seek professional help right away.

Finally, as you read this book and apply its principles, may you do so with complete dependence on the One who has created you and desires that you live a more complete and anxiety-free life. My approach throughout will be informed by the wisdom of the following words, written nearly two thousand years ago:

> Don't worry about anything; instead pray about everything; tell God your needs and don't forget to thank him for his answers. If you do this you will experience God's peace, which is far more wonderful than the human mind can understand. His peace will keep your thoughts and your hearts quiet and at rest as you trust in Christ Jesus. (Phil. 4:6–7, LB)

DR. ARCHIBALD D. HART
Pasadena, California

ACKNOWLEDGMENTS

I am again deeply indebted to many for their assistance in bringing this book to completion. I am especially thankful to:

- My wife, Kathleen, for her loving support and constant encouragement. Without her understanding and help, a project like this would be impossible to complete.
- My secretary, Nova Hutchins, for her dedicated service and constant patience while typing manuscripts and making revisions.
- My administrator, Bertha Jacklitch, and the other office staff, especially Kathy Ralston and Freda Carver, who have supported me as I try to do too many tasks.
- My many clients over the years who have helped me become a more mature psychotherapist. I have taken great pains to preserve confidentiality, so while the specifics of many of the stories I tell are true, the names are fictitious, and I have changed enough details so that no one person is represented in any story. Yet even though I do not tell any one person's real story, life stories you entrusted to me have given me the insights needed to write this book.

To all of you I express my deepest and heartfelt gratitude.

Part 1

UNDERSTANDING ANXIETY

The first half of this book will focus on developing a clear understanding of the nature of anxiety and will identify the various types of anxiety. While the twentieth century has been termed the "age of anxiety," anxiety and fear are as old as humanity itself. Before the present century, however, anxiety, as distinct from fear, was not fully recognized nor was it seen to be a distinct and problematic condition. Today there are very clearly definable anxiety disorders and in this part I will provide some simple tests that will help you to identify your specific form of anxiety experience.

While in these chapters I will focus on diagnosing and understanding anxiety, I cannot avoid providing some guidance on how to overcome anxiety where it seems appropriate. A more complete guide for overcoming anxiety is provided in part 2.

ANXIETY—CENTRAL PROBLEM OF OUR AGE

1

Few emotional problems are more common nor more debilitating than anxiety. Most of us realize, on the basis of personal experience as well as observation of fellow humans, that anxiety is a pervasive and profound phenomenon in our society. As we approach the end of the twentieth century, its devastation seems to be on the increase. We are anxious as individuals, and an air of anxiety pervades our nation, too.

There is even some anxiety—or at least confusion—about anxiety itself. Our understanding of this emotion and its related disorders is currently undergoing considerable change. New ideas on its nature have emerged, and new treatments are emerging. While there is broad agreement in scientific circles about some aspects of anxiety, many differences still exist, and there are enough competing theories and unsubstantiated treatment strategies to confuse professionals in the mental-health disciplines—not to mention lay people!

Picking one's way through the maze of theories and treatments can be very frustrating. And this is especially true for the Christian believer, because most research approaches the problem of anxiety purely from an evolutionary framework, totally ignoring the profound effect that the spiritual dimension can have on our emotional well-being. Humans are more than physical organisms, and nowhere does this impact the human condition more than in the arena of anxiety.

I am convinced that one reason so many continue to suffer from acute anxiety in our society is that people fail to make this important connection. Not even our most sophisticated technology, medical or psychological, can free us from an important but painful facet of our existence—our built-in need to be reconnected with our Creator. This need overrides all others, and when it is unmet there is much cause for anxiety. Because most researchers and therapists ignore this reality, they tend to place too much emphasis on the physical world as a cause of anxiety and fail to address deeper spiritual needs.

Another important reason many who suffer from anxiety are not helped is that only a very small fraction of those who suffer from disorders of anxiety actually seek treatment. Instead, most suffer stoically through their torment, becoming disenchanted with life and spending most of their energy avoiding anxiety-producing circumstances.

I doubt it is necessary for me to "prove" that anxiety is pervasive in our society, since you have probably felt its impact personally. But anxiety has always been a part of human existence. What makes it different today? There are several reasons, and a review of them may help you pinpoint a source of a specific anxiety that has been bothering you:

- *The fast pace of today's life.* The stress of life in the "fast lane" is creating unique forms of anxiety less known in previous times.

A CASE OF ANXIETY

Sue is only nineteen, and a freshman in college. She is conscientious, attractive, popular—an "all-American" girl. Always at the top of her class, she plays tennis, enjoys all types of outdoor activity, and captains her swim team. She is also the victim of an acute anxiety attack.

One day recently I received a frantic phone call from Sue's mother, a client of a few years back. "Sue is in a terrible state. She thinks she's going crazy. I've asked her to come home right away. Can you see her?"

When Sue entered my office, she was visibly trembling and quite pale. "I don't know what's happening to me. I can't stand being alone, but I don't want to speak to anybody, either. I feel afraid all the time, and I jump at the slightest sound. All I want to do is curl up and sleep forever."

About three weeks before, Sue had begun studying late at night for an important exam in chemistry, the one subject she felt unsure of. Gulping coffee to keep awake, she pushed herself to study until she fell asleep with exhaustion. This happened again the next night, then the next. Early in the morning of the third night, about 3 A.M., she suddenly woke up with an acute feeling of fear; she felt she was dying and that doom was about to befall her and all her loved ones. Dreadfully afraid, she ran to a friend's room and remained there the rest of the night.

Throughout the next day, Sue felt panicky. At times her head pounded, her heart thumped and raced; her lungs felt tight. "I couldn't get enough air, so I kept away from closed places. I couldn't concentrate or remember anything, and all I wanted to do was cry." Sue's friend persuaded her to go to the school's health center, where a nurse reassured her that there was nothing seriously wrong—just a case of "the nerves." The nurse said, "You are working too hard," and urged Sue to slow down.

But the next night the panic hit Sue again, so she called her mother right away. Mom was wise! She recalled having had the same experience herself some years back, which was why she had first gone to see me. She told Sue to come home right away: "You're having a bad anxiety attack. If you don't take care of it now, it will only get worse." Sue was sensible. She sought help for her problem immediately and saved herself from a lifetime of panic anxiety.

- *Workaholism.* The need to work constantly in order to feel worthwhile prevents people from allowing adequate time for physiological and psychological rejuvenation.
- *"Contagious" anxiety.* "Covert" anxiety (where people keep their fears to themselves) has now given way to "overt" anxiety (where people freely share their fears and pass them on to others).
- *Increased global conflict.* Threats of atomic annihilation and terrorist attack are taking their toll on our sense of security.
- *Environmental insecurity.* The very earth we live on is being threatened. Overpopulation, diminishing resources, and ecological disasters are all creating intensified "existential" anxieties.
- *Decreased sense of community.* The breakdown of the family unit and the increased mobility of the population have resulted in inadequate "support" systems (such as friends and extended families) that help individuals cope with the inevitable stresses of life.
- *Increased sense of meaningless.* The loss of capacity and opportunity to experience faith and believe in a meaningful and orderly creation with an omnipotent Creator who is in control inevitably provides a seedbed for anxiety. The twentieth century may well become known as "the century of anxiety," and perhaps the theologian Paul Tillich was correct in describing anxiety as "man's reaction to the threat of *nonbeing.*" By *nonbeing* he meant more than just the threat of physical death; he was speaking of the threat of *meaninglessness* in one's existence.

ANXIETY—FRIEND OR FOE?

Perhaps the biggest debate about anxiety right now in philosophy, psychology, and religion is whether it is a friend or foe.

There are those who would make anxiety central to every act of the human person, creative or destructive. All behavior involves some element of anxiety. Anxiety, they would argue, has its source in the fact that human beings are both finite and free—finite in that we must search for (or work for) food and other necessities, but free in that we have the capacity to transcend our finiteness by anticipating perils and reflecting on our human condition. The result of our freedom is the ability to fear the unknown and anticipate with dread every threat, real or imagined—in other words, anxiety. And all of this has a ring of truth about it. It means that some anxiety is inevitable and even necessary for a healthy existence. A certain amount of anxiety about death keeps us in the appropriate lanes on the freeway and helps us obey traffic laws. Anxiety about failing helps motivate us to study for an exam or make that extra effort in our job. Anxiety with people keeps us polite and civilized. Anxiety is necessary to stimulate change in human behavior and is almost always necessary in psychotherapy. Without a modicum of anxiety, society would most likely plunge into chaos, and personal and spiritual growth would stagnate.

But is anxiety always a friend? Clearly not. By the term "anxiety disorder," we clearly signify anxiety that is abnormal and emotionally destructive. In this book we will encounter many illustrations and case descriptions of anxiety that has gone wrong and become a destructive force.

How do we reconcile the idea that anxiety can be our friend with the clear evidence of so much pathological anxiety in our age? Very simply, I believe. We are using the same word to describe *different human experiences*. Although they have some features in common, the two kinds of anxiety are essentially different. Anxiety over whether or not your biopsy will turn up a malignancy is both quantitatively and qualitatively different from a *panic attack* or an incapacitating fear about leaving the safety of your home—I'm not even sure the two experiences are in the same ballpark! In the one case the feelings are normal and act to mobilize corrective action. In the other, something has gone wrong in the complex biochemical system of tranquilizers that the brain manufactures and uses. The differences between the two will become clearer as we proceed.

OUT OF THE BLUE

Before our third bundle of joy arrived, I was busy with life—serving God in outreach to neighbors, working in ministry with young mothers, and rearing the two little girls who have given us so much joy. [So writes a mother in a letter to me recently.]

My life was full of exciting activities. I was learning about computers, studying how to teach the Bible, running long distances, and witnessing to my club members. There was no crisis in my life. I did not come from a dysfunctional home, and my marriage was as happy as any human marriage can be.

But suddenly, one day, it all changed. I felt a strange excitement. I couldn't sleep that night or the nights that followed. My adrenaline kept pumping—nothing would switch off. For the next two months I experienced incredible anxiety and emotional discomfort. It gripped me around the throat; my heart pounded, and I couldn't breathe properly. I became afraid of everyone and every place. If it wasn't for the medication my doctor gave me to help me relax and sleep, I would have gone berserk.

This letter describes a very clear example of anxiety gone wrong. The onset of anxiety problems "out of the blue"—sudden fear, seemingly inexplicable and overpowering—is characteristic of a very common form of anxiety disorder. To say to such a person, "Your anxiety is normal. All you have to do is pray and trust God more and everything will come right," is both callous and misleading. Yet this is often the advice such a person gets when he or she consults a clergyman or a lay Christian counselor.

Anxiety is often assumed to be a sign of spiritual or psychological weakness, but nothing could be further from the truth! Very often, those who suffer from a sudden and incapacitating attack of anxiety are competent, responsible, and normally healthy individuals. This may be part of the problem, in fact. Because they *are* competent and able to do so much, they tend to be highly driven, deeply committed, and overly *stretched* people. Their anxiety disorder is the penalty for overusing their normally strong bodies and minds. It is the consequence of too much wear and tear on basically efficient biological and mental systems.

The mother's letter I quoted earlier goes on to show this clearly: "In retrospect, I can see how I pushed myself too far. I thought I was capable of anything and didn't need much rest. I was invincible! I was also happy, fulfilled, and excited with everything I was doing and thought I had the world by the tail." Hardly the words of a person who is weak, cowardly, or incompetent!

As in so many areas of human weakness, there is not one of us who does not need to heed the apostle Paul's advice: "Therefore let him [or her] who thinks he [she] stands take heed lest he [she] fall" (1 Cor. 10:12, NKJV). Not one of us is so strong or resilient that anxiety cannot reach up and pull us down. The only "safe" person is the one who is on guard, who sets up precautions against anxiety by understanding how it works, and who then keeps it under control.

BUT WHAT IS ANXIETY?

Because anxiety is multifaceted and, unfortunately, we only have one word to describe all its manifestations, allow me to briefly define it and outline its *major forms.*

Webster's New World Dictionary (second edition) defines *anxiety* as: (1) a state of being uneasy, apprehensive, or worried about what may happen; concern about a possible future event; (2) an intense state of this kind, characterized by varying degrees of emotional disturbance and psychic tension; (3) an eager but often uneasy desire, such as "an anxiety to do well." Its synonyms include *distressed, disturbed, worried, troubled, fearful, uneasy, fretful, restless, nervous,* and *antsy,* to name just a few.

Personal Inventory 1
TEST YOURSELF: HOW ANXIOUS ARE YOU?

	Yes	No
1. Do thoughts that you can't stop keep moving through your mind?		
2. Do you often feel you must take tranquilizers or drink alcohol before social engagements or performances?		
3. Do you spend a lot of time worrying that bad things may happen to you?		
4. Do you become extremely uncomfortable when you find yourself the center of attention?		
5. Do you worry intensely about dying or about having something terrible happen to you?		
6. Do you find it difficult to relax or fall asleep at night?		
7. Do you avoid open spaces, crowded places such as shopping malls, or closed places?		
8. Are you afraid to leave home without being accompanied by someone you know?		
9. Are you afraid of airplanes or flying, even on major airlines?		
10. Do you experience a sudden racing of the heart, difficulty in breathing, sweating, dizziness, or light-headedness?		
11. Are you sometimes suddenly overcome by an intense fear that something terrible is going to happen?		
12. Have you gone to an emergency room or doctor at least once in the past six months, fearing a heart attack, only to have the medical examination reveal no problem?		
13. Are there things that you feel you must do repeatedly— such as wash your hands, check the front door or windows —despite your efforts to resist?		
14. Do you worry a lot about your body or feel sure you have a disease, even though doctors say you are in good health?		
15. Do you tend to urinate very frequently, or suffer from frequent indigestion or abdominal discomfort?		
16. Do you suffer from numbness or coldness of your hands, or do you experience strange feelings such as crawling or itchy sensations on your arms or legs?		
TOTALS		

If you answered yes to *any* of these questions, you may be suffering from some form of anxiety. The more yeses you checked, the greater your "anxiety score"; more than four yeses suggest that you should seek professional help for your problem right away.

8

All these descriptions and equivalents for anxiety are correct. Anxiety of all sorts will produce these characteristics in varying degrees. The differences between the various forms of anxiety lie not so much in the end product (the emotional distress) as in the *causes*. Many different causes can produce the same consequence, namely, anxious feelings.

Sometimes the causes have to do with more basic *fears*, such as the fear of death, strange objects, pain, rejection, or separation. The important difference between fear and anxiety, however, is that fear is usually caused by tangible objects or threats. Anxiety picks up where fear leaves off and is mostly directed toward *imagined* or *unrealized* objects or conditions. Anxiety is more vague and more pervasive.

It is possible for an experience to have components of *both* fear and anxiety. If you are going to the dentist for a root canal, for instance, you may have a legitimate fear of pain; it is unpleasant and hurtful to have someone poking about in your mouth. But you may also have an unfocused feeling of dread that is based on imagination and is excessive in relation to the amount of pain you are likely to experience. This is anxiety.

Sometimes anxiety has no fear component; the emotional discomfort is rooted entirely in the imagination. For instance, I remember going through a period as a child of seven or eight years of age when I did not want to go to sleep because I feared I would not wake up again. I suppose I was just beginning to realize what death is all about. But it was my imagination that fed this acute apprehension, and the response to such an imagined danger is more accurately described as anxiety, not fear.

But not all anxiety is of this sort—fed by vague fears and vivid imaginations. A lot of anxiety discomfort is caused by disturbances in the brain's complex chemistry, and it is the ignorance of this component that produces most misunderstandings about anxiety.

The brain produces its own natural tranquilizers, which are used to block certain chemical receptors in the brain that receive them as "signals" to produce a state of tranquillity. In fact, it is *because* the brain has its own tranquilizers that artificial agents (and we call them tranquilizers as well) can do their job. We merely replace what is missing in the brain—and anxiety subsides.

I will have more to say about this phenomenon later, but for now I want to establish that anxiety has these two origins:

- *Psychological*—in which thoughts, imagination, and the ability to evaluate and understand cause us to be concerned about our welfare or safety and give rise to anxious thoughts and states of mind.

- *Biological*—in which the complex chemistry of the brain is unbalanced and normal tranquilizers of the brain are dislodged, causing anxious thoughts and states of mind.

So, you see, there are at least two major roads to our anxieties, each of which needs to be clearly understood and treated appropriately.

FORMS OF ANXIETY

All of this suggests, as I have already indicated, that there are different forms of anxiety. Unfortunately, modern psychology lacks a clear differentiation of these various *forms* of anxiety. Oh, we have clearly categorized the different *disorders* of anxiety; these are set out in the *Diagnostic and Statistics Manual* published by the American Psychiatric Association. But this categorization does not really help us in understanding the differences among various forms or *expressions* of anxiety.

I happen to believe that the differences in the various forms of the experience called "anxiety" are not just subtle, but quite major and very clear. While a given sufferer may experience many *forms* of anxiety at the same time, this does not prevent us from differentiating between the forms so that we can better understand how anxiety works and thus treat the anxiety more effectively.

To help in differentiating the various types of anxiety, I have prepared the chart presented in figure 1 entitled "Forms of Anxiety." It is by no means the final word in how to differentiate the various forms of anxiety, but I have found it useful in guiding my therapy.

The first form of anxiety is what I call *worry anxiety*. This term describes the excessive use of worry to cope with life. A worrier ruminates often and long about imagined or unlikely threats. Strangely enough, this form of anxiety seems to pay some sort of emotional dividend in that the worriers somehow feel as if they are controlling their world by worrying about it.

The second form of anxiety, which I have already described, is what I term *fear anxiety*. Here the anxious feelings involve real fears, threats, or demands. Fear anxiety is overconcern that may have some basis in reality, but is excessive and debilitating. A good example would be a fear of examinations, public speaking, or the dentist. There may be some pain involved (failing the exam, bombing out on the speech, or having a tooth broken during the extraction), but the anxiety is exaggerated. It also stops when the threat is past—unlike worry anxiety.

The third form of anxiety, also alluded to above, is *existential anxiety*. In my opinion, this form of anxiety has not been given enough

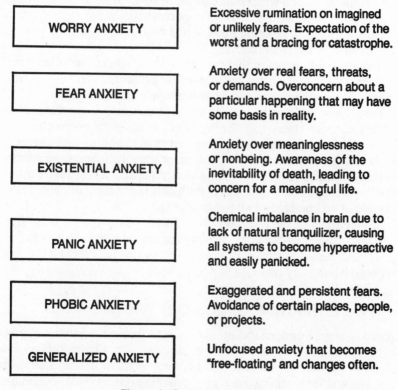

WORRY ANXIETY	Excessive rumination on imagined or unlikely fears. Expectation of the worst and a bracing for catastrophe.
FEAR ANXIETY	Anxiety over real fears, threats, or demands. Overconcern about a particular happening that may have some basis in reality.
EXISTENTIAL ANXIETY	Anxiety over meaninglessness or nonbeing. Awareness of the inevitability of death, leading to concern for a meaningful life.
PANIC ANXIETY	Chemical imbalance in brain due to lack of natural tranquilizer, causing all systems to become hyperreactive and easily panicked.
PHOBIC ANXIETY	Exaggerated and persistent fears. Avoidance of certain places, people, or projects.
GENERALIZED ANXIETY	Unfocused anxiety that becomes "free-floating" and changes often.

Figure 1: Forms of Anxiety

attention, especially by cognitive or behaviorally oriented psychologists. It involves the concern that all humans feel about our existence—especially about finding meaning and purpose for our lives. When we become fully aware of the inevitability of our death, we experience this anxiety.

In many ways, existential anxiety can be a creative and healing force in our lives, because it helps us to evaluate our values and face our mortality in a realistic way. It moves us toward spiritual maturity and the freedom to live out the unique life to which God has called us.

Of course, even this creative anxiety can deteriorate into a "worry anxiety" when one becomes excessively preoccupied with the fear of dying. (Comedian Woody Allen has built a lucrative filmmaking career on satirizing what happens when existential anxiety degenerates into neurosis.) Existential anxiety may require the expertise of a skilled psychotherapist or a wise counselor for it to fulfill its purpose of helping us grow and mature. It is so important that it warrants separate treatment, if not a separate book, and I will have something more to say about it in the final chapter.

Panic anxiety refers to that cluster of disturbances, including panic attacks, which are mostly brought on by prolonged stress or overdemand. As I explain elsewhere in this chapter and later in this book, I believe it is brought on by loss of natural brain tranquilizer that accompanies chronic stress and the body's becoming "superreactive." A panic attack can be a prelude to more chronic phobic or worry anxiety.

Phobic anxiety refers to the phobias, or unrealistic fears, we develop of things, places, or people, leading to extreme and unreasonable avoidance of these places or objects. Agoraphobia is one form of phobic anxiety and often combines with panic anxiety.

Generalized anxiety, the last form listed, has no focus. It is "freefloating"; it comes and goes, changing often without serving any purpose. Sufferers describe it as a vague uneasiness they feel all the time without having any real idea of why or what causes it.

CONSTRUCTIVE VERSUS DESTRUCTIVE ANXIETY

Another way of understanding anxiety is to understand that it can become either a *constructive* or a *destructive* emotion. Figure 2 shows how this can happen. At the root of all anxiety is the organism's need for survival and for meaning. *Fear* is the "warning system" that goes off like a fire alarm whenever there is a threat to either meaning and survival.

In addition, fascinating research has recently begun to illustrate the interaction of threatening life events with "unpredictability" or "uncontrollability." As humans, we desperately need to feel in control of our environment. But more than this, we need to feel that we can predict how things will turn out. Take away our ability to control our lives, or upset things so that we cannot predict with any certainty what is going to happen, and you create a fear that leads to anxiety of the most disturbing kind.

For example, a child who cannot predict when a parent will be pleased or displeased will suffer excessive anxiety. Many parents contribute to this problem by sending conflicting messages. "I always want you to tell the truth," a father will tell his son. But when the son does tell the truth (say, after damaging the family car), the father invokes the most severe punishment. The son cannot see the value of telling the truth when it only leads to more severe punishment and so may develop a lot of anxiety about telling the truth.

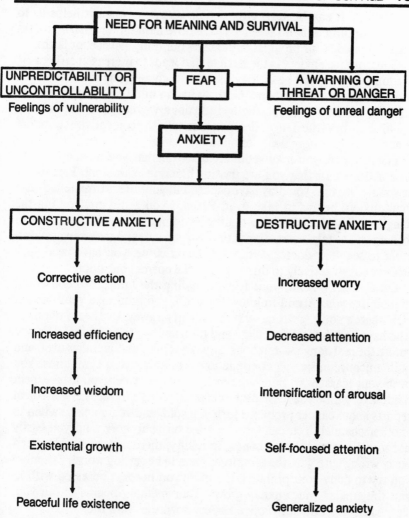

Figure 2: Constructive versus Destructive Anxiety

Similarly, we also have a need to "control" our environment. Uncontrollability leads to severe feelings of apprehension, and chronically anxious people develop the perception that "this terrible thing may happen again at any time, and I can't control it." With no sense of mastery or ability to avoid the terrible thing (even if it is only imagined), an intense state of fear is created. Anxiety is the exaggerated and unreal dimension of this fear. It can become either *constructive* (as when it helps us to change our direction or take steps to remove a threat) or *destructive* (as when it impedes our progress or damages our body, psyche, or faith).

Constructive anxiety is the anxiety that leads to increased efficiency, wisdom, growth, and peaceful existence. It gives us the freedom to become completely the persons "God has had in mind for us to be" (Rom. 5:2, LB). When we are constructively anxious, we recognize the warning signal, see where the danger lies, and then take the corrective action that is necessary to restore peace of mind.

For instance, you may suddenly discover that you have a lump in your abdomen or that you are passing blood in your stool. Fear arises as you realize that you may have cancer and your life is threatened, and then anxiety begins to take over. Perhaps you avoid confronting the danger at first, but then you realize how important your anxiety is in forcing you to take corrective action. So you call and make an appointment to see your doctor. Whatever the outcome, you have used your anxiety constructively to direct you to the correct behavior.

On the other hand, your fear at finding the lump or blood could immobilize you. Afraid to know the truth, you minimize your danger: "Oh, there's nothing wrong with me. It will go away. I've heard of others who have had the same problem and it turned out to be benign." So you ignore the real danger—but not really. Your imagination takes over, and quite unconsciously you continue to worry about your symptoms. You push your fears away, but they sneak up on you when you least expect them. Every time you drive past a hospital, your heart races. TV medical reports about cancer problems turn you cold, and you quickly switch to another channel. You can't concentrate on your work, and you easily become distracted. Even though, in reality, there may be nothing seriously wrong with you, the symptoms seem to be getting worse. The more you try to deny your problem, the more you become obsessed with it, and the greater your anxiety grows. Your memory begins to fail you, sleep is elusive, and destructive anxiety now rules your life.

Anxiety that motivates you to take corrective action is *always healthy*. Anxiety that increases avoidance and intensifies your fear of imagined circumstances is *always destructive*. Whether your anxiety is constructive or destructive is very much a matter of choice—and you control the choice.

THE BRAIN'S NATURAL TRANQUILIZERS

The ability of the brain to produce its own natural tranquilizer is an important, but often overlooked, phenomenon of the brain. Our brains are prolific drug factories, producing very complex and effective chemicals that aid in its control and function. One group of brain chemicals, identified only during this past decade, consists of morphine-like substances called "endorphins." "Endorphin" is short for "endogenous morphine"—so called because one of its prime functions is to help us control pain.

But endorphins do more than this. Consider the following range of emotions and activities: crying, laughter, depression, compulsive gambling, labor and delivery, appetite, immunity to disease, near-death experiences, runner's high, and the thrill of music. Each, it is claimed, is somehow involved with the sloshing around of endorphins in our brains, spines, and bloodstreams.

Research on these fantastic brain chemicals began with the unexpected discovery that there were opiate receptors in the brain, receptors on which morphine acted to reduce pain. If we have such receptors, it was reasoned, then it is likely that the brain also produces the same sort of morphine-like substance itself. Lo and behold, that's what was found. Biochemicals dubbed "opioid peptides" or *endorphins* were discovered that actually have molecular shapes which fit into the shapes of the receptors in the brain—very much as a key fits into a lock. When this occurs, pain is reduced.

But not only are there receptors for pain reduction; there are also receptors for substances that calm and tranquilize the brain and body. This is why tranquilizing pills of the newer variety work so well. They fit like keys into the brain's receptors, performing the same duties as the brain's own natural tranquilizers. In states of severe (and perhaps even moderate) anxiety, I believe, there is a depletion of these natural brain tranquilizers. This throws the system into a panic or anxiety state until the tranquilizer can be replaced—either through natural replenishment or by taking an artificial agent. Prolonged stress is one of the major causes of this natural tranquilizer depletion, which is why such stress almost inevitably causes panic conditions.

While the use of an external tranquilizer may be necessary to calm the brain and restore tranquillity in cases of extreme anxiety, the use of such tranquilizers is helpful only on a temporary basis. This is because there is a "feedback" system controlling the centers that produce the body's natural tranquilizers. Long-term use of external tranquilizers, which block the receptors created for the internally manufactured tranquilizers, causes signals to be sent back to the "manufacturing centers" of the brain, shutting down production.

The result is that a person taking an external tranquilizer over a long period of time becomes dependent upon this chemical, and the vicious cycle of addiction begins. If the sufferer tries to stop the external tranquilizer, the system panics, because there is a gap between the time the receptors open up and the time the body is up to speed in producing its own tranquilizer to fit those receptors. The result is severe withdrawal symptoms—acute anxiety.

This phenomenon must be clearly understood both by those who prescribe tranquilizers and by those who take them. And as we will see later, it explains why so many struggle to come off the helpful but powerful tranquilizing drugs that we have available today. Overcoming dependence on tranquilizers is difficult; the only effective way is to reduce the drug *very slowly*—so slowly that one literally shaves a fraction off the pill each time with a razor blade. I describe a method for doing this in chapter 14.

THE CHRISTIAN'S EXPERIENCE OF ANXIETY

Throughout this book, the question will continually arise: Where does anxiety fit into the experience of the Christian believer?

Christians are by no means free of the problem of anxiety. Many are even at greater risk than the general population, because trying to live a holy life in an unholy world is far from easy. Trying to raise godly children in a society that glorifies sex, violence, and greed; struggling to keep families together in a culture where fragmentation is becoming the norm; endeavoring to keep ethical standards in a dog-eat-dog business world; fighting to spread the gospel in an uncomprehending civilization—all these stresses and more take their toll in terms of anxiety. In addition, married Christians worry about their spouses' fidelity; employed Christians worry about their jobs; Christian singles about getting a partner; pastors about church growth; and teenagers about whether their peers will reject them if they take a Christian stand on sex or drugs. Potential for anxiety permeates the Christian world as much as anywhere.

But are sufficient resources not already available to help Christians cope with their worries and anxieties? I believe not. Some very fine books have been written on the topic, but quite frankly most of them either have a very limited application or are grossly out of date. Much progress in our understanding of anxiety—particularly of panic disorders and agoraphobia (fear of leaving a safe place or going out in public)—has been made in the last two or three years. I believe this help needs to be passed on to the average man or woman who is trying to live a balanced Christian life. And that is the kind of help I hope to present in the chapters to come.

WORRY AND THE CHRISTIAN — 2

"Christians who worry don't have faith."

"Anxiety is sin. Confess it and get back in touch with God."

"God doesn't like anxious people—He won't answer their prayers because they don't please Him."

"God's providential care and concern make *all* anxiety unnecessary."

These are actual statements I have heard through the years from Christian teachers and preachers who meant well but only intensified the hurt and pain that a child, parent, or friend was feeling. Anxiety is disruptive enough without adding the shame and guilt of feeling rejected by God. Feelings of guilt and worthlessness abound among Christian believers who suffer from anxiety because they incorrectly assume that their problem is a sign of personal failure or of God's disapproval.

Take Suzanne, for example. Since her earliest years, she can recall feeling anxious about one thing or another. Even as a young girl, she worried about her mother's being left alone at home while Suzanne was in school. When she bought a new dress or new shoes, she worried for days that she had bought the wrong thing. When she went out of the house, she worried about whether all the doors were locked or whether she had left a window open. Suzanne worried about her pets, her school grades, her reputation, and her future.

At nineteen years of age, Suzanne became a Christian, mainly through the influence of a college friend. For a period of about three months, she felt a great freedom from her tendency toward anxiety. She learned how to pray and read Scripture and found much hope and reassurance in these resources.

Then one day Suzanne woke up to find that her newfound sense of peace had simply vanished. All her old anxieties returned, but greatly intensified. "What's happened to me?" she asked, shortly after starting therapy. "Why has the anxiety come back? I believed that God had freed me from all that pain. Have I failed God somewhere? Has He abandoned me? Am I doomed to be a failure all my life?"

Suzanne's experience is a common one. After conversion often comes a wonderful sense of comfort and release from anxiety. It is the honeymoon phase of faith, and often there is great excitement over a newfound prayer life and the insights Scripture can bring. God's Spirit seems very close and His comfort very real.

But anxiety can become deeply rooted in a personality. And while God sometimes provides a miraculous removal of these roots, more often He calls upon us to begin and continue the process of sanctification that has been opened to us through salvation. God expects us to continue and maintain our spiritual growth. He provides the tools from which to shape our maturity, the power to use these tools, and the courage to be determined, but we have to learn how to use them. God seldom provides a shortcut to sainthood.

"God has not abandoned you," I reassured Suzanne. "It is now that He calls on you to continue your walk with Him and to learn how His resources are sufficient for all your anxieties. If you feel guilty because you are afraid you've failed God, then confess that guilt and use it to turn yourself back to Him. Don't ever let your guilt feelings drive you away from God."

Suzanne and I then spent the next few sessions exploring the idea that times of anxiety are not necessarily times when we have no faith. Feelings of anxiety certainly don't cancel out our salvation. In fact, some of the greatest saints have known the deepest darkness and have had to fight through to overcome their dread. Even Jesus Himself once felt deserted by God, and His experience in Gethsemane was as full of abandonment as anyone has ever experienced in life, but Jesus nevertheless remained faithful to His Father's plan.

Severe anxiety disorders have their roots so far back in life that many years of "faith building"—and perhaps professional therapy—may be required before the problem can be brought under control. It is important therefore, that we not reproach ourselves (or others) for being slow learners. Doing so only adds to our misery—and may stand in the way of our growth.

WAS JESUS EVER ANXIOUS?

The question of whether Jesus felt anxiety during His earthly ministry is, I believe, an important one, because it gives us an idea of just how intrinsic anxiety is to the human condition. While Jesus was the Logos, the Word, the Son of God, He was also fully human—He had to be in order to be the sacrifice for all of humanity. We look to Him, therefore, as the model of our humanity, as someone who came to demonstrate how we should live.

We know that though Jesus was fully human, He was *not* guilty of sin—that He was tempted but did not succumb. In order to be the

Messiah, Jesus *had* to be guiltless, spotless, undefiled. So we can say that, for Jesus, being human did not have to mean being sinful. And by the same token, I would suggest, being completely human did not have to mean being *neurotic*. I believe Jesus could have met all the conditions of humanness by being totally healthy, free of neurotic defenses and all we associate with emotional disturbance.

This is not to say that Jesus was emotionless! The biblical account shows that Jesus was fully human in His emotions. We know, for example, that He *wept* and was *sad* on a number of occasions, including His visit to the garden of Gethsemane (Matt. 26:37). Being emotional is not the same as being neurotic; the human body is designed to be a feeling organism. The ability to feel honest emotions is as much as part of Jesus' full humanity as His ability to experience pain (Mark 8:31), hunger (Luke 6:2), sleepiness (Luke 8:23), and fatigue (John 4:6).

Yes, the Scripture accounts show that Jesus was *fully human*—but not neurotic. No Scripture even hints at an unhealthy emotional adjustment. Jesus had no need to repress His feelings, deny them, or sublimate them. Unlike most if not all of us, Jesus was a complete and healthy human being.

I would further suggest, therefore, that while Jesus was capable of feeling genuine fear—after all, His body had the same glands, hormones, and fear mechanisms as ours—He was able to keep His fear from becoming unreasonable or uncontrollable. The fact that He was capable of fear does not mean He was fearful, nor that His fear alarm-signals were allowed to become anxiety driven. Remember, He was able to withstand a boat trip in a severe tempest (which would have made most of us extremely afraid), yet sleep through it and then ask the disciples (in the form of a rebuke): "Why are you fearful, O you of little faith?" (Matt. 8:26, NKJV).

Scriptural evidence, therefore, supports the belief that while Christ's body was capable of experiencing fear—and hence anxiety—Christ was *not* anxious. He did not worry as we do. He was not neurotic as we are. He never panicked—and yet He was fully human!

The model of Christ's life, therefore, clearly points to the way we are to follow and demonstrates how we should live. But even more important is the power He gives us to live free of neurotic tendencies. He comes to dwell in us through the Holy Spirit, to encourage us and help us see through our problems and understand our insecurities. *Together* with Him we can become whole persons. And while there will always be some tendency toward anxiety on our part—we will never achieve perfection in this life—Christ is always ready to forgive, heal, and restore us in our struggle. So don't think you have to overcome your anxiety by yourself. You have a Partner who is greater than yourself to help you.

DOES SCRIPTURE CONDEMN ANXIETY?

There is no doubt in my mind that Scripture clearly condemns anxiety. But as we have already established, there are many different *forms* of anxiety. Before we rush in to condemn anxiety generally as "bad," therefore, we should first examine each of these forms and determine *which* of them is tabooed by Scripture.

As I showed in the previous chapter, we have only one word for anxiety in English, and this sometimes limits our understanding of it. Remember, there are many varieties of anxiety, and not all of them are neurotic or negative. It is the neurotic forms of the emotion of anxiety that I believe the Bible condemns. Scripture uses the word *anxiety* to primarily mean worry or fretting. *Worry anxiety*, therefore, is the form of anxiety uniformly condemned by Scripture.

Jesus sometimes used the expression "taking thought" to refer to this form of anxiety. In the Sermon on the Mount, for example, Jesus refers again and again to "taking thought" for the future or for what will happen (See Matt. 6:25–34, KJV). And His lesson is clear: Worrying, or "taking thought," doesn't help birds get their food nor lilies to grow. And worrying about tomorrow is also pointless and useless. There is plenty to be concerned about right now to occupy your energies, and worrying about tomorrow will not keep its evils away.

The apostle Paul was a very intense person who at times experienced "fear and trembling" (1 Cor. 2:3). Nevertheless, his position regarding the uselessness of our worries is very clear. In Philippians 4:6, he tells us to "be anxious for nothing," reminding us to pray "with thanksgiving" (NKJV). The apostle Peter joins Paul at this point, telling us to cast "all [our] cares upon him; for he careth for [us]" (1 Pet. 5:7, KJV).

Worry anxiety is portrayed in Scripture as an evil that chokes God's Word: "Now he who received seed among the thorns is he who hears the word, and the cares of this world and the deceitfulness of riches choke the word, and he becomes unfruitful" (Matt. 13:22). The "cares of this world" (KJV) in this verse can also be translated as "the worry of the world" (NASB); this clearly implies that excessive preoccupation with life's uncertainties is like a bed of thorns that choke God's word and constrict the development of our faith.

Worry anxiety is also seen as hindering us from doing God's work. Second Timothy 2:4 suggests that soldiers of Jesus Christ should not get overly entangled in or become worried about the affairs of everyday life, because this distracts and detracts from their spiritual warfare. And Luke 21:34 proposes that *worry anxiety* gluts the soul and weighs us down so that we cannot be alert to impending perils.

Even our relationships suffer when we give in to *worry anxiety,* Scripture tells us. *Worry* causes a brother to hate a brother, robbing us of love and setting us up in competition against each other (Gen. 32:6-12).

Worry anxiety, therefore, is characterized by a lack of trust in God and a failure to fully understand His plan and provisions for us. It is clearly harmful to us and therefore displeasing to God.

But this does not mean we should not be unconcerned about our lives (I will discuss the difference between "concern" and "worry" later). Neither does it mean that we have committed the unpardonable sin just because we spent a sleepless night worrying about a wayward child or an unhappy friend. Paul tells us to "stop *perpetually* worrying about even one thing" (Phil. 4:66 and 7), but also gives us a prescription for our worry: We are to bring our requests to God, with an attitude of thanksgiving, expecting that what awaits us is the "peace of God which surpasses all comprehension" (Phil. 4:6-7).

Worry anxiety, you see, is what happens when God's creatures try to live their lives independently from God. When we refuse to be joined to our Creator, even when He has provided a way back to Himself through Jesus Christ, we settle down into the bog of our own anxiety.

Still, it is hard for us as believers to "stop worrying perpetually" and to reach out for the resources God makes available. I have met very few Christian believers so perfect in their walk with God that they are free of anxiety. Because of this, scriptural antidotes for anxiety have been prescribed by the Great Physician. These include reliance upon God's Spirit (Mark 3:11), appropriating God's provisions (Luke 12:22-30), and resting in God's care (1 Pet. 5:6,7). What medicine could be more complete?

The problem, of course, is not with the medicine but with the patient—you and me. We are rebellious children by nature and gag at our "medicine." We are disobedient; we love to run away when God calls. So we shouldn't be surprised if, while wallowing in the pigpen like true prodigals, we also suffer from incapacitating anxiety.

The responsibility for getting up and leaving the pigpen lies with us, as we will see shortly.

DIFFERENTIATING "CONCERN" FROM "WORRY"

Perhaps the most confusing aspect of worry anxiety for most of us is that we do not distinguish it from a healthy (but related) emotion or reaction which can best be labeled "concern."

It is very helpful to separate worry from concern. The one is unhealthy; the other is healthy. To put them both in the same category is to increase our confusion—and heaven knows, life is confusing enough already.

Simply put, the word *worry* should be reserved for that kind of fruitless mental activity which keeps thoughts revolving endlessly but takes no action to solve the problem—either because no action is possible or because we refuse to take action. Such fretting is pointless; it goes nowhere. When we worry, we cause an emergency reaction throughout our body, and as a result we become exhausted, disorganized, and disoriented—without moving one inch toward solving our problem.

Concern, on the other hand, refers to that kind of mental activity that focuses on a problem with a view toward taking action to resolve the problem. Concern springs naturally from love and caring and is directed toward an end.

Now, worry and concern often coexist and cannot be separated easily. And worry sometimes grows out of concern—when we let our feelings get out of hand. The important issue then becomes a matter of which predominates—worry or concern.

Let us suppose, for example, that a loved one is about to undergo surgery. I know the feeling well because just a few years ago my wife, Kathleen, had major surgery. I recall sitting in the waiting room with my stomach all tight and my hands sweating. Was what I felt worry or concern? I must admit that there was an element of worry when I allowed my imagination to get away from me. But a lot of my feeling was nothing more nor less than concern. Because I love my wife, I wanted her to feel comfortable, the surgery to go smoothly, and the outcome to be satisfactory. This concern helped me to focus my prayers and to pray for the surgeon and for my wife.

Here's another example that may clarify the difference between concern and worry. If my teenaged daughter does not return at 11:30 P.M., as she said she would (this happened a lot when my girls were growing up), I naturally become "concerned." Once again, this "concern" is a sign of love—a symbol of my care. Only by being indifferent and unloving could I avoid being concerned for the well-being of someone I love.

Now, concern over my daughter's lateness might prompt me to take corrective action. I could call the friend she is visiting or someone at the meeting she is attending and make sure she is okay. I might, in some circumstances, get into my car and retrace her route to see if perhaps her car has broken down. Or I might simply entrust her to God's keeping and tell myself, "She is a responsible person, and she will telephone me if she needs help." *All* these actions are healthy and are usually an expression of my love.

On the other hand, rather than taking any of these courses of action, I could simply stew and fret over my daughter's lateness—imagining possible tragic scenarios and growing progressively more upset. That would be worry—clearly a dead-end street!

Now, because the boundaries between worry and concern are not always clear, it's possible for us to deceive ourselves into believing that our "worry" is merely "concern." It's true that, to a certain extent, "concern" is in the eye of the beholder; many wives, for instance will probably accuse their husbands of calling their "concern" worry, and vice versa. But honesty with oneself in this area is very important, because self-deception only brings more worry.

Since worry often follows closely on the heels of concern, allow me to suggest some ways you can avoid worry and use your "concern" in a healthy way:

(1) *Clarify what it is you are "concerned" about.* Ask yourself, "What is the *real* issue here?"

At this point, it is important not to force the concern out of your mind by denying or minimizing it. Denial or minimization will almost certainly transform your concern into worry.

In the case of my daughter's not being home on time, for example, I could simply avoid looking at the clock or convince myself that "It's really not that late." This would be *denial,* refusing to believe that there is a difficulty. The problem with denial is that it only pushes the concern below the level of consciousness, where it continues to fester as worry.

Alternately, I could tell myself, "There's really no need to worry. Despite what the newspapers say about girls' traveling late at night by themselves in Los Angeles, no one I know has had any problems." This would be *minimizing* the problem, another strategy for reducing anxiety that only causes it to "go underground."

When attempting to clarify the issue, it helps to write down your concern or to discuss it with someone else. This will restore your perspective and help you be more objective. Concern always must be objective if it is not to become worry.

(2) *Decide on a course of action.* Setting out the problem or concern as clearly as possible will help in the next step, which is to ask yourself: "What can I *do*?" The purpose of concern is to alert you to a problem so that you can take action. Turning your concern into action will stop that concern from degenerating into worry.

Sometimes the only action possible is to pray and consciously commit the problem into God's hands. Very often, however, there are other steps you can take as well. A telephone call, a visit, a change in plans—anything that moves you to action—will help to overcome worry.

I once heard an astronaut—a man of obviously superior gifts and remarkable resilience—talk about his experience of blasting off into space. He was asked about what he felt as he sat there on top of the huge rocket that was about to propel him into orbit. Now, this is not an experience many of us would wish to go through; only a robot could fail to feel a certain amount of concern.

So what would a person do with concern in such a situation to prevent it from becoming worry? The astronaut's reply was quite insightful. "I have so much I must *do,*" he replied, "I don't have time to worry about what might happen to me."

(3) *Honestly evaluate the possible outcome of that which you fear.* Ask yourself, "What is the worst possible outcome?" And then, "Can I live with it?"

Evaluating the worst possible scenario usually serves the function of bringing us back to reality. When we take the time to ask ourselves what could really happen, most times we'll end up saying, "I *can* live with it." If we can say this honestly, worry is minimized.

Let me illustrate. I tend to be a person who is preoccupied with time. I like to be on time (in fact, I'm always early), and I don't like being delayed.

One morning, on my way to work, I discovered I had a flat tire. My concern level jumped sky-high. "What am I going to do? It's going to take fifteen minutes to change the tire—and I will be late for my first patient's appointment."

When I opened the trunk, I had a further blow; the spare tire was flat. Now my concern jumped even higher (to the nearest star at least), and I felt it starting to turn to worry. "I'm not just going to be late for the appointment, I'm going to miss it altogether, because it will take me another twenty minutes to get the spare pumped up with the little compressor I keep in the tool kit."

Then I stopped myself. "Wait a moment," I said. "What is the worst thing that can happen as a consequence of my getting a flat tire?" I forced myself to come back to reality. The *worst* thing I could come up with was that my patient would not understand the circumstances for my not showing up and would cancel out on seeing me altogether. "Is this a catastrophe?" I went on to ask myself. It depends on how you look at it. If my patient was that easily put off, perhaps it would be better that he see another therapist anyway. As it turned out, my patient was most understanding, and the worry I was about to embark on was quite unnecessary.

Now, the purpose of imagining the worst possible outcome is *not* to help bring that outcome about, but to free you from the tyranny of worrying about it. Even if the outcome you imagine is very painful, facing it realistically can keep you from imagining even worse possibilities. And you can use your anticipation of the worst possible scenario to build your confidence that with God's help you can cope with *any* circumstance.

One patient I worked with had a strong tendency to convert her concern into worry. Most of her concern revolved around her husband of thirty years, who throughout their married life had shown little real affection for her and had treated her with no real respect. But she had always responded with love and had faithfully performed her duties as a wife because she felt deep down that he really did love her in his own way. She was convinced that the problem, deep within his personality, was that he was unable to show love and affection to anyone because he feared abandonment.

Still, my client felt continual concern for her relationship and feared that one day her husband might leave her. At one time in their marriage, this possibility became very real, and her concern shifted quickly into intense worry over her future. She couldn't sleep at night, and all day she walked on eggshells, trying to avoid any action that might upset him. The stress was taking its toll, and she was on the verge of a nervous breakdown.

So I asked this woman, "What is the worst thing that could happen if your husband left you?" She gave it some thought and then wrote down all the possible outcomes she could think of. After reflecting on her list for a while, she concluded that not one of them was catastrophic. As a couple, they were well off, so money would not be a problem. Even if she had to go to work, she could adjust; in fact, she suspected working might be good for her. She wouldn't really mind having to move; she was tired of staying in her present home. And if her husband refused to be friends with her, she would not lose much, because he had never treated her as a friend anyway.

"So what's the worst thing that could happen?" I pressed her. "Nothing," she replied. "Absolutely nothing. I'd probably be a happier person."

This awareness changed my client's attitudes and freed her from a prison of her own making. She no longer lived in fear of her husband's constant rejection. Interestingly enough, when this woman became stronger, her marriage improved, and her husband's respect increased dramatically. I think he came to realize how much he would lose if *she* left *him!* Their marriage continues to improve to this day.

THE SIN OF WORRY

In calling worry a "sin," I do so more to make a point than to be judgmental. Worry anxiety, as Scripture clearly shows, is bad for us—and therefore runs contrary to God's good plan. It involves relying on self rather than on God, and it gets in the way of faith. As such, it is sin. When we worry, we are in need of God's healing and forgiveness, just as we are when we lie or commit adultery.

In addition, worry is an intriguing problem from a clinical point of view. We all have an inherent tendency to anticipate or prepare for future events by thinking about them in advance. We use thoughts and images to help us either understand or solve our problems. But worry is more than just thinking about things; it seems to take on a life of its own. It becomes an "enemy within," distracting us from our work with its relentless flow of bothersome thoughts. While it may fool us into thinking that it is directed at solving problems, it never delivers the goods. We never get closure on anything we worry about.

One research group at Pennsylvania State University has defined worry well as "a chain of negative and relatively uncontrollable thoughts and images." Another person has described worry as "interest paid in advance on a debt you may never owe," and this description probably captures it best of all. Most worry focuses on the future (what will happen tomorrow, next week, or next year) but a lot of it also focuses on the past.

Most worry follows a circular path; it starts nowhere and ends up back where it started. "I've got to meet that deadline. . . . Deadlines are important. . . . My boss puts a lot of store in meeting deadlines. . . . If I don't meet the deadline I won't get a raise. . . . My promotion will be dead, too. . . . Maybe I'll even get fired! . . . What will happen to me? . . . This is the only job I know. . . . How will I make the house payments? . . . What will my kids do? . . . If I don't stop thinking like this, I won't get this assignment finished. . . . And I won't meet the deadline. . . . I've got to meet that deadline!"

About 15 percent of the population are *chronic worriers*. That's a little less than one person out of seven. But what is a chronic worrier? Researchers tend to think that if you worry for less than one and a half hours a day, you do not have a worry problem. Amazing! But then, you see, a lot of worry goes on unconsciously; it is not until you catch yourself putting shaving cream on your toothbrush that you realize you've been worrying.

What are some of the consequences of worry? Misery, for sure, but there are many other consequences as well—headaches, lack of sleep, loss of appetite, overeating, lower tolerance of frustration, irritability, and bad disposition. There is even some suggestion that it might create high blood pressure, heart disease, and ulcers. While there is no hard evidence yet, worry is even suspected to be an aggravating factor in cancer.

HOW WORRY "FEEDS" ON ITSELF

Even chronic worriers are known to have periods when they don't worry. This phenomenon—times of worry, followed by periods of no worry—has led to some interesting and useful discoveries.

Research has shown that short periods of worrying (say, for less than ten minutes) or very long periods (greater than thirty minutes) tend to cut down on the tendency to worry. It is the "middle" range of worrying, between ten and thirty minutes, that produces the worst consequences. This effect is called "incubation" and is thought to explain why worry tends to "feed on itself." We don't worry *all* the time. If we did, we would probably extinguish the worry. Nor do we tend to worry for just a brief period and then set it aside; this would also extinguish the worry. Instead, we worry enough to entrench our anxious feelings, then we leave our worry alone for a while so it can incubate. Later, we return to our problem to find that it is ready and waiting for more worry. This pattern entrenches the worry and makes it very resistant to extinction.

It's very much like painting a barn door. Put on one thin coat of paint and leave it, and the paint will wear off quickly. Put on a very thick single coat, and the paint will drop off quickly because it doesn't dry properly and therefore doesn't adhere well. But put on just the right amount of paint, give it time to "set," add a second layer and let it dry, then add another and another, and you build up a strong, impermeable, almost indestructible covering.

Now, this process may be good for painting barn doors, but it is not good for protecting the psyche. When worry is entertained in just the right amount and repeated at just the right interval, it will build up to become an entrenched habit that is resistant to almost any therapy and to the Holy Spirit as well. That is why, I'm convinced, that Scripture pegs worry anxiety as sinful.

HOW TO BREAK THE WORRY HABIT

"Don't worry." It's easy to say. I've even seen it on T-shirts and bumper stickers, as if it's the greatest discovery ever made. But it's not really helpful just to tell people not to worry. That's a little like telling a person who is overweight, "Just don't eat so much." It's true, but it's not really helpful! To overcome worry anxiety, we need to understand *why* we worry, come to see how useless it is, and learn how to turn worry into action.

While I will discuss ways of breaking the worry habit in a later chapter, I'll make a few suggestions at this point that can help you avoid the "incubation" pattern that causes worry to feed on itself.

Remember, first of all, that there is enormous help available to us in the Christian faith. My own faith in Christ has helped me survive many times when I thought worry would do me in! God understands how we are made, and whatever practical help I might offer from a psychological point of view must be taken with a *massive dose of spiritual renewal.* I am convinced that the first line of defense against worry must be an understanding that God gives us power to live meaningful lives and sustains us through every experience we face and every challenge we must cope with.

God can deal with *every* situation that gives us cause for worry—of this I am certain. Do you remember Joseph's saying to those who plotted his death, "You meant evil against me, but God meant it for good" (Gen. 50:20, NASB)? Begin each day trusting that this is as true for you as it was for the young Joseph, and the need to worry your way out of predicaments will diminish.

Still, there are times when worry is overpowering and no amount of praying or believing seems to enable us to withstand it. Remember, God understands this also, so take heart and try the following process for handling your worry:

(1) *Monitor your thinking to cut out worry.* As soon as you catch yourself worrying, postpone the act of worrying to a given "worry period." Write down the worry so you won't forget it. (This will also help your mind to "let go" of the worry until the appointed time.)

(2) *Make a date to worry.* This "worry period" of no more than five minutes (use a timer if necessary) should take place at the same time each day and preferably in the same place. For example, you can do it at the table right after lunch, before you go back to work or fetch the kids from school.

(3) *Concentrate on worry when the time comes.* When your appointed "worry time" arrives, pull out your notebook, start a timer,

and begin to devote the next five minutes to worrying. Force yourself to use the time for worrying. Don't allow yourself to be distracted. Get everything out in the open. Focus on the task, and try to separate your concerns from your worries

(4) *Put away your worries when your worry time is up.* At the end of the five-minute worry period, pull your concerns together and decide on actions to be taken, again writing them in your notebook. Commit your concerns to God in prayer, then go about your business, ignoring any worries that might linger in your mind.

This technique, while not perfect, has helped many to lessen the frequency and intensity of their worry. It can help you worry less by preventing the development of an "incubation" pattern. It also can help you separate your legitimate concern from pointless worries and encourage you to take action on your concerns. Finally, it will give you a structure to follow as you learn to "release" your worries and give them over to God, which is by far the best way to handle your worries.

THE TWELVE STEPS TO OVERCOMING WORRY

The twelve steps to recovery that were devised by Alcoholics Anonymous (AA) have been lifesavers for many people over the years. They have been used as a model by many self-help groups including Overeaters Anonymous, Gamblers Anonymous, and Cocaine Anonymous. Perhaps we need a group call Worriers Anonymous. The only problem is that we would probably all have to join!

Chronic worry can be very much like an addiction—we come to depend on it and we can't stop doing it. As a bad habit, it can be as debilitating as alcohol. With due apology to AA, therefore, I would like to present *twelve steps to overcoming worry.* Work through them, one step at a time, and you will find they help you control your worry tendencies. Take your time over each step and make sure you have mastered it before moving on to the next one.

Here are the twelve steps:

(1) *Admit you are a worrier and that you are powerless to overcome worry entirely on your own strength.* Admit that worry is unmanageable for you most of the time, even when you exercise the greatest willpower.

(2) *Believe that God, through Christ, is able to help you overcome your worry.* Accept that you can "do all things through Christ which strengtheneth [you]" (Phil. 4:13, KJV). This includes controlling your thinking and eliminating wasteful worry.

(3) *Turn your life over to God.* Present your body (including your mind) as "a living sacrifice, holy, acceptable unto God, which is your

reasonable service" (Rom. 12:1, KJV). This will help to renew your mind (v. 2) and give it foundational peace.

(4) *Make a list of everything that worries you.* Never allow any worry to remain in your mind without writing it down so that you can read it, understand it, and see how ridiculous it is. Instead of avoiding your fears, face them courageously and get them out into the open.

(5) *Find someone you can talk to about your worries.* Talking your problems out helps restore perspective and good sense. Trying to explain your worries points up their inconsistencies and the inaccuracies inherent in all worry. Talk to God about what is worrying you, too. He can help you see them more clearly also.

(6) *Be willing to "let go" of your worries.* For many, worrying pays dividends; when we worry, we avoid having to take action, deal constructively with problems, or face inadequacies. Worry can be comforting in its own strange way. It's like the child's security blanket—worn, tattered, and useless—but somehow it makes us feel safer.

(7) *Trust God to give you the courage you need to take action and abandon the safety and comfort of your worry.* Move away from the safety of the shore and launch into deeper and riskier waters. God knows your shortcomings and will not abandon you.

(8) *Review all your past worries and see how they never came to pass.* Try to recall everything you worried about, say, last week or last month. Make a list of them. Go back to last year or even your childhood. Try to recall as many worries as possible and then write down next to them what the actual outcome was. Did the things you worried about actually happen? Many probably did not. If they did, then ask yourself: *Did it really devastate me? Did I survive?* Try to reinforce the idea that most, if not all, things we worry about never come to pass—and that you can survive the ones that do.

(9) *If anything you worried about in your past actually did happen and was devastating to you, ask yourself what you could have done to avoid it.* Could you have changed something, or was the situation not entirely up to you? If you could have avoided what happened, then write down the steps you could have taken. This will help you the next time you face a similar situation and aid in showing you where and what you can control.

(10) *Continue to take personal responsibility for your life.* Don't shirk making decisions, and certainly don't avoid the tough times. If you fall into a bout of worry, don't punish yourself. Instead, promptly admit your error and take control of the worry.

(11) *Spend a part of each day strengthening your personal relationship with God.* Do this through prayer and quiet meditation on His

Word, and maintain an attitude of continual trust in His protection. Pray for daily strength and the courage to take each day one moment at a time.

(12) *At the end of each day, take a few minutes to review the accomplishments of your day.* Thank God for each worry you deflected and for every fear you did not give a foothold in your mind. Remember each moment of comfort you received and every word of encouragement God gave to you through the day. Thank Him for every friend who passed your way and encouraged you, for each shoulder you cried on or ear that listened. Count each of these blessings, and thank God for them. Then go to bed knowing that tomorrow's challenges and concerns will be lighter to bear and easier to master.

Some years ago, I heard a story of a woman who had learned to do just that. A reporter visited this unusual woman, a widow, who had raised six children of her own and had adopted six others in order to give them a home.

"How have you been able to raise all these children by yourself—and do it so well?" asked the reporter.

"It's been very simple," replied the widow lady. "You see, I'm in a partnership."

"A what?" asked the surprised reporter.

"A partnership," replied the widow calmly. "One day a long time ago I said to the Lord: 'Lord, I'll do the work if You will do the worrying,' and I haven't had a worry since."

Try this partnership yourself. I think you will be pleasantly surprised at how well it works!

3
UNDERSTANDING YOUR ANXIETY

Anxiety is such a common problem that everyone should know how to recognize it. I would even suggest that it should be possible for you to diagnose your particular form of anxiety yourself. You may need to see a professional to get help for a more serious anxiety problem. But even then, the more you know about anxiety the better, because your understanding of anxiety may help you get the right sort of professional help.

Many anxiety sufferers who have struggled with emotional pain for years—engaging in therapy that doesn't work, taking pills that make them dependent, watching helplessly as their careers and families fall apart—could reduce their pain by taking the time to understand their problem. At the very least, they might avoid adding to their misery with a sense of inadequacy or guilt. "If only I were stronger, I could get on with my life," I have heard so many say. "This problem must be a sign that I am totally hopeless."

Most people who suffer from panic attacks, for instance, are so embarrassed about their condition that they refuse to seek treatment. They see their problem as a sign of weakness and even failure, and this is especially true if they are Christian believers. Anxiety, for them, is not only a sign of personal weakness but evidence that they have also failed as Christians.

Being able to diagnose your own condition is especially helpful in counteracting the fear that your problem is purely a psychological one. Our culture tends to stigmatize "emotional" problems; we see them as "failures" or signs of weakness—unlike "real" physiological disorders.

There is "good news" for most anxiety suffers: Many anxiety problems are *not* just in your head—and even those that are primarily psychological are both real and treatable. So if anxiety is a problem for you, stop blaming yourself. Stop writing yourself off as "weak" or the victim of a mixed-up childhood. Even if treatment has failed for you, take heart! That failure may just mean that you haven't yet discovered the real cause for your anxiety. Exciting new discoveries are being made all the time, and our skill in applying these discoveries grows steadily. The cure for your anxiety problem may be just around the corner.

RECOGNIZING ANXIETY SYMPTOMS

There are two steps to developing our understanding of anxiety. The first is to increase our *recognition* that anxiety is present and to differentiate it from other problems such as depression. The second element, *diagnosis,* then tries to pinpoint the particular form of the anxiety disorder so that the appropriate treatment can be applied. This will be discussed later in the chapter.

Recognizing anxiety is easier if the signs or symptoms are thought of as falling into three categories: physiological, behavioral, and emotional. The symptoms of different forms of anxiety tend to be concentrated in different categories. The list of symptoms is very long, but table 1 shows the most important ones.

Now, before you rush out to persuade your doctor to prescribe a tranquilizer, let me caution you not to overinterpret this long list of

Table 1
SYMPTOMS OF ANXIETY

Physiological Symptoms

Headaches	Vague aches and pains	Skin eruptions
Dizziness/faintness	Strange sensations/tingling	Breathlessness
Insomnia	Excessive perspiration	Flushing
Fatigue	Heartburn/chest pain	Pounding heart
Trembling/shaking	Hyperventilation	Tense muscles
Frequent urinating	Nausea/choking sensations	Palpitations
Dry mouth	Ringing in ears	Lump in throat

Behavioral Symptoms

Lack of concentration	Lack of motivation
Speech disruptions/hesitations	Increased reactivity to stimuli
Compulsive behavior	Obsessive behavior
Loss of memory	Loss of problem-solving ability
Increased restlessness	Shakiness
Fidgetiness	Quick onset of fatigue

Emotional Symptoms

Fear of dying	Morbid self-awareness	Fear of "going crazy"
Overconcern	Increased fearfulness	Increased irritability
Tearfulness	Increased shame and guilt	Excessive worry
Nervousness	Emotional instability	Tendency to panic

symptoms. Obviously, we all have times when we experience some of these symptoms.

Take dizziness, for example. Dizziness can indeed be a symptom of anxiety. But you can also feel dizzy if your inner ear has been disturbed by infection, lack of sleep, medication, or even car travel. Dizziness alone is not an unmistakable sign of anxiety. In fact, no single symptom should be taken too seriously.

In recognizing your problem as one of anxiety, you must take into account three variables: the *number* of symptoms you recognize (and whether they can be attributed to other causes), the *length of time* you have experienced the symptoms, and their *intensity*. But if you have experienced several of these symptoms for some length of time and no other physical cause has been identified, then you may be justified in suspecting anxiety.

The *intensity of the symptoms* is an especially important consideration. The more intense the symptom, the more likely it is to be significant. (Intense symptoms of this sort may require treatment even if the source proves to be something other than anxiety!)

If you become concerned when reading this list of symptoms, I suggest you consult your general physician as a starting point. He or she will be able to tell you what your next step should be. One of the unfortunate characteristics of anxiety is that it can severely accentuate feelings about itself. Being anxious makes your fear or concern *about being anxious* worse—if you follow me! Anxiety feeds on itself in a self-defeating way, so don't hesitate to get help in stopping the cycle if you feel it getting out of control.

TESTS FOR YOUR ANXIETY

The list of symptoms associated with anxiety covers many varieties of anxiety disorders. As we proceed, we will clarify the specific symptoms associated with each disorder. For our immediate purposes, however, I would like to present two short tests—one to help you determine whether or not there is enough *general* anxiety present to be of concern, and another to help you assess the specific type of anxiety you suffer from.

Personal inventory 2 is a general questionnaire designed to measure how much anxiety you are currently feeling. The questionnaire is drawn from a number of clinical tests, and while it has not been subjected to rigorous study, I have found it to be quite valid in determining the degree of general anxiety present.

Personal Inventory 2
GENERAL ANXIETY QUESTIONNAIRE

This questionnaire is designed to measure the general level of anxiety. Score each item according to the following scale:

0 = I never or rarely experience this.
1 = I sometimes experience this, but it doesn't bother me.
2 = I often experience this, and it bothers me a little.
3 = I often experience this, and it bothers me.
4 = Most of the time I experience this.

	Score
1. I have dizzy spells.	
2. My stomach gets tied up in knots.	
3. I feel nauseous.	
4. At times I cannot breathe normally or must go to the window to get air.	
5. I am afraid of heights or closed places.	
6. I cannot stay alone for long.	
7. I cannot go far away from home.	
8. I have difficulty going to sleep.	
9. I wake up early and cannot go back to sleep.	
10. I fidget and am restless.	
11. I don't feel confident and am afraid of the future.	
12. I am afraid of dying.	
13. My thoughts run wild and cannot be controlled.	
14. I experience spells of panic or terror.	
15. I avoid large crowds or public places.	
16. I seem to be having a heart attack at times.	
17. My insides feel shaky or nervous.	
18. I use tranquilizers or antidepressants.	
19. I have strange sensations in my body or skin.	
20. I have difficulty relaxing or doing nothing.	
TOTAL SCORE	

To take the test, read each item of the scale and give yourself a score from 0 to 4, according to the description presented at the top of the test. Be as honest as you can, and if you don't want anyone else to see your score, write it down on a separate sheet of paper. Don't spend too much time pondering your answers, but give the score you believe most generally fits your condition. At the end, total your score.

As you can see, the higher your score, the higher will be your general experience of anxiety. The highest you can score is 80, and the lowest is 0. In my opinion, no one should score zero on this test. Only the dead are free of all anxiety!

The following ranges of response for the total score can generally be accepted:

0–15	A very low anxiety score.
16–25	Your anxiety score is mildly elevated.
26–60	Your anxiety score is moderately elevated.
61–80	Your anxiety score is severely elevated.

A score of 26 or higher warrants some attention. Above 61 is quite severe and should receive immediate professional attention. For those who score below 26, your anxiety level may be a problem only during a specific life period or if you are going through a stressful experience. Overall, however, you seem to have your anxiety under control.

The next test, presented in personal inventory 3, will help you pinpoint the more specific form of anxiety that seems to be your problem. It is *not* a comprehensive diagnostic tool and is designed only to give a general idea of the type of anxiety present.

Because of space limitations, this test concerns itself with only five types of anxiety. There are other types also, including variations of these five, and the various types of anxiety also overlap each other. For example, stress-related anxiety and panic attacks are very closely related. Forms of anxiety in which certain behaviors or psychological defenses prevent the overt expression of anxiety (such as in denial or obsessive-compulsive behaviors) do not lend themselves to "self-diagnosis" so cannot be reduced to a simple questionnaire. They need professional evaluation and will be discussed later.

In this test, answer yes or no to each of the questions, then total the number of yes answers (abbreviated as Y) under *each* of the five categories.

The interpretation of this test can be a little tricky, especially since, for many anxiety sufferers, more than one type of anxiety often exists.

Personal Inventory 3
PINPOINTING YOUR TYPE OF ANXIETY

This questionnaire is divided into five sections, each corresponding to a particular type of anxiety. Answer yes (Y) or no (N) to each question and then total the number of Ys for each section.

I. STRESS-RELATED ANXIETY

	(Y)	(N)
1. I have problems with sleep (falling asleep or staying asleep).		
2. I have ulcers or severe stomach acidity.		
3. My blood pressure is higher than normal.		
4. I often experience a "racing sensation" or excitement, even without cause.		
5. My heartbeat seems to be fast a lot of the time.		
6. My heart seems occasionally to skip beats, or give an extra jump.		
7. I often experience diarrhea.		
8. I often have headaches.		
TOTAL NUMBER YS		

II. FEARS AND PHOBIAS

	(Y)	(N)
1. I have a fear of closed places, elevators, or being in strange places.		
2. I have a fear of birds, blood, or animals.		
3. I have a fear of cemeteries, germs, or sick people.		
4. I have an intense fear of high places, deep water, or airplanes.		
5. I hate speaking or performing in front of people.		
6. I dislike social settings or having to make small talk.		
7. I believe that most of my fears are irrational.		
8. I have had my fears since childhood.		
TOTAL NUMBER YS		

Personal Inventory 3 *(Continued)*

III. PANIC ATTACKS

		(Y)	(N)
1.	I have had an apparent heart attack that turned out to be nothing serious.		
2.	I experience shortness of breath or a smothering sensation from time to time.		
3.	I have experienced choking sensations and had difficulty swallowing.		
4.	I periodically experience chest pains or discomfort.		
5.	I sweat a lot.		
6.	I have become dizzy or faint and felt very unsteady.		
7.	I have been overcome with trembling and shaking.		
8.	I have had times when I feared I was going to die, go crazy, or do something I couldn't control.		
	TOTAL NUMBER YS		

IV. AGORAPHOBIA

		(Y)	(N)
1.	I fear being in places or situations from which escape is difficult.		
2.	I cannot travel too far from home without becoming very fearful.		
3.	I prefer having someone to accompany me to the supermarket, church, or other public place.		
4.	I intensely dislike traveling in a bus, train, or car.		
5.	I worry a lot about being alone or not having a companion who can assist when I need help.		
6.	Gradually through my life I have become more and more restricted in what I do or where I go.		
7.	I anticipate with dread all activities that I associate with anxiety.		
8.	I am becoming increasingly dependent on others to do my shopping or other chores.		
	TOTAL NUMBER YS		

Personal Inventory 3 *(continued)*

V. GENERALIZED ANXIETY   (Y) (N)

1.	For longer than six months I have been bothered by unrealistic or excessive worry.		
2.	I tremble, twitch, and feel shaky a lot.		
3.	I suffer from muscle tension, aches, or soreness.		
4.	I easily become fatigued.		
5.	I experience dry mouth quite often.		
6.	I experience diarrhea quite often (or more than occasionally).		
7.	I react when startled with an exaggerated response.		
8.	I have great difficulty concentrating, or my mind goes blank when I'm troubled.		
	TOTAL NUMBER YS		

Generally speaking, however, one type will predominate. Whichever of the five types of anxiety, identified with Roman numerals I through V, has the highest number of Ys is likely to be the *dominant form* of anxiety you suffer from. The next highest number of Ys will be the second dominant form, and so on down the list. If two (or more) have the same number of Ys, they may be codominant, or you may have a "mixed" form of anxiety disorder—which as I have already indicated, is quite common.

Please remember that these tests are merely guides to help you understand your unique form of anxiety. If they disturb you in any way, don't hesitate to see a professional (physician or psychologist). It is just possible that you are overinterpreting your responses. If you have calmly and honestly answered the tests, you should now have a much clearer picture of just how anxiety prone you are. As we proceed it will become clearer to you whether you need to make changes to your life or personality and where and how this can be done.

SPECIFIC FORMS OF ANXIETY

In addition to the general anxiety features already described, there are several very specific forms of anxiety that are quite common. They are worthy of brief discussion so that you may determine whether any or all of these are a problem to you:

(1) *Separation anxiety.* This is an anxious response to the absence of familiar people or places. It often occurs in children who are separated from parents for more than a few days or when older children are sent away to summer camp or boarding school. When young children are abandoned by parents or even when they are left alone a lot, they develop an anxiety reaction to this separation which may stay with them well into adult life.

I have personally been very aware of my propensity toward anxiety separation. As a young adult, I noticed that whenever I went on a business trip or to a convention without my wife, the experience of being in a strange city, in a strange hotel, and with strange people set up a high level of restless tension that I could not fully understand. I found myself going back to the hotel bedroom at various times through the day for no real reason other than to relieve my vague feelings of anxiety. Later in my life, I identified these feelings as related to separation from my wife and children and realized how this anxiety had been created in my early childhood.

Not too surprisingly, as soon as I recognized and labeled the problem it decreased dramatically. When I would begin to feel restless about being away from home, I would simply remind myself that my childhood feelings had no real substance now. There was no loss or separation to fear, nor would my loved ones abandon me just because I was temporarily away from them. Slowly the tendency toward separation anxiety has gone away. Often, all these feelings need is to be recognized—and then ignored!

(2) *Stranger anxiety.* Now, this is not a problem I suffer from, but there are many who do. Most children between eight months and two years go through a period of stranger anxiety in which they pull away from and are even frightened by strange faces. My granddaughter Nicole is now fifteen months old, and she is just getting over her fear of strangers—even of me, since I see her only once or twice a month. I suspect that if she lived further away, so that I only saw her once or twice a year, I would be even more of a stranger!

But stranger anxiety does not always stop in the second year of life. Some children continue to fear strangers all the way through to adult life. And this anxiety is more than just being shy in the presence of strangers. It is an acute sense of uneasiness that begins the moment one anticipates meeting a stranger and continues through until the stranger has gone away.

This type of anxiety reaction can be quite debilitating; the sufferer will often set up a complicated system of behavior so as to avoid encountering anything or anybody out of the ordinary.

(3) *Anticipatory anxiety.* Also known as "signal anxiety," this reaction occurs when one anticipates some event which is perceived to be threatening. Many of us experience this kind of anxiety when we think about going to the dentist. (Poor dentists! They are blamed more often than parents for causing neurotic behaviors.) Some feel it when they go for a driver's test or take an examination. Actors feel it before opening night and brides (and grooms) before their wedding day.

Much anticipatory anxiety is quite normal and easily coped with. We don't enjoy the feeling, but it does not prevent us from doing what must be done.

But for some people anticipatory anxiety becomes acute. The future situation is so feared that the anticipation of it is incapacitating. At the last minute, people like this will cancel the flight, the dental appointment, the examination, or even the wedding.

The question in such a situation becomes: Does the anxiety-based behavior have a justifiable reason behind it? Is it within the normal range of experience? For many who suffer from acute anticipatory anxiety, the answer is clearly no.

I suppose, for instance, that if you have experienced an airplane accident and escaped unharmed but very shaken, you could understandably cancel out on the next one or two flights. But if you feel this way four or five years later, your anxiety has clearly become abnormal.

So as you evaluate your own propensity toward anticipatory anxiety, keep in mind whether or not there is justifiable reason to feel this way. If there is, then chances are high that you will quickly recover from it. If there isn't, then you have a problem that needs to be worked on.

(4) *Excellence anxiety.* Now this is a new one, brought on in recent years by our culture's preoccupation with success and the pressure to be as "competent" as you possibly can be.

These days "excellence" is in! Everyone is concerned about it and, in many cases, desperately searching for it. Business organizations are conducting research on the achievement of excellence as a motivational force and how workers (usually more for the benefit of the company than for the individuals) can be helped to reach their "excellent" level.

This preoccupation with striving for excellence inevitably creates anxiety: "Will I make it?" "What if I fail?" "How can I know I'm being excellent?" "What if I turn out to be only second-best and someone else is better than me?" These are the questions of *excellence anxiety,* an uneasiness and tension that occurs when we fear we just might not make it or that someone else is going to win over us.

The mental and physical consequences of excellence anxiety are far more serious that most would think. This anxiety creates an intensified striving to succeed that feeds workaholism and is a major source of stress in the workplace. Certain personalities thrive on this challenge but don't realize just how damaging it can be to their minds and bodies.[1] The need for excellence and achievement is very threatening to some. Most people, even when they are being highly competent, never develop a feeling of "being excellent." Instead, they feel inadequate and inferior, and they fear someone will "find them out."

These feelings and fears have been exacerbated by changes in the American business climate over the past several decades. In an age of mergers, buy-outs, and "streamlining," many very competent middle-aged men and women have been let go by businesses and industries as a way of making room for younger (and often cheaper) executives. This has created an even greater load of excellence anxiety, and natural insecurity has been heightened. I know quite a few extremely capable and thoroughly excellent men and women who for arbitrary reasons have had their lifelong ambitions and accomplishments yanked away from them. Long service and faithful dedication to one's job no longer count for much in today's business world. The consequence is that the diseases of stress and anxiety are on the increase, and this trend promises to continue into the next decade.

(5) *Free-floating anxiety.* Not all problems with anxiety are tied to specific issues or life events. Very often the fear stimulus is unknown, or at least is not readily recognizable.

George, who serves as an associate pastor for a large suburban church, is a good example of someone with a free-floating anxiety problem. George has never been overly ambitious, but he has always sought to be conscientious and sincere, and no one has criticized the way he performs his duties. Nevertheless, he has a sense that perhaps he isn't quite up to the expectations of his senior pastor and some of the church leaders.

Of course, George will concede that he has always felt this way—that he doesn't quite measure up. And for years he has suffered from a variety of uncomfortable physical and mental symptoms.

George hates making mistakes, for example, and he spends a lot of time fantasizing how he would have done certain things differently. Occasionally he breaks out in a sweat, develops a dry mouth, and has some difficulty breathing. He develops headaches almost every Monday and feels weak all over after a busy Sunday. Frequently he feels lousy, and he tends to worry about things that never come to pass.

---

[1] For a more complete treatment of this topic, see my book, *The Hidden Link Between Adrenalin and Stress* (Waco, TX: Word, 1985).

Almost every staff meeting causes him anxiety because he doesn't know what is coming up. He hates surprises since they always throw him off balance. All this is capped with a tendency to be forgetful, to be easily distracted from what he should be doing. Most frightening of all to George are the frequent nightmares that disturb his sleep.

George suffers from a *free-floating* anxiety that has fastened itself to his work. He can't pinpoint any specific fear or reason for his feelings, but he lives with a general feeling that something is terribly wrong.

Other symptoms of this disorder include occasional pounding heart, intestinal disturbances, irritability, mild depression, and "freezing"— locking up emotionally to the point that thought or action is impossible. While most of these symptoms are not very severe in themselves, put together they can make life pretty miserable.

(6) *Generalized anxiety disorder.* The last of the specific forms of anxiety I wish to discuss here is that known as *generalized anxiety disorder.* In many ways it is very similar to that of free-floating anxiety, but there are enough differences to warrant putting it in a separate category. The symptoms are listed in Table 2.

Table 2
SYMPTOMS OF GENERALIZED ANXIETY DISORDER[2]

Frequency of symptoms in 100 cases of Generalized Anxiety Disorder:

Physical Symptoms	Percent	Psychological Symptoms	Percent
Inability to relax	97	Difficulty concentrating	86
Muscle tenseness	86	Fear of losing control	76
Fear	79	Fear of rejection	72
Jumpiness	72	Inability to control thoughts	72
Unsteadiness	62	Confusion	69
Overall weakness	59	Blurred mind	66
Sweaty hands	52	Inadequate memory	55
Terror	52	Fear of being attacked	35
Racing heart	48	Fear of dying	35
Flushed face	48	Stuttering	24
Difficulty breathing	35		
Frequent urination	35		
Nausea	31		
Diarrhea	31		
Faintness/dizziness	28		

[2] D. H. Barlow, ed., *Clinical Handbook of Psychological Disorders* (New York: Guilford Press, 1988).

I tend to believe that free-floating anxiety is tied to one's personality. If you suffer from free-floating anxiety, you tend to be that way all your life. You see *every* life event as a potential threat and consequently respond with worry and anticipation of pain or discomfort. Free-floating anxiety attaches itself to whatever object it pleases; you have no choice but to follow where it leads with worry and concern.

Generalized anxiety disorder, on the other hand, is not tied to your personality, but is the price you pay for being "overstretched." When things go wrong at a certain point in your life and you can't cope, your anxiety may become "generalized." You feel it everywhere from motor tension and trembling to feeling "on edge" and having difficulty in sleeping.

In free-floating anxiety, you attach the *meaning* of threat to everything. In generalized anxiety, the *symptoms* are attached to *all* parts of your mind and body.

Technically speaking, for "generalized anxiety" to be a "disorder," the symptoms must persist for at least six months, and the focus of worry must not be attached to any life circumstance. Also, the anxious feelings must not be related to any physical disorder. (I will discuss how physical disorders can cause anxiety reactions in the next section.)

PHYSICAL CAUSES OF ANXIETY SYMPTOMS

There is clear evidence that modern medicine often misdiagnoses biological disorders as anxiety reactions and vice versa. Between seventy-five and ninety-five physical conditions can mimic psychiatric disorders, and over fifty conditions specifically cause prominent anxiety symptoms. No discussion of anxiety can be complete, therefore, without recognition of these disorders.

Here is a short list of some major physical disorders that can mimic anxiety reactions:

- *Hyperthyroidism:* overactive thyroid gland,
- *Hypoglycemia:* low blood-sugar levels,
- *Thyrotoxicosis:* excessive thyroid hormone in blood,
- *Caffeinism:* overuse of caffeine (as in coffee, etc.),
- *Diabetes Mellitus:* disturbed insulin balance,
- *Depression:* serious mood disturbances,
- *Schizophrenia:* serious mental disturbance,
- *Psychomotor epilepsy:* epilepsy affecting one part of the brain,
- *High blood pressure:* elevated pressure in arteries,
- *Cerebral arteriosclerosis:* hardening of the arteries in the brain,

- *Alcohol withdrawal:* all withdrawals are anxiety producing,
- *Cocaine abuse:* overuse of cocaine,
- *Mitral valve prolapse:* a disorder of a heart valve,
- *Hyperventilation:* a disturbance of regular breathing.

This is by no means a complete list, so please consult your physician if you suspect that your problem may have a physical cause. (At any rate, most of the conditions listed require medical attention of some sort.)

It stands to reason that if you have a physical problem known to produce an exaggerated anxiety reaction, you should *first* have this problem attended to. It may very well be the *sole* cause of your anxiety problem. Even if it isn't the sole cause, it may be contributing directly or indirectly to the anxiety by weakening your tolerance for normal tensions.

An excellent example of how physical factors can bring on anxiety symptoms was reported recently in a psychiatric journal. The case concerned a woman (let's call her Evelyn) who loved diet colas, especially those sweetened with a particular artificial sweetener. Normally, she drank several cans a day. But then one day Evelyn took a job as a cook in a restaurant. The kitchen where she worked was unusually hot, and she perspired a lot, so she boosted her consumption of diet colas to twenty cans a day.

About a week later, Evelyn began to suffer anxiety attacks. She felt dizzy; her chest was tight, and it was hard to breathe. She knew enough to realize that her overconsumption of diet cola might be the problem, so she immediately cut back to three or four a day, and her symptoms disappeared. To test that this was really the reason for her anxiety, she went back up to twenty a day—and her symptoms immediately returned.

Evelyn was wise to be alert to possible physical causes for her anxiety. She saved herself a lot of trouble and money in not having to seek treatment. More important, she avoided being conditioned by her first few anxiety attacks into being an anxiety neurotic.

It has been estimated that up to 20 percent of patients under psychiatric care today are actually suffering from a *physical condition* of one sort or another. Who knows how many devout Christians are blaming themselves and their lack of faith for the psychological problems that may have a biological basis?

Help for your anxiety problem begins by honestly looking for the *primary* cause—whether that is physical, psychological, spiritual, or all three. As our discussion continues, I hope you will be able to sort out more effectively the cause and cure of your particular problem.

4 ANXIETY, GUILT, AND DEPRESSION

An understanding of the nature of anxiety is incomplete without consideration of its relationship to guilt and depression. The emotions of anxiety, guilt, and depression intermingle to such an extent that one cannot cope—or help someone else cope—with any one of them without explaining how the other two either aggravate or mask the first. In health and illness, anxiety, guilt, and depression are always experienced together to some degree. Those who seek psychological help frequently complain of feeling these emotions together. One may dominate over the others in the clinical picture, but the others are there either as shadows or mirror images.

There is something paradoxical about the coexistence of the three, at first glance. Anxiety seems to be directed at the future, while guilt feelings and depression point to the past. Anxiety seems to heighten nervous vitality, while the other two emotions seem to lower or remove it.

Actually, however, there is nothing mysterious about this. The human mind and body mingle emotions all the time, and the presence of one never rules out the presence of the others. Untangling the three of them is often necessary in order to gain mastery over each one. You need to know *when* you are dealing with each, *how* they differ, and *what* they do when you are caught in their trap. Freedom from their clutches can only come from taking control of their game!

It is not my purpose in this chapter to discuss either guilt or depression at any length. My primary emphasis is on anxiety, and I will limit my discussion of the other two emotions to showing how they relate to both healthy and unhealthy forms of anxiety.

First, I will discuss how *guilt* is caused and then how it creates anxiety. Then I will do the same for *depression*. Following this I will show how neurotic guilt and depression (as distinct from true guilt and depression) can interfere with healthy and constructive anxiety. Understanding this sequence is vital in achieving freedom from incapacitating anxiety, especially to those of us who are Christian believers. The creation and perpetuation of neurotic forms of anxiety, guilt, and depression is rife within our Christian subculture, and a turnaround of this situation is long overdue. We have a glorious and healthy gospel.

Let us preach and teach a healthier version of it to an age that is beleaguered by anxiety and guilt.

CAUSES OF GUILT

Guilt, like anxiety, is part of the price we humans pay for our superior psychological, spiritual, and intellectual abilities. To the best of our scientific knowledge, guilt is a specifically *human* emotion.

Now, you may have a much-loved cat that you believe you understand well. Occasionally, after you have caught her in the act of sharpening her claws on your best sofa and meted out the appropriate verbal or physical reaction, you may think you detect a glimmer of guilt in her eyes just before she scampers behind the piano or escapes into the garden. But don't trust your wishful perception. Your cat may have *looked* guilty, but in reality she lacks the mental capacity to know what is right from what is wrong. The look on her face (and her running away) is the result of conditioning, not conscience. True guilt is the blessing (or curse) of being human.

Guilt, in part, is a function of that part of the mind we call the "conscience," which, like a computer that has been programmed, plays back to us the way the brain has been programmed to judge right from wrong. But our conscience is more than a fantastic computer. I suppose it would be possible to program one of our modern large computers to become a "conscience." It could judge right from wrong and tell us what decision to make or direction to take in our lives, if it had all the right information. But no matter how sophisticated it was, such a computer would still lack one important feature: it would not be able to *feel* guilt.

And here is where humans are different, whether from cats or from computers: *They can feel their guilt*. They don't just "know" they are guilty in their brain; they hear guilt's throbbing in their hearts, they sense its condemnation in the pit of their stomachs, and they see its message in the tremor of their fingers. "I have done something that violates my integrity," they can say to themselves, and the evidence fills their being from top to toe. This is human guilt.

And we *do* feel it—when we disobey the law, when we fail to conform to the social expectations of our culture, when we violate those internalized rules of life that our parents bred into us, when we think we've displeased God, or when we refuse to give in to the request of some demanding friend.

The sense or "feeling" of guilt is evoked whenever an action or even a thought violates whatever authority we have identified with—or *internalized.* In other words, each of us constructs a set of standards for what is right or wrong out of our early experiences. We *learn* moral behavior; it is not programmed into us, although God has given us minds with the built-in *capacity* to know right from wrong.

Unfortunately, this "knowledge" or conscience is not always programmed consistently or correctly, so we can arrive at adulthood with all sorts of guilt distortions. Some people feel guilty about almost everything—how they talk, eat, relax, or even cross the street. Others have few guilt feelings about not paying their debts or even about robbing a bank. Consequently, our conscience or "feeling" of guilt is not very reliable; many adults have to set about reprogramming it to feel the appropriate amount of guilt.

The apostle Paul understood very well how unreliable the conscience can be. For instance, in 1 Corinthians 8:7, addressing the issue of eating food sacrificed to idols, he writes:

> However, some Christians don't realize this. All their lives they have been used to thinking of idols as alive, and have believed that food offered to the idols is really being offered to actual gods. So when they eat such food it bothers them and hurts their tender consciences. (LB)

Such a "tender conscience" is *not* God's voice of conviction. It is the product of environmental programming, of being taught what is right and wrong. And there are many parallels to this in modern-day Christianity.

On the other hand, a conscience can be "hard" or "seared." It can be programmed never to send a signal of violation, so that the person never knows he or she is doing wrong. So Paul writes to Timothy: "These teachers will tell lies with straight faces and do it so often that their consciences won't even bother them" (1 Tim. 4:2, LB).

Fortunately, God does not depend on our consciences to convict us or to teach what is right or wrong. First Timothy 4:1, which immediately precedes the verse quoted above, reminds us, "But the Holy Spirit tells us clearly. . . ." Jesus taught that one of the functions of the Holy Spirit is to guide us into all truth (John 16:13). In a nutshell: The Holy Spirit becomes our conscience and makes up for the deficiencies in our upbringing or our distorted consciences. What remains is for us to turn our spiritual ears to His voice.

UNDERSTANDING NEUROTIC GUILT

Much misunderstanding about guilt arises because we don't separate guilt as an emotion from guilt as a legal concept. The first is a "feeling," the second is a "state."

For example, if I accidentally drive through an intersection with a stop sign (as I have done a few times in my life), I may not "feel" very guilty. I could argue to the officer who stopped me (as I have done) that the stop sign was partly hidden behind a bush and that the road paint was mostly worn off. "If I had seen the sign I would have stopped," I could say in defense of my not feeling very guilty.

"I am sorry, sir," I would hear (and have heard) from an officer, "but you are still guilty. You have broken the law." He, of course, is referring to my *state* of guilt, which is different from my *feeling of guiltiness.*

Most times I *feel* guilty when I am in a *state* of guilt. This is normal and healthy. Let us suppose we were able to measure, quite independently, both our *feeling* of guilt and our actual *state* of guiltiness according to a scale ranging from 0 to 100 percent and then plot those measurements alongside each other on two vertical lines. The result would be a chart something like figure 3.

If we plot the example given above, where I didn't *feel* very guilty (let's give it a score of 10 percent) but was guilty to some extent (let's give it a score of 90 percent allowing for some bush covering and paint wear), we get the line marked "A."

Suppose, on the other hand, that I had a supersensitive conscience and drove through an intersection where there is no longer a stop sign, but where the road markings are such that I fear I *may* have broken the law. Afterward, I lie awake worrying, asking myself whether I should report my negligence to the local police, just in case I did something wrong. In such a case, my *feeling* of guilt could be 90 percent but my state of guilt may be zero. This would be line B.

Now, neither line A nor line B is healthy. Line A represents someone who is not owning up to true guilt. A person whose lifestyle is based on such a state would be described as "sociopathic"—lacking any conscience at all.

Line B, on the other hand, is "neurotic." The *feeling* of guiltiness far exceeds the *state* of guilt, and a lifestyle based on this kind of guilt will clearly be one in which anxiety is high and happiness low or nonexistent.

Ideally, we should seek to develop the relationship represented by line C, which shows a close correspondence between our *feeling* of guilt and our *state* of guilt. When these go together in harmony, we have a healthy conscience.

Paul understood this need for feelings to correspond to the state of guilt and described it clearly in Romans 2:12–15:

> He will punish sin wherever it is found. He will punish the heathen when they sin, even though they never had God's written laws, for down in their hearts they know right from wrong. God's laws are written within them; their own conscience accuses them, or sometimes excuses them (LB)

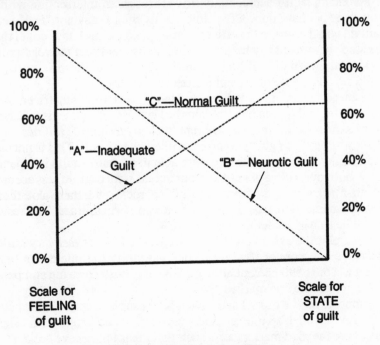

Figure 3: Understanding Guilt

God gave us a conscience, the ability to learn and know right from wrong. It is our responsibility to develop that ability in a healthy way, guided by the Holy Spirit, so that we might be faithful followers of His laws.

HOW GUILT CREATES ANXIETY

Because feelings of guilt are the result of violating our internalized sense of right and wrong, we might ask: what is it that directs us to change our behavior? Or, to put it another way, if I know I have done something wrong, what forces me to change? The answer: *anxiety.* The state of guilt sets up an emotional disturbance (anxiety) that is designed to move us forward in growth and change. Unfortunately it doesn't always do this. Often, because the conscience is "too tender" or is focused on exaggerating insignificant violations, it bogs us down in incapacitating anxiety, not the healthy kind of anxiety that prompts change.

Let me illustrate. I once counseled with a middle-aged man who, despite his competence in business and his success in accumulating a small fortune, was riddled with guilt feelings. He felt guilty when he threw away a half-eaten slice of toast, when he became slightly angry at someone, or when the conductor on a commuter train didn't take his ticket. He even felt guilty when he accidentally tramped on a spider and squashed it out of existence!

As we explored the origin of this man's overly tender conscience, we saw clearly that it had started in his childhood. His parents had been very strict, punishing him severely for every minor infraction. (Most times, they were reacting to their own guilt-ridden consciences.) Even though these people were Christians, they never taught or showed their son any forgiveness.

As a result of this guilt-inducing condition in childhood, my client was fragmented and distraught in middle adulthood. His anxiety reactions became severe. For instance, when he made a mistake like overcharging someone, he would be overcome by guilt and anxiety. But instead of letting this anxiety move him to make amends (returning the overcharge), he worried about further repercussions: "What if they tell the police?" "What if they think I did it deliberately?" This fed further anxiety into his system, until he finally collapsed with chest pains and had to be taken to the hospital. Of course, the "heart attack" he suffered was nothing more than a classic panic attack, although he often wished it would have been be fatal just to relieve his misery.

Severe forms of anxiety in reaction to guilt are experienced generally by people who are unable to receive forgiveness and whose consciences have been programmed to demand punishment. When their *feelings* of guilt exceed their *state* of guiltiness, the anxiety they feel is called "neurotic" or "false" guilt.

When the feeling of guilt matches the state of guilt—"true" guilt—and the person is able to respond to the anxiety of guilt by making amends and/or accepting forgiveness for the violation, the result is a "healthy" conscience and a happy person. I will have more to say about this later, but let us thank God that His plan of salvation brings to us a healthy program of forgiveness and restoration.

ANXIETY AND DEPRESSION

Psychologists have long been aware of a close connection between anxiety and depression in clinical populations. Often psychologists and psychiatrists inappropriately diagnose anxiety as depression, and vice versa. The relationship between depression and anxiety is complex. Sometimes the depression is part of the stress that creates the anxiety. At other times, anxiety sets up the depression, creating confusion, loss of confidence, and a feeling of hopelessness. It is also possible that both depression and anxiety have common denominators.

Broadly speaking, depressions fall into three categories depending on how they are *caused:* psychological (the mind and emotions are reacting to some event in one's life), biological (something is wrong with the body chemistry), and disease (some illness is causing the body to become depressed to aid in the healing process).

The first of these, the psychological, also includes spiritual causes of depression and is the one I am focusing on here. Biological depressions (sometimes called "endogenous depressions") are understood to be caused by defects in the body's biochemistry, especially the neurotransmitters, and are best treated by combining antidepressant medications with psychotherapy.

Disease-induced depressions are dealt with by treating the illness causing the depression. For example, once the "flu" passes off, the accompanying depression also lifts.

Psychological depressions are generally called "reactive," because they are reactions to what is going on in a person's life. For instance, if I am a farmer and experience a drought during a critical growth phase for my crops, I am likely to become depressed. If I am fired from my job or a friend leaves to live in another country or my elderly mother dies, I am also likely to become depressed.

These life experiences all have one thing in common: They are experiences of *loss.* And loss—recognized or unrecognized—is the root cause of all reactive depression. This loss can be a real and tangible (such as loss of income from being fired), abstract or symbolic (such as the loss of respect or esteem I might feel when I am fired), or a combination of both. The normal purpose of the depression is to slow our bodies down and give us time to accept and adjust to the loss.

I drove to a store recently to buy some clothing. Being in a hurry, I jumped out of the car without bothering to lock the doors and rushed into the store. It was only after selecting my items and going to the cashier counter that I realized I was missing the leather case in which I carry my checkbook, glasses, credit cards, and some cash. Abandoning my purchases, I rushed back to the car, but the case was not there.

I was devastated. I had lost my case once before, and I knew how inconvenient and time-consuming the consequences would be. My mind began to race. Could I have left the case at home? I rushed to a telephone to call my wife. No case there.

I started to feel depressed (for me, depression usually starts in the pit of my stomach). I might as well face it—the case was gone! Then I also noticed that my anxiety was up. What about the checkbook and credit cards, I worried? If the case had been stolen, could I be robbed even more? How quickly could I stop the thief?

My anxiety, fortunately, won out over my depression and mobilized me into action. I returned to the telephone and, preparing for the worst, canceled credit cards, made a police report, and notified the bank. The next day the store found my case complete with credit cards, checkbook—everything except the cash. My depression and my anxiety then began to subside—but that's another story!

The connection between depression and anxiety is similar to that between guilt and anxiety. All three are designed to help us know when something is wrong. If we do something wrong, we respond with guilt and then anxiety. If we suffer a loss, we react with depression and anxiety. Anxiety mobilizes us to try to restore the loss. Depression starts the grieving process to help us come to terms with the loss.

GUILT, DEPRESSION, AND DESTRUCTIVE ANXIETY

As long as the anxiety triggered by guilt and depression moves us toward constructive action, it is normal, healthy, and necessary. The *message* of anxiety may be very important in these instances and needs to be heeded because it is constructive and positive. Unfortunately, however, there are times when anxiety paralyzes us and makes us ineffective, when it creates intense fear and emotional pain. In such cases, the anxiety is destructive.

Under what conditions are we likely to experience this destructive form of anxiety? My observation from years of psychotherapy suggests that destructive anxiety results from "neurotic" forms of guilt or depression.

Let's take the example of neurotic guilt. I suggested in an earlier section that neurotic guilt is characterized by an inability to receive forgiveness. When we experience neurotic guilt, we don't really *want* to be let off or forgiven; we unconsciously desire to be punished for our sin (real or supposed).

I know of a case in which a Catholic woman felt compelled to go to confession six or seven times every week because she felt guilty about almost everything she did. If she walked past a beggar without giving something, she felt guilty. If she drank a cup of coffee, she felt guilty. Getting on the train, going shopping, doing her taxes, going to see a movie—you name it, she would be overcome with guilt about some aspect of the experience.

This lady's experience of guilt was clearly neurotic. Its effect was illness, not health. This woman was not a devout Catholic seeking to be righteous; she was a neurotic seeking to punish herself. The anxiety she felt was as unhealthy as her guilt, because it moved her only toward obsessional preoccupation with herself, not toward making amends.

Depression can also be neurotic, and can breed destructive anxiety. Let me hasten to remind you, however, that both depression and anxiety can be biologically based. The label of "neurotic" *does not* apply to every experience of depression or anxiety—or even most of them. Neurotic depression, in fact, is really not depression at all, although it may have started as depression. What I term "neurotic depression" is learned behavior, a lifestyle in which the victim tries to avoid life's realities.

Let's take Mary as an example. When her husband first brought her to see me, she sat quietly in the reclining chair, only giving a brief yes or no to my questions. She refused to talk, and whenever I pushed her to respond to something her husband said, she would simply reply, "Whatever he says!"

Mary certainly seemed depressed. She acted lethargic and appeared to take no interest in anything. Her husband explained that she hardly ever got out of bed, except for very basic necessities. When he came home from work, she would still be in her nightclothes, and very seldom did she prepare a meal.

After meeting with Mary alone for a few sessions, I came to understand that Mary had slowly developed this lifestyle as a defense against the demands of her husband, who was the authoritarian type. In the early days of their marriage, he gave her long lists of things to do, then ranted and raved if she did not complete the list. Mary, convinced she could do nothing to please him, became depressed. And then she found that her depression relieved the intense anxiety she felt about trying to live up to her husband's demands. She discovered that if she stayed in bed and did nothing at all, less was expected of her. So she literally just "copped out" of life as her way of avoiding anxiety.

Unfortunately, however, Mary really did not escape her anxiety at all; her neurotic depression merely turned her anxiety against her. Lying in bed all day, she had time to think, and her vivid imagination only turned up more anxiety—but the depressive lifestyle she had developed prevented her from acting on that anxiety. As a result, she became more and more immobilized and trapped by her condition. She was unable to move or take any constructive action because her foot was on both the brake and the accelerator at the same time.

Both neurotic guilt and neurotic depression remove from us a healthy anxiety that would spur us to corrective behavior and replace it with a destructive anxiety that immobilizes us or sabotages change.

They become a way of relating to the world that prevents us from becoming mature—either psychologically or spiritually! And because these states of being easily become entrenched in our personalities, they usually require intense and prolonged psychotherapy. The earlier in life they are recognized and corrective steps initiated, the better the prognosis. If someone you knows suffers from either neurotic or excessive guilt or depression, encourage that person to seek professional help as soon as possible.

5

Of all anxiety disorders, panic attacks have received more attention than any other. This is partly because they are the easiest of the anxiety disorders to understand—their symptoms are more or less consistent from person to person—and partly because they are so common—their incidence increases dramatically each year. Recent research by the National Institute of Mental Health shows that in North America anxiety disorders of the panic variety are the *number-one* mental-health problem among women and are second only to drug and alcohol abuse among men.

Some four to ten million Americans, mostly women in the childbearing years, experience panic attacks every year.[1] And these are mostly high achievers—highly educated and very competent people. They have histories of strong personalities, above average abilities, and a high tolerance for stress—until their first attack of panic.

Peter's experience is typical. At twenty-eight years of age, he was completing an advanced degree in engineering. One fine spring day, he sat down with a group of other students to take an examination. Little did he realize how that day would change the course of his life. Just as he was nearing completion of the examination, which up to that point was going well for him, Peter felt a sudden surge of fear:

"For no apparent reason and right out of the blue, I felt overwhelmed by an intense panic feeling. Something very bad, very evil, was going to happen," he related afterward. "My heart started to race. I could hardly breathe; it felt like someone was shutting off the air to my lungs. My chest was tight, like a steel band was around it. I got scared. Man, did I get scared!"

A friend helped Peter to his car and took him to the hospital, fearing he was having a heart attack. (Very often a panic attack simulates a heart attack: pain in the chest, difficulty breathing, and a sense of impending death.) But after a thorough physical evaluation Peter was sent home; there was nothing wrong with his heart!

For months Peter worried about this experience. Was he going crazy? Was he simply a weak person? Would he have another attack?

---

[1] *Psychology Today* (March 1989), 80.

56

Personal Inventory 4
ARE YOU EXPERIENCING A PANIC ATTACK?

This inventory can help you decide if you are experiencing a panic attack. It can be used to evaluate a previous experience, but its primary purpose is to examine a set of feelings you are presently experiencing. If you suspect that you suffer from panic attacks, make a copy of this test and carry it with you. As soon as you feel the attack coming on, take out the test and score yourself on each item according to the following scale.

0 = Not at all—or can't tell.
2 = Slightly—not enough to be bothersome.
3 = Severely—I am afraid of the symptom.

	Score
1. Is your heart palpitating?	
2. Are you having difficulty breathing?	
3. If you hold your breath, do you feel an immediate urge to breathe?	
4. Do you feel dizzy or lightheaded?	
5. Do you feel detached from any part of your body?	
6. Are you sweating?	
7. Do you feel shaky, or are you trembling?	
8. Do you have an urge to urinate?	
9. Do you feel some terrible thing is about to happen?	
10. Do you feel nauseous?	
TOTAL SCORE (Maximum is 30)	

Score   Evaluation

0-5   You are not likely to be experiencing a panic attack.

6-10   You may be experiencing a mild panic attack, or the attack is only in an early stage.

11-15 You are experiencing a mild to moderate panic attack. Be on guard in case it gets worse, and get help if you feel out of control.

16-20 You are experiencing a moderate panic attack. Since it may get worse, seek help right away.

20-   You are experiencing a major panic attack. You should seek professional help immediately.

These are questions that plague all panic attack sufferers. Fortunately, the outlook is good. With early identification and aggressive treatment that includes both drug therapy and psychotherapy, Peter can look forward to a life relatively free of any recurrence.

There is a price to be paid, however. Peter will have to work conscientiously at overcoming his problem and pursue the right form of treatment. If he doesn't, chances are that over time he will suffer recurrent and worsening panic attacks or even develop agoraphobia (the fear of being in places or situations from which there is no escape).

A BRIEF HISTORY OF PANIC DISORDERS

The origin of the word *panic* is interesting and may tell us something of the history of the disorder. Pan was the mythical Greek god of fertility. He was depicted as a merry but ugly man with the horns, ears, and legs of a goat. The ancient Greeks believed that when this god was feeling fractious, he loved to frighten unwary travelers. Therefore, the traveler who feared going on the road again after a frightening, unexplained experience was thought to have been visited by Pan in one of his ill-tempered moods—hence the word *panic.*

The very existence of the word suggests to some that panic attacks have been around a long time. This is possible, of course, but I am convinced that the nature of panic attacks has changed significantly in recent years. Recognized at least since the era of the Civil War, the modern panic anxiety disorder was first linked to the exhaustion that overtakes soldiers when they are subjected to life-threatening events and prolonged physical exertion—hence one of its best-known names, "soldier's heart." During the First World War, soldiers who suffered from panic disorders were devastatingly numerous, presumably because the nature of that war was such that it created intense fear in soldiers. The Vietnam War had a similar profound effect on soldiers. Wherever hand-to-hand combat predominates, so does panic disorder.

What is interesting to me is that, apart from war, there is little evidence of panic anxiety in earlier times; it does not seem to have been a problem of ordinary life. I know of no record of a panic anxiety attack in the Bible, for instance, and peacetime references to them in other literature all postdate the industrial revolution.

What this says to me is that our modern lifestyle has taken on the character of warfare. The battles being raged are more symbolic than physical in their threats, and the struggle is more with achievement and status (on the one hand) or survival in a drug-infested ghetto (on the other) than with surviving an enemy's sword. But to our bodies and emotions, war is war! Despite our relative safety and the relative absence of real physical threats in modern life, panic disorders are on the increase. The reason: The stress of modern life is as devastating as fighting a battle. It certainly feels that way to me.

WHAT CAUSES A PANIC ATTACK?

Despite our dramatic progress in *treating* panic disorders in recent years, we still don't know a lot about precisely what causes this disorder. The fact that certain drugs can block and relieve panic attacks suggests they have a strong biochemical component, but at the moment we know more about *which* drugs work than about *why* they work.

We also know that psychological (and possibly spiritual) factors play a role in setting up the disorder as well as in precipitating a given attack. The mind and body are one unit, and it is almost impossible to separate emotional factors from physical ones. In every emotional problem, the body contributes something and the mind contributes something. Like a pair of dancers, they move together to fashion a pattern of feelings. In panic attacks, these dancers combine their movements into an intricate ballet of emotional pain and physical discomfort.

All this is to say that while in this chapter I will focus at times on the biochemical mechanisms at work in panic, we should not forget the significant role of the psychological and spiritual dimensions. While a given hormone may take the starring role at times, the supporting cast is made up of how life is being lived and how thoughts are evaluating the action offstage.

The key to long-term recovery from a panic disorder may initially lie with the relief that medication can bring in substituting for a missing natural tranquilizer and in suppressing our adrenaline response, but sooner or later we must give attention to changing how our mind works and reorganizing our values and life pursuits. As shown in chapter 1, one cannot live on antianxiety drugs forever.

Even though we don't know exactly what causes a panic attack, two factors seem to contribute to the onset of panic:

- Prolonged life stress, not necessarily of the catastrophic kind but including the stress of high demand, continued excitement, and sustained overarousal of the adrenal system.
- The development (sometimes inherited) of increased sensitivity of a number of important receptors within the body and brain.

Since both of these have implications for understanding panic attacks, as well as for designing a management strategy, I will discuss each of them in more detail.

(1) *Life stress.* For many years, researchers have been fascinated by the connection between stressful life events and the onset of panic attacks. Many studies assessing their relationship have found an abnormally high incidence of stressful life events immediately preceding the first panic attack. One study reported that 91 percent of these attacks had been preceded by stress. Another found an incidence of 96 percent.

The main problem with this research (even though the findings are conclusive) is that there is still a tendency to think of "stress" as relating only to the unpleasant or catastrophic events of life. As I tried to show in my book, *The Hidden Link between Adrenalin and Stress,* the stress that kills us is not the stress of crises; these are short lived and unpleasant enough that we try to avoid them. The stress that does us in is the stress of challenge, high energy output, and overcommitment. These demand as much adrenaline as do fears and threats. And because we enjoy the arousal they bring, we may actually become adrenaline addicts—and move closer to the point where panic may become a possibility.

Prolonged stress—pleasant or unpleasant—wears down the system. It exhausts our supply of adrenaline (an important hormone for fighting stress) and, most important of all, depletes the *natural tranquilizers* in our brain that help us keep calm and go about our business in a controlled manner. When this happens, we become prone to panic.

I have already given a brief explanation of how these natural brain tranquilizers work (see chapter 1), but allow me to expand briefly on this topic here since it is so relevant to understanding why we slip into a panic mode.

Perhaps the most famous of all external tranquilizers is Valium. Since it was first introduced, this drug has been a godsend in many ways, a bringer of peace to troubled minds. It has brought problems, too, as many who became dependent on it will attest. Nevertheless, it has worked miracles in helping people cope with anxiety disorders.

At the time Valium was discovered and released, we did not fully understand why it worked. It was several years before researchers cottoned on to the reason: Valium calms the brain because the brain has receptors that are sensitive to a *natural* substance within the brain that resembles Valium. The human-made substance works because it is identical (or nearly so) to a natural brain substance.

This realization revolutionized our understanding of brain medications. It also pointed toward a probable cause of panic attacks: Since Valium (and now more potent tranquilizers such as Xanax) block receptors and stop panic attacks, it is very possible that the attacks are brought on in the first place by a deficiency of natural tranquilizer. One way of looking at panic disorder, therefore, is to see it as a "deficiency" disease, much like diabetes, which is a deficiency of insulin.

The deficiency of natural tranquilizers, in turn, can likely be caused by the body's being preoccupied with prolonged stress and "emergency" living. It follows, therefore, that stress needs to be brought under control before any "cure" for panic disorders can be effected.

(2) *Increased receptor sensitivity.* Interacting with the decrease in natural brain tranquilizer brought on by life stress is another phenomenon that seems to contribute to the onset of panic attacks: Certain important receptors (known as "chemoceptors") within the body show increased sensitivity. They become "raw" and easily aggravated.

It is here that genetics may contribute some influence. Studies of the families of those who suffer from panic suggest that relatives are more likely to suffer similar attacks than are those with no family history of such attacks. Also, identical twins, who share the same genetic makeup, are more likely to suffer from similar panic attacks than are fraternal twins, who share parentage and life circumstances but have different genetic combinations.

The tendency for certain individuals to develop increased receptor sensitivity in response to stress or as the result of genetic influence accounts for why stress may produce panic attacks in some people and not in others. The next three sections will elaborate further on this idea of "receptor sensitivity."

PANIC AND HYPERVENTILATION

Hyperventilation is an involuntary reaction in which one breathes either faster or more deeply than normal, raising the oxygen level in the blood. The connection between uncontrollable hyperventilation and panic attacks is well established. In fact, many of the symptoms of a panic attack are the same as those for hyperventilation. Both can occur after muscular exertion or while falling asleep or waking up. One hardly ever sees a panic disorder without also seeing a tendency toward hyperventilation.

What causes hyperventilation? There are several mechanisms. One natural mechanism is an inordinately high concentration of carbon dioxide in the blood, as when one is exercising excessively. Stepped-up breathing follows, and this brings more oxygen into the blood to counteract the carbon dioxide. When there is no actual physical need to fight or flee, the body is left with too much oxygen, and hyperventilation may result. There are three possible ways in which hyperventilation can be connected to panic:

(1) *Hyperventilation can cause panic.* Many panic-prone people can actually trigger a panic attack by deliberately increasing the rate and depth of their breathing. I have sometimes done this with a patient to show how a panic can be triggered—and how it can be stopped by breathing into a brown paper bag to increase the level of carbon dioxide in the blood.

(2) *Panic can cause hyperventilation.* This is just as possible. The inhalation of carbon dioxide (the reverse of hyperventilation) is also known to cause panic attacks in certain subjects. When these people panic, they don't breathe in more oxygen, but less, and this upsets the balance of gases in the blood, starting a panic attack. Research at Massachusetts General Hospital has shown that even moderate amounts of carbon dioxide can cause panic attacks in certain individuals who are so predisposed. Normal subjects are not affected. Does this contradict the first cause mentioned above? Not at all. I believe it merely indicates that we may have two *different* forms of panic attack—the one triggered by too much oxygen, the other by too much carbon dioxide.

(3) *Both disorders have a common cause.* The striking similarity between panic and a predisposition to hyperventilate most likely points to both having a common cause. In other words, the same physical or genetic mechanism that causes a person to be panic-prone also makes that person likely to hyperventilate.

PANIC AND EXERCISE

Exercise is another factor that has been linked to certain kinds of panic attacks. This is important to recognize, because panic sufferers often assume that what they need is more exercise—and this can have disastrous results for some people.

Here's a typical scenario: Tom is a thirty-five-year-old engineer. His work is quite demanding, with periods of intense stress when he has to prepare designs and cost estimates to meet bid deadlines. About once every month for the past year, he has had a severe emotional and physical reaction whenever he tried to do physical work such as heavy gardening or when he tried to exercise for fitness. Usually the bad reaction to exercise occurs after a period of intense work, late nights, and travel. He feels he should exercise—but the more he tries to do something physical, the more he experiences the panic reactions, which leave him feeling weak all over, panicky, and dizzy.

At first Tom thought he was having heart problems, but extensive physical tests ruled this out. Tom finally concluded that he just had a low tolerance for physical exertion and would have left it there if his wife hadn't insisted that he come to see me.

Tom suffers from an interesting form of panic attack characterized by a very low tolerance for physical exercise. Any exertion beyond even a mild level produces a panic reaction accompanied by lethargy—an important signal that many should heed. During the 1940s, several researchers observed that exercise intensified the symptoms of panic in people with chronic anxiety. These patients also had higher levels of lactic acid in their blood. The higher the level of lactic acid, the greater the discomfort of the anxiety. People without the tendency to high anxiety experienced no such discomfort with exercise.

Many years later, Dr. Ferris Pitts of the University of Southern California used these findings to show that injecting sodium lactate (the same as lactic acid) into the bloodstream of both chronic-anxiety sufferers and those without chronic anxiety produced panic in the chronic-anxiety group, but did nothing to the non-anxious group. When he set up a steady flow of sodium lactate to anxiety sufferers, he discovered he could start and stop the panic merely by turning the flow on and off.

This discovery provided a useful way of researching panic anxiety and opened up a technique for diagnosing this particular type of panic disorder. The use of sodium lactate to provoke a panic attack is sometimes referred to as a *challenge test*. The procedure begins with the infusion of a placebo (saline). Then at a given moment, unknown to the patient, sodium lactate replaces the placebo. A panic attack following the infusion of the sodium lactate confirms the diagnosis of this particular disorder.

Since vigorous exercise produces lactate buildup in the blood, any sensitivity to exercise, low exercise tolerance, or obvious evidence of a panic reaction following physical exertion should be taken as evidence of a possible lactate-sensitive panic disorder and referred to a physician, who may require severe restrictions on exercise. Treatment needs to focus on the underlying lactate sensitivity and a very carefully controlled and gradual program of increasing exercise designed to raise the tolerance for physical exertion. Careful management of stress and avoidance of stimulants is essential.

PANIC AND CAFFEINE

Panic attacks have been associated not only with hyperventilation and sodium-lactate sensitivity, but also with certain common chemical substances that have been shown to aggravate the problem when they are present in the bloodstream. King among the suspects is caffeine—that ingredient of coffee, tea, and cola drinks that has the power to hook us in a form of addiction we don't readily admit. Caffeine is so powerful that it should be considered a drug of the stimulant class.

It is believed that caffeine, lactate, and carbon dioxide act on sensors called *chemoceptors*. These sensors work like smoke detectors to monitor conditions such as the acidity of the blood. Normally, these detectors sound their alarms and produce changes to restore chemical balance whenever there is a buildup of a toxic substance. Panic is part of this "alarm" system; in "normal" situations the chemoceptors create panic as a warning that something is seriously wrong with the chemical makeup of the blood.

In someone who suffers from a panic disorder, however, there may be a faulty or oversensitive chemoceptor that "sounds the alarm" and creates panic when there is no reason for it—much like a faulty smoke detector. I know all about this! Just recently I had to replace all the smoke alarms in my home because they kept giving me "false signals." If only we could replace the faulty chemoceptors in panic disorders!

Another substance that is thought to increase the sensitivity of the chemoceptors and thus worsen panic is progesterone, the sex hormone. Since the level of progesterone in the blood increases in menstruation, this link may explain why women suffer more from panic attacks than men and why "premenstrual syndrome" (PMS) is characterized by many of the symptoms of panic attacks: anxiety, irritability, nausea, headaches, and lightheadedness (see discussion on PMS below).

The connection between panic and progesterone is just speculation at this point. However, the evidence against caffeine is much stronger. Clearly it is a major aggravator, if not precipitator, of panic attacks in panic-prone subjects. Furthermore, it inhibits the effect of commonly prescribed tranquilizers and so can work against medical treatment for panic attacks. Caffeine can even produce panic attacks in people not normally subject to them—all it takes is approximately ten cups of coffee. While the research is still formative, it seems very clear that panic-disorder patients should be advised to restrict or eliminate their caffeine consumption.

Caffeine may not affect normal subjects at lower levels of ingestion, but a study by the National Institute of Mental Health has shown that as few as four cups of coffee can sharply increase blood levels of a stress hormone called cortisol, as well as sodium lactate, the substance already known to cause panic attacks. (It can also produce a "caffeine buzz" and a slight tremor.) And while the study showed that the rise of these substances is substantially greater for panic-prone people, it happened in non-panic-prone people as well. It would therefore seem advisable for all of us to limit or at least monitor our intake of caffeine, particularly during times of stress.

Despite caffeine's powerful connection with anxiety in general and panic attacks in particular, its use is so common and acceptable, that few people have any idea how much caffeine they consume each day.

One patient I was seeing for minor panic attacks insisted that his consumption of coffee was normal. His attacks, which had begun about three months before, were now occurring two or three times a week and were so severe that they were interfering with his work. I suggested to him that he had increased his coffee intake about the time the attacks started, but he refused to see any connection, insisting, "I don't drink that much coffee."

After I insisted that he record on a three-by-five card every cup of coffee he drank, we discovered (to his surprise) that he was consuming about twelve cups of strong coffee a day. He was so wrapped up in his work that he paid no attention to his coffee-drinking habit.

My client found out, in addition, that the person who used to make the coffee in his office had left about three months before without telling the office she always made decaffeinated coffee. The person who took over the chore only drank "real" coffee, and similarly never bothered to tell anyone of the change.

Switching back to decaffeinated coffee stopped the panic attacks for my client, although he continued to work with me for awhile on other lifestyle issues that affected his panic problem.

Coffee and tea, of course, are major sources of caffeine in many people's diets. One serving of instant coffee contains 66 milligrams of caffeine per serving, while percolated coffee contains 110 milligrams —the drip method pushes it up to 146. But coffee is not the only caffeine-loaded substance we ingest. Tea provides a little less caffeine —about 23 milligrams of caffeine after one minute of brewing or 46 after five minutes. Cocoa and many soft drinks also contain relatively high amounts of this drug, as do many nonprescription medications. One "over the counter" stimulant, for example, has 200 milligrams of caffeine in each capsule (why do you think it keeps you awake?); many painkillers and cold medications also contain it. It's important to read the label on the bottle before you buy!

To control your caffeine intake, either eliminate all foods, beverages, and medications containing it (if necessary, switch to decaffeinated coffee, tea, and soft drinks). Or carefully write down all you ingest during the course of a day and limit your quota. You can then see how closely caffeine relates to your anxiety and then make the changes you think are necessary.

I would add a word of caution. Stopping caffeine is like stopping any drug—you can have withdrawal symptoms. You may want to gradually reduce your intake over a week or two rather than go "cold turkey."

PANIC AND DIET

Most of us have a great appreciation for how diet affects physical health, how it causes high blood pressure and heart disease, and how it affects our sleep. But there is not a lot of understanding of how diet affects our moods and emotions, especially anxiety. And we are not talking here about overeating, but how food directly affects our moods. Some people are so affected by certain foods or food additives or preservatives that even small amounts can cause anxiety symptoms. Whether or not this is some form of "allergic response" is not known at this stage, but the cure is obvious: avoid these foods.

For many people, sugar is a prime culprit in anxiety. This is because insulin, the substance which helps the body process sugar, is also a major biochemical correlate of anxiety. Anxious people often seek out foods high in sugar content, such as candy and cake. Not only do they crave the taste of sweet things, but they boost the level of sugar in the blood, triggering the release of insulin needed to counteract that high blood sugar. In many people, anxiety symptoms accompany these blood-sugar changes, which appear to impact mood. Therefore, controlling blood sugar is an important key to controlling anxiety in many sufferers. If you feel you have a problem in this area, consult your physician and ask for a diet that will stabilize your blood sugar. Your physician may suggest a "glucose tolerance test" as a way of ensuring that your system is working properly before starting you on any diet.

Sugar is not the only dietary substance that can contribute to anxiety in general and panic attacks in particular. People differ widely in their ability to tolerate dairy products such as cheese and buttermilk; canned, cured, or processed meats containing nitrates or nitrites; peanuts and peanut butter, marinated meats; yeast extracts; and MSG (monosodium glutamate, a "flavor enhancer" often used in Chinese food and found in many processed foods).

The only way you can find out if any of these substances affect you is to carefully observe the connection between eating any of them and the emergence of panic or anxiety symptoms. Experiment by omitting certain foods and see if you can avoid the anxiety symptoms. If you can—you have your answer, so abstain! The expert help of an allergist may also be a wise step.

Finally, much has already been published about the undesirability of both tobacco and alcohol. Both are used as tranquilizers, but neither are helpful in anxiety. Besides, the addictive properties of nicotine and alcohol far outweigh any minor beneficial effect they provide, and the emotional stress of addiction can aggravate a panic problem.

PANIC AND PREMENSTRUAL SYNDROME (PMS)

It seems that between 30 and 95 percent (depending on whose statistics you believe) of all healthy females may experience an increase in irritability, anxiety, and depression, in addition to physical discomfort, prior to menstruation. Usually the problem starts between five and seven days prior to the onset of menstruation, during what is known as the premenstrual phase, although it has been known to commence as early as fourteen days prior. The symptoms disappear during the week following the onset of menstruation.

There is no known cause of PMS, though it clearly has a biological basis and is an acknowledged syndrome. Stress seems to be a significant aggravating factor in *some* cases, but not all.

Of the two categories of symptoms that accompany PMS, physical and psychological, the psychological are the more devastating. Many women have been inappropriately branded as neurotic because the complexity of their body's function has not been understood. Failure to recognize the biological factors underlying mood changes at menstruation has caused much unnecessary suffering and inappropriate self-labeling. Professionals who fail to diagnose PMS correctly and label it as panic disorder can aggravate the problem.

How can one rule out PMS or differentiate PMS from panic disorder?

(1) *Keep careful records* of both your menstruation and your supposed panic or anxiety episodes. By matching the times of anxiety with the menstrual cycle, a clear picture of their connection should emerge after a couple of months.

(2) *See your physician* if you notice increased tenseness, restlessness, anxiety, instability, depression, crying, fatigue, confusion, forgetfulness, and difficulty in concentration during the week before your menstrual period

Even if you have a genuine panic disorder not directly due to PMS, it is possible that the stress of menstruation can be the precipitating factor. Many patients report a greater frequency of panic attacks during the menses. It is very possible, as indicated above, that hormonal changes underlie these attacks and increase the sensitivity of certain chemical receptors within the body. If you notice this connection, ask your physician for advice on your treatment.

PANIC AND DEPRESSION

While depression can sometimes accompany a panic disorder, they are usually distinctly different disorders. However, depression may complicate the panic and slow the recovery. Any depression lasting longer than two or three weeks, therefore, should be treated as a separate problem.

Fortunately, the use of antidepressant medication in lower doses has proved to be an effective way of treating panic attacks. If depression coexists, then, the physician may recommend that the antidepressant dosage be increased so as to treat both the panic disorder and the depression. Also, one of the tranquilizers used in panic disorders, Xanax, is also an antidepressant.

Depression can be the *consequence* of a panic disorder—a reaction to the loss of a sense of control over life—not just a coexisting condition. Such depression in turn tends to create a pervasive sense of personal worthlessness, negative outlook, and self-rejection that feeds the anxiety. Helping someone overcome anxiety when they have adopted a depressive attitude is difficult. They feel inadequate, hopeless, and unmotivated to change. In such a situation, there is only one advisable course of action: help from a competent therapist. Fighting depression *and* panic at the same time is more than any normal person can hope to cope with.

PANIC AND HYPOGLYCEMIA
(LOW BLOOD SUGAR)

There is much controversy in medical circles about this disorder. Although many people believe they suffer from hypoglycemia, it is really quite rare and is found mainly in diabetics. Symptoms include great physical discomfort, as well as increased anxiety and irritability, whenever the glucose level in the bloodstream is lower than normal (for example, just before the next meal).

When the symptoms of hypoglycemia are severe, they are indistinguishable from those of a panic anxiety: perspiration, anxiety, irritability, fast heartbeat, trembling, lightheadedness, weakness, and panic. They occur because the adrenal glands, in response to the low blood-sugar, release adrenaline to help the release of stored glucose. This adrenaline acts as a stimulant, creating the "fight or flight" emergency response. The result is a condition similar to, but not identical with, panic anxiety.

Hypoglycemic panic attacks often occur in the morning on waking, when blood sugar is lowest, or just before mealtimes. If you notice any pattern here, or if consuming sugar in some form (fruit juice, candy, or cake) seems to relieve the symptoms of an attack, you should report this to your physician. Hypoglycemia may be a complicating factor in, or possibly the sole cause of, your problem.

A positive diagnosis of hypoglycemia will at least point to the primary cause of the disorder.

COMPLICATED AND UNCOMPLICATED PANIC DISORDERS

Yet another facet of panic that must be understood is the fact that panic does not always exist as a "pure" phenomenon—a so-called "uncomplicated" panic disorder. More often, it is a "complicated" panic disorder—and oh boy, is it complicated!

The possible "complications" to panic include phobias, unreasonable fears such as agoraphobia, and other emotional problems such as obsessions, compulsions, and paranoia. The more complicating secondary problems there are, the more difficult it will be to bring the primary problem under control and the more essential it is to seek professional help.

The complicating factors of phobias and agoraphobia are less of a problem because they are likely to be linked directly to the panic problem. Phobias develop following panic attacks as the victim develops avoidant behaviors. If, for example, an attack occurs in a supermarket, the victim may come to associate supermarkets with bad feelings and will in the future avoid going into a supermarket. (Imagine if your wife or husband had an attack around you and believed you were the cause! It's a frightening thought—but I know of such a case.)

I will discuss these complications in more detail in chapters 6 and 8.

THE FEAR-OF-FEAR REACTION

Perhaps the most complicating factor of all in managing panic disorders is that the experience of a panic attack can be so frightening, even to the strongest and most resilient among us, that it sets up its own cycle of anxiety. In other words, the sufferer becomes so afraid of reexperiencing the panic attack that this fear itself becomes the source of further anxiety. This is known as the "fear-of-fear" reaction.

I have seen this reaction in many patients. One gentleman, a thirty-seven-year-old industrial chemist, became so afraid of his panic attacks that he would go nowhere—not to the supermarket, the post office, or even to the garage next to his house—unless he was accompanied by his wife. Her presence gave him comfort and helped quell his fear of his fear.

It is not hard to understand how this can happen. The sudden onset of the first attack is so frightening and the intensity of the experience so great that a sufferer never wants to repeat such an experience. When it does happen the second time, the fear of fear combines with fear that is inherent in the attack itself to create an ever-accelerating fear loop that almost guarantees that there will be a third, attack, a fourth one, and so on. Fortunately, this does not happen to every panic attack victim; if it did, few would ever recover.

How can this fear-of-fear reaction be prevented? I will cover this in detail in part 2, but here are the basic steps:

(1) *Reinforce the belief that nothing serious can happen.* Clearly the *first* and most important step is for the panic sufferer to obtain as much information as possible about the nature of the panic disorder and to frequently reinforce this understanding. For most panic sufferers, the most salient facts are that there are many variations of panic attack, that the mechanisms that trigger an attack can be identified and corrected, and—most important—that *no one dies from a panic attack.*

Again and again I hear myself saying this to a panic attack sufferer. It's true. If you suffer from a panic attack, you may wish you were dead, but the attacks themselves do not kill. Panic attacks are self-limiting; even if you hyperventilated until you were blue in the face (actually, it is lack of oxygen that turns you blue, not hyperventilation) the worst that can happen is that you might faint!

I tell my patients who suffer from panic attacks, therefore, to just keep reassuring themselves between attacks—to keep drumming away at the idea, "*Nothing serious can happen to me.*"

Many victims will end up in the emergency room repeatedly because they fear the worst. I would say that if you need that assurance, then by all means go to the trouble of getting it. But once you have clearly established that you have a panic disorder, try to reinforce your belief that nothing can happen and move to the next step.

(2) *Master panic-stopping techniques—and take your medicine!* The *second* step in preventing the fear-of-fear reaction is to master one of the techniques for stopping a panic attack that I will describe in part 2. In

addition, it is crucial to take any medication that has been prescribed! (We'll look at the issue of medication compliance a little later.)

TREATMENT CONSIDERATIONS

While I will provide a more extensive discussion of the treatment of anxiety disorders in part 2, it is appropriate that I provide some general guidelines here specifically for dealing with panic attacks. These guidelines should be taken in the context of part 2 and combined with the larger issues I will discuss there.

First, remember that achieving a reduction in the symptoms of panic may just be the first step toward a final cure, not a cure in and of itself. Relapses can and will occur and must be accepted as "par for the course." Faithful and persistent adherence to the principles of treatment is absolutely necessary. Most sufferers fail to find relief simply because *they give up too soon* or because they jump from one treatment to another. Make sure you give each strategy a fair chance. You will learn more quickly what the most effective treatment for your particular problem is if you follow through on each component before moving to the next.

Second, it is important to carry out any suggestions I make in this book in cooperation with whoever is treating you. If you suffer from a panic disorder, you need the objective guidance of a trained professional to coach you to success. The ultimate goal is to bring about a change in lifestyle so that the suggestions I will make become an essential part of your normal life. They should become so natural that you don't even have to think about them.

This means, among other things, cooperating with your physician in terms of medication. Panic attacks are so frightening and they so easily set up a fear-of-fear reaction that it is often necessary to bring the attacks under control with appropriate medication so as to reduce this fear and to facilitate healing.

There are several possible dangers in medication, of course. One is that the victim may feel so good on the medication that he or she loses interest in further addressing the underlying causes of the panic attacks. Lifestyle stress, immoral or abusive behaviors, or other issues may need to be evaluated, and without the "urgency" of the pain anxiety brings, the pressure may diminish. Even if you find relief in medication, *don't neglect these other important issues; if you do, you may find yourself in greater trouble later on when the medication must be stopped.*

An opposite danger is that a panic sufferer may resist taking the prescribed medication. Many well-meaning believers who suffer from panic attacks simply do not comply with their physician's prescriptions —to their own discomfort. Some are caught up with fears about becoming addicted to the medication. Others see their need for medication as a sign of spiritual failure or weakness and therefore resist taking their medicine.

Listen to me. These beliefs can easily be satanic in origin in that they are designed to keep you suffering and not help you master your affliction. God understands why you are suffering and wants your wholeness and happiness as much as you do. If a competent physician has prescribed appropriate medication and this medication will help to prevent an attack or ultimately cure you of your panic disorder, then you owe it to yourself and your loved ones not to sabotage the treatment. You play right into the hands of Satan if you continue to allow yourself to suffer and remain ineffective and miserable. As far as your fear of becoming addicted to the medication is concerned, I will have more to say about this later. While there may be a few who will abuse the medication and thus create a major dependency, most do not. Discuss your fear with your physician, if necessary, to be reassured on this point!

Of course, there are always those who refuse to take their medication because they are just plain stupid and self-destructive! They know they need the medication. They can see what happens when they neglect to take it. But they prefer misery to tranquillity, pain to calmness, and confusion over peace. They don't like being told what to do, and they resist every attempt to solve their problems. I can only hope that none of my readers are in this category, it is impossible to help a person who simply refuses to be helped!

One final note. Medication cannot remove or cure phobias when they are a complication of panic. These are *learned* fears, by and large, and pills won't fix them. Psychotherapy is the preferred form of treatment.

WHAT TO AVOID IF YOU ARE PANIC-PRONE

Here are a few closing suggestions on what to avoid in order to reduce the frequency of panic attacks (part 2 will provide more details on developing a panic-proof lifestyle):

- *Avoid exercise*—if you are lactate sensitive. Otherwise, try a safe form of exercise to improve your fitness level and reduce the stress in your life.
- *Avoid caffeine.* Go cold turkey if necessary and get over your addiction.

- *Avoid alcohol.* Alcohol is a depressant that plays havoc with your systems. If used as a tranquilizer, it can often be addictive (alcoholism), which simply complicates a panic problem.
- *Avoid smoking.* Nicotine is addictive and aggravates panic attacks.
- *Avoid unnecessary stress.* Making room in your life for plenty of sleep and relaxation will help restore natural brain tranquilizers and reduce or eliminate panic reactions.
- *Avoid any foods or food additives that seem to make your symptoms worse.* By experimenting, find out what food products can increase your anxiety—or consult an allergist.
- *Avoid seriousness!* Try to be less intense. Try laughing at yourself, your mistakes, and your life circumstances. Humor helps to restore the brain's natural tranquilizers and releases us from physical and emotional tension. It's hard for the body to maintain a state of anxiety in the face of laughter. Humor also helps to restore our perspective—to help us see life as less threatening. Believe me, "a merry heart doeth good like a medicine" (Prov. 17:22).

6
FEARS AND PHOBIAS

Irrational fears—and those extreme form of anxious fears known as phobias—are nothing new. Historians, philosophers, and poets down through the ages have described the unreasonable terrors that sometimes plague human beings—famous and ordinary.

King James I of England, for instance, broke out in a cold sweat whenever he saw an unsheathed sword. Frederick the Great, king of Prussia, feared water, so his servants rubbed him clean with dry towels. Napoleon Bonaparte, who conquered most of Europe, couldn't conquer his fear of tall buildings. He was so obsessed about them that he would stand in front of the building and count the windows one by one—a typical obsessional strategy for reducing anxiety.

The famous escape illusionist, Harry Houdini, who built a legend out of his ability to escape from chained trunks, padlocked cells, and underwater barrels, was actually claustrophobic—terrified of enclosed places. As long as he was in control, his problem never bothered him. But twice in his life he panicked—once in a telephone booth and again in a bathroom stall. He became violently hysterical, and after that never left home without a special set of lock picks that could free him if he were trapped anywhere.

Anecdotes of this sort abound, and they all make the same point: Fears and phobias are nothing to be ashamed of. Many strong and capable people experience them. In fact, I suspect that *everyone* has a secret fear—a fear so strong that we may even block it from our consciousness.

My discussion in this chapter will focus on three types of phobias: simple phobias, social phobias, and agoraphobia. Before launching into a discussion of these specific phobias, however, it will be helpful to review how phobias come about and how they are different from ordinary fear.

THE ORIGIN OF PHOBIAS

Fear, as we all intuitively know, is a basic reaction to threat. It serves us well in the normal course of events because it keeps us from harm. We either avoid that which will hurt us (I don't deliberately touch a hot

74

stove), or we run away from it. Fear, therefore, serves an important biological function. When we feel fear, the adrenaline level in our blood goes up, our muscles tense, our heart beats faster—all to prepare us for survival. We may need to fight a dangerous animal or flee from a falling tree.

Almost anything that can harm us can also become something we fear. One famous early psychologist, G. Stanley Hall, as far back as 1897 described over six thousand fears people suffer from. (This is hardly surprising, given fear's protective function and the number of possible dangers in the world.) Furthermore, some human fears are also seen in lower animals. For instance, the fear of snakes, which is so universal in humans, is also seen in primates. Fear is a God-given provision for an imperfect and dangerous world.

But like so many healthy functions, fear can be distorted and become an enemy rather than a friend. Imagine, for example, that while at the beach one day with your young son you see a lifeguard pulling an unconscious figure from the water—a teenager who has fallen off his surfboard, knocked his head on it, and nearly drowned. Later in the day, as you take your child to the water's edge, you notice a strong sensation of fear within yourself. You instinctively pull your child back for a moment, then you realize there is no real danger. So you relax and let your child play in the water—keeping a close watch on him, of course.

All very normal. The sight of the young man being pulled from the ocean only served to remind you that water can be dangerous, so you should be careful.

Contrast this with another scenario. This time, when you see the teenager being rescued, you are overcome with an intense fear. You begin to have horrible fantasies of your own child drowning. Your heart races; sweat gathers on your forehead. *I can't let my child stay here,* you say to yourself as you gather up clothes, towels, beach chair, umbrella, and child and rush home to safety. This would be an excessive fear reaction. Perhaps if it died down in a day or two, it could still be considered normal. But if you are never able to take your child to the beach again, you have created a phobia.

Simply put, a person who reacts with unreasonable fear or dread in a harmless situation and begins to avoid all similar situations has developed a *phobia*. Phobias are fears that do not respond to rational thinking. They operate blindly, forcibly, and without reason.

Figure 4 illustrates the origin of phobias in a more general sense. Most phobias have their beginnings in early childhood experiences and then are fed by four conditions:

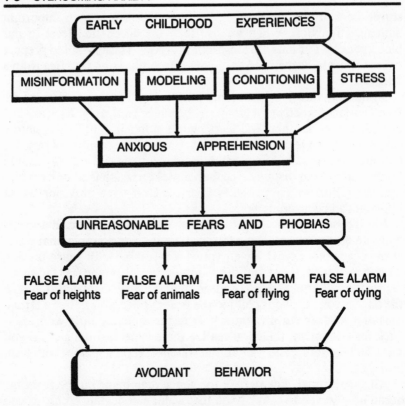

Figure 4: The Origin of Phobias

(1) *Misinformation and Faulty Logic.* In order for a phobia to de-velop, there has to be some distortion of the facts. In the previous exam-ple, you would have to draw a lot of false conclusions from the teenager's accident to develop such a fear of the beach. When you saw the lifeguard drag him in, for instance, you might falsely assume (not knowing about the surfboard) that he was injured simply because he went in the water. Or you might hear someone say that the same kind of accident has happened often at this particular beach. And from all this you might conclude that your child is automatically in danger any time he is in or near the ocean. Misinformation and illogical reasoning underlie the *beginnings* of phobia.

One reason phobias tend to develop in childhood is that inexperience often causes children to get the facts wrong. Sometimes parents even deliberately feed misinformation to children as a way of controlling them. This is particularly true in the area of sexuality: "If you kiss a boy, you can become pregnant." "If you masturbate, God will never forgive you." Statements like these are made by well-meaning parents with little thought as to how such false statements could eventually create phobic responses to areas of sexuality.

(2) *Modeling.* Modeling is also an important factor in feeding phobias. The repeated expression of alarm by a fearful parent is a common cause of phobias.

In the beach incident cited above, you would be much more likely to develop a phobia about the beach if your mother had been like the mother of a client of mine. This woman refused to take her children to the beach. She often preached to them about how dangerous the ocean was, and every time a drowning or a shark attack occurred she would cut out the newspaper report and put it up for her children to see. Now, at age thirty-two, her son is also ocean-phobic and likely to model this in turn to his children.

(3) *Conditioning.* Conditioning is a well-known psychological phenomenon based on our ability to associate one event with another. When two things happen at the same time, the one tends to "condition" the reaction of the other.

Suppose, for instance, that every time you answer the telephone, an unpleasant message awaits you. Very soon, every ring of the telephone will cause you to react as if something unpleasant has happened—before you even hear the message. The telephone ring is the "stimulus" and the unpleasant feeling is the "response." The message itself may get lost in the process.

Some conditioning serves the useful purpose of allowing us to react to our environment without having to reason every situation out. If I burn my finger every time I place it in boiling water, I will soon learn not to put my finger in boiling water—and I won't have to carefully think through my reasons. Just the thought of it causes me enough pain to stop me from doing it.

But conditioned responses are not always that logical or healthy. Many adult phobias have their origin in conditioned responses to painful childhood events they cannot even recall. One famous case history, described by another early psychologist, John B. Watson, concerned a young woman who ever since she could remember had feared running water. She could remember no precipitating incident. no bad experience with running water. All she knew was that the sound of running water made her afraid. When she took train trips, they had to cover the window so she couldn't even see streams, let alone hear them.

Then, when the young woman was in her early twenties, she had a visit from an aunt, who reminded her of the event that had triggered the phobia. At age seven, she had gone on a picnic with her mother and aunt, but the mother had returned home after lunch. That afternoon, while walking with her aunt in the woods, the girl had disobediently run off. The aunt found her wedged between two rocks in a stream, screaming hysterically, with a waterfall noisily pouring over her head. The girl begged her aunt not to tell her mother of her disobedience, and in a few days had "forgotten" the incident.

The aunt had religiously kept her promise and never told the mother of the incident. Since the mother did not know, she could not help her daughter understand the phobia that subsequently dominated both their lives. Many phobias, especially claustrophobia and phobias about specific objects or animals, probably have such a conditioning origin.

My youngest daughter, at age six, had an experience which could have conditioned a phobic response. At school one day she went into one of the school toilets which at that time had full-length doors (now they have gaps in the bottom) and could be locked from the inside. She closed the door and turned the latch to lock it, but when she was finished, she could not unlatch it; her hands were too small to overcome the reverse friction. She started crying hysterically.

Her panic reaction brought a teacher, who calmly talked her back to calmness and then called the school janitor, who removed the door at the hinges to let her out. Needless to say, the school had to change the type of latch, but for several days my daughter would demand that the toilet door at home remain wide open when she was in the bathroom. By slowly teaching her how to lock and unlock the door and staying by the toilet with her at first, we gradually helped her overcame her fear. Under different circumstances, however, my daughter's fear of closed doors could have developed into a conditioned response—a phobia.

(4) *Stress.* Stress must also be considered to be a precipitator of phobia. Stress weakens our resources and makes us more vulnerable to our fears, partly because it depletes our natural brain tranquilizers. The longer the stress lasts, the less objective we are able to be, and the more easily a frightening experience can be transformed into a phobia.

PRISONS OF FEAR

The essence of a phobia is *anxious apprehension*. Each of the above conditions, or combinations of any of them, can set up this apprehension or anticipation that something terrible will happen. This in turn gives rise to a whole range of *false alarms,* which is what a phobia really comes down to.

In essence, a fear is an *alarm.* It alerts us to a danger and mobilizes us to deal with it (fight) or escape from it (flee). *Real alarms* are our allies. They protect us from harm. But phobias are *false alarms.* There is no real threat—at that moment. There may have been a real threat long ago, when the phobia originated, but right now there is really nothing to fear.

Our conditioned response to the *false alarm* raised by a phobia is to try to escape the danger. Since there is no real danger, escape is pointless, but we try to avoid the threatening circumstance nevertheless. This leads to *avoidant behavior,* or a tendency to keep away from those situations that provoke the phobia.

This avoidant behavior is the final and most devastating consequence of the chain of events we call a phobia. It is this tendency that traps us into social isolation or imprisons us in our home and causes us to miss out on many activities.

Phobias, because they lead to avoidant behavior, create prisons as real as steel bars do. They cause us to avoid pets, people, places, and privileges that could make life richer for us. They rob us of inner peace. Saddest of all, they diminish our capacity for a rich spiritual life and prevent us from reaching our full measure of stature as God's children.

While I don't want to suggest that phobias in any way reflect a failure on our part to appropriate all of God's blessings, I do know that they rob us of a full life. Fortunately, however, there is hope for people who suffer from irrational fears. So if you are handicapped by a phobia, read on. Together I hope we will find a way out of your prison cell.

COMMON FEARS AND SIMPLE PHOBIAS

As I have shown, *fears* are different from *phobias.* Before we proceed, let us take a moment to make this distinction a little clearer.

When a *fear* is widely shared, it is referred to as a *common fear.* Most of us, for instance, fear that one day there may be a nuclear war. The very thought sends chills up and down my spine—and so it should. The devastation and wholesale destruction that would follow such an eventuality is almost too frightening to contemplate. It is natural that we fear such a happening.

Other examples of *common fears* include fear of walking close to the edge of a cliff, fear of fire, or fear of walking through tall grass in an area known to be infested with snakes. These fears are natural. They are reasonable in light of the real risk. Most important of all: They don't incapacitate us in any way.

Personal Inventory 5
ASSESSING YOUR FEARS

Taking a periodic inventory of your fears is a helpful practice because it helps you keep track of whether they are on the increase or going away. An inventory also helps you face your fears with courage—the first step toward mastering them. Rate each fear listed below according to the following scale, then date your inventory and file it away for future reference:

0 = This is not a fear for me.
1 = This fear causes me mild or no discomfort.
2 = This fear bothers me, but I can face it.
3 = This is an intense fear for me; I avoid its object at all costs.

Fear	Score	Fear	Score
Accidents		High places	
Airplanes		Injections	
Animals		Knives	
Being alone		Mental illness	
Birds		Public speaking	
Blood		Sick people	
Boat on ocean		Spiders	
Buses		Snakes	
Cats		Strangers	
Cemeteries		Suffocation	
Closed places/cupboards		Surgery	
Crowds		Thunderstorms	
Darkness		Trains	
Dead people		Woods	
Death		Dogs	
Dentists		Guns	
Elevators			

DATE: _____

But many fears are *unreasonable*—not so much because they are uncommon as because they are blown out of proportion to the point that they keep us from living a normal life. Take, for example, a fear of having one's house burgled or of being beaten up by a gang of hooligans. These fears are natural. But if they prevent us from leaving the safety of our homes, or cause us to sweat profusely or shake uncontrollably when we take a neighborhood stroll, they clearly go beyond the bounds of normality and incapacitate us to a certain extent. These fears go beyond the bounds of reasonableness—they are out of proportion to the real risk. After all, we don't live in Lebanon or certain countries in South America, where such fears are entirely reasonable. The person who must take two days to travel a thousand miles by train because he fears flying is going to be severely limited in life.

A fear that is persistent, excessive, and unreasonable is termed a *phobia*. When one fears just one object or situation, it is a *simple phobia*. Specific animals, such as cats; one of the natural elements, such as water; or even a given person can all be triggers for *simple phobias*. Examples of simple phobias include claustrophobia (fear of closed spaces), acrophobia (fear of heights), aquaphobia (fear of water), astraphobia (fear of lightning), ophidiphobia (fear of snakes), and zoophobia (fear of animals). Other frequently feared objects are germs, poison, crowds, and the dark.

The treatment of simple phobias—and of phobias in general—is basically one of desensitization. Gradually and systematically, first in imagination and then in real life, the victim is exposed to the feared object. If the patient knows what originally conditioned the phobia, then reliving the experience in a carefully controlled situation under professional supervision can help in desensitization. *Under no circumstances,* however, should a layperson attempt either to facilitate recall of a frightening childhood experience or to assist someone to relive the experience. Considerable skill and experience are required to "bring out" these kinds of memories without reinforcing the phobia and entrenching it even further.

SOCIAL PHOBIAS

Another category of phobias is termed *social phobias*. In these instances, the victim fears and avoids situations that could lead to public humiliation or embarrassment. One patient I knew could never use a public toilet because he feared other people could "hear" him. But this particular phobia was not his most troublesome one. He could never speak when more than two or three people were present, and this meant he had to go to great trouble to avoid being caught in situations where he would have to speak, ask directions, or respond to questions. The elaborate planning that had to go into this man's every activity is characteristic of many phobics' lives.

Fear and avoidance of social situations tend to be common in adolescence and may cause truancy from school. Fortunately, the problem usually diminishes as the child grows older, although some shyness and social reticence may remain as part of the personality.

Other social phobias include fear of authority figures (such as older people or professors), fear of public speaking, fear of crowded rooms, and even fear of the opposite sex. In more severe cases, the social phobia can begin to merge with a panic disorder.

What is the origin of a social phobia? In some cases, an actual frightening event earlier in life, usually childhood, can be pinpointed. Extreme humiliation by a parent in front of one's peers or adult company, devastating failure (such as "going blank" while performing in front of an audience), or receiving intense criticism while trying to help someone can all be causes of social phobias later. Life-threatening incidents or actual physical harm can also "condition" a social phobia. Encountering a robber, being raped or mugged, or simply imagining these events while young can create a phobia for places and certain people that can be deeply rooted and may be triggered at the slightest provocation.

In many cases of social phobia, however, no specific trigger event can be pinpointed. No matter how deeply and far back one searches, there doesn't seem to be any frightening event to account for the phobia. This is not to say that no such event occurred—just that there is no recall.

In such cases, the psychologist or counselor often has to make a determination of just how important recall is for healing of a phobia to take place. In some cases, such as early childhood sexual abuse, it is probably very important; in other cases, recall may not be vital. In many cases, people can be desensitized without the causes' being known.

The treatment of social phobias is pretty much the same as for simple phobias—gradual and systematic desensitization. In addition, assertiveness training can be helpful, because many social phobics also have an underlying problem with assertiveness. They shy away from many human interactions, avoid eye contact, mumble instead of talking clearly, and refuse to stand up for themselves.. While assertiveness itself doesn't cure a social phobia, learning assertiveness can go a long way toward helping someone cope with unpleasant circumstances or achieve some necessary goal.

Assertive behavior is a *skill* that can be learned. When practiced regularly, it builds confidence and *reduces* social fears. Assertive people feel in control—rather than controlled by others.

Many Christian believers are confused about assertiveness, however; they feel it is selfish or unbecoming of a Christian. And it's certainly possible to assert oneself in a selfish, un-Christian manner! But assertiveness is not necessarily the same thing as selfish aggression. When practiced in a Christian way, assertiveness creates trust, honesty, and openness. Rather than alienating people, it draws them together in mutual respect and commitment. Cowardice is the opposite of assertiveness, as are dishonesty, distrust, and disharmony. A healthy assertiveness knows when to sacrifice its rights—but does not do so for the wrong reasons.

A number of books have been written in recent years about *Christian assertiveness* to counteract the selfish, one-sided approach that has characterized some secular approaches to the subject; I commend these resources to you. Two excellent books on assertiveness are *Beyond Assertiveness* by David Augsburger and *Speak Up!: Christian Assertiveness* by Randolph Sanders and Newton H. Malony.[1] A Christian psychologist can also be helpful in teaching you how to be assertive without being hostile or selfish.

AGORAPHOBIA

Agoraphobia is the most serious form of all the phobias. Since it is now quite a widespread problem and likely to continue increasing, I will devote the remainder of this chapter to it. It is such a complex problem that it must be viewed as different from all other phobias.

Agoraphobia literally means "a fear of the marketplace." Since in times past public gatherings tended to center around the market, the term is now used to describe a fear of public or open places. At any given time, as many as one out of two hundred people in the general population could be agoraphobic—terrified of crowded public places, especially where escape is threatened or cut off, and also of being alone. Activities are restricted to home or to a very clearly defined perimeter around the home. As a result, the sufferer is eventually housebound and unable to move far from "safety" and help.

One of my agoraphobic clients, for instance, only felt safe within a literal perimeter of three blocks from his home—in every direction.

[1] Augsburger, *Beyond Assertiveness* (Waco, TX: Word, 1980). Sanders and Malony, *Speak Up!: Christian Assertiveness* (Louisville: Westminster, 1985).

Once he crossed the intersection of the marked block, he would begin to panic, but taking one step back would stop the panic. When blindfolded so that he could not tell precisely where he was, however, he could be driven several blocks beyond the permitted perimeter without panicking. This shows just how dependent the disorder is on perception and belief. It also points to the key in treating this disorder—changing the perception of danger and the belief about threats.

The worst cases of agoraphobia involve people who will not leave a certain room in an otherwise safe house. Obviously, this can be very disruptive and inconvenient to the whole family.

Since panic attacks frequently accompany agoraphobia, some have suggested that they are key to understanding the origin of agoraphobia. This may be true in some cases, but certainly not for all of them. Sometimes, in addition, a panic disorder sufferer will become housebound and may therefore seem to be agoraphobic as well, but the two conditions are sufficiently different to be considered as separate disorders.

One difference between pure panic disorders and agoraphobia lies in where and how the attacks occur. Agoraphobic panic attacks strike

Table 3
SIMILARITIES BETWEEN PANIC DISORDER AND AGORAPHOBIA[2]

Agoraphobia (or fear of public places) is generally considered to be a different disorder from anxiety panic attacks, although a panic disorder sometimes develops into agoraphobia as the victim becomes more and more afraid of leaving the safety of home. Research conducted at the University of Iowa College of Medicine, however, indicates that agoraphobia is a more severe variant of panic disorder. A comparison of the clinical features follows:

Clinical Features	Agoraphobia	Panic Disorder
Mean age (in years)	42.4	42.8
Percent who are female	74.6	75.9
Age of onset (years)	23.8	27.6
Sudden onset (percent)	59.7	42.5
Percent with precipitating events	57.1	71.2
Percent with previous anxious traits	44.3	32.9
Percent with complicating depression	40.3	27.7

Agoraphobia tends to start earlier in life and has a more sudden onset than panic attacks, which are more likely to have a precipitating event. Agoraphobics have a slightly greater tendency to be anxious in their personality.

---

[2] "Relationship between Panic Disorder and Agoraphobia" *Archives of General Psychiatry* 43 (March 1986):227-32.

when the "boundaries of safety" are violated; they do not occur so much within the boundary of safety. They are therefore "conditional panic attacks" and quite different from the general attacks of the other panic disorders, which tend to come upon the victim unexpectedly and can occur anywhere. Another important difference between agoraphobia and pure panic attacks involves the *beliefs* that sustain the fear. Fundamentally, I believe that the pure panic attack disorder (without agoraphobia) is much more a stress-related dysfunction, whereas agoraphobia is connected to psychological phobias. The agoraphobic sufferer normally has a complex belief system, developed over many years, about what constitutes danger. Panic attacks, on the other hand, can involve fear reactions without any conscious recognition of danger. Beliefs play a stronger role in agoraphobia, therefore, than they do in pure panic attacks.

Sex Differences in Agoraphobia

One aspect of agoraphobia that remains very puzzling to clinicians is the fact that it is found disproportionately in women. Eighty-five percent of agoraphobics are women, and there are no clear-cut explanations as to why this is so.

Some researchers have attributed the disproportionate numbers to differences in the ways boys and girls are taught to face the world. They point out that parents often don't do as good a job preparing daughters for independent living as they do their sons. Women may therefore be more prone to anxiety, self-doubt, and overdependence. A similar theory holds that males are taught to confront fearful situations more directly, thereby desensitizing themselves to these situations, and that men may therefore learn coping mechanisms that prevent anxieties from building into panic. Still another idea is that, since males are focused outwardly on work and sport more than on the home, they avoid the close attachment to home that some women develop. They are therefore less likely to associate the home with security and the outside world with threat.

In addition to these environmental differences, there may be biological factors that play a role in increasing the female's susceptibility to panic. For instance, many women develop their agoraphobic symptoms after childbirth—a time of great hormonal change. This has led some researchers to suspect that hormones may play a part in the development of agoraphobia. (Women also suffer from a higher risk of depression and a greater frequency and severity of headaches—all of which may have a hormonal basis.) This evidence is far from conclusive; after all, the postpartum period is also a time of increased responsibility and elevated stress, and this in itself could influence the anxiety level. Still, the role of hormones and blood chemistry in agoraphobia cannot be ruled out.

Common Themes in Agoraphobia

Agoraphobia is a complex problem. Sorting out the relative influences of biological and psychological factors is no easy task, and it may be a long time before we have clear-cut answers to many of the questions it raises. Still, there are some common denominators among agoraphobics that give us clues as to the nature and solution of the problem. Certain themes—characteristic ways of thinking and feeling—appear again and again among agoraphobics. A brief discussion of these themes can help point out those areas of personality that may contribute to agoraphobia and also help provide better understanding of the complex nature of the problem:

(1) *"I've always felt inferior."* The reason I emphasize the value of making very small gains and being content to achieve very small steps in one's progress toward healing is that many agoraphobic symptoms are maintained by the sufferer's *self-image*. Most agoraphobics have an "inferior interior"; they feel useless, and they constantly criticize their own actions. While they constantly seek approval from others, they quickly reject this approval as insincere or not applicable. They decline to accept compliments and reflect an attitude of basic self-distrust.

Now, it is easy to understand how the agoraphobia itself can erode self-esteem and destroy self-confidence, but many sufferers have had these tendencies long before agoraphobia set in. The following story illustrates this:

Betty is forty-six years old now and has suffered from agoraphobia for the past twenty years. She has three children and a very tolerant and kind husband. For most of the agoraphobic years, Betty has also suffered from bouts of depression which she attributes to her frustration over the phobia. At times she has even thought about suicide, but the love of her husband and the idea of leaving her children has kept her from ever trying to take her life.

Betty's first anxiety attack occurred just after the birth of her third child. Since then, the intensity of her disorder has fluctuated from being so bad she could not leave her bedroom to brief periods when she was totally free of any problem. During these periods of freedom she would "binge" on her outings, making the most of her freedom before the prison doors slammed shut again.

The most prominent symptom that Betty experiences when she's away from home is a fear of losing control. Thoughts like, *If I stay here,*

I'll humiliate myself, or *I'm going to go crazy if I don't get back home,* flood her mind. She can't think clearly, and she feels as if her mind were going to run away from her body, as though in a dream. The moment she returns home, she feels safe again. But then the guilt sets in: *Why can't I just trust God and stay out? Why do I allow this problem to control me? I suppose I must be a terrible person—God must be very disappointed in me.*

Over and over again, these thoughts punish Betty, making her more and more depressed and eroding her self-esteem. She has come to feel absolutely useless and of no value to herself, to God, or to anyone else. As we explored Betty's past, however, we discovered that these feelings existed long before the agoraphobia set in. Betty's parents had divorced when Betty was six. She had been raised by her mother, a very dominating person who repeatedly reminded Betty of the tremendous sacrifices she had made for her and accused her of being the most ungrateful creature on God's earth.

Betty learned very early to feel guilty for things she never did. Over and over, she tried to please her mother, only to be blamed for something that she had overlooked. If Betty washed up after dinner, her mother would complain because she didn't empty the trash. If Betty brought her mother a flower on Mother's Day, she would be told it was the wrong color. Nothing Betty did was right—and she was never allowed to stand up for herself or explain her actions when something went wrong.

Betty tried to ignore her feelings, but deep down she came to believe that she was useless, incompetent, and an inferior person. Her mother had done a first-class job of setting the stage for agoraphobia. All it needed now was the right hormonal or other biochemical disruption—and it would blossom.

Betty also discovered through her therapy that her agoraphobia was closely tied to her *fear of being abandoned.* All through her childhood, she had felt an irrational fear that her mother would not be at home when she returned from school—that she would abandon Betty and possibly run off with some man. The thought of being alone or having to live with her father (who had remarried and had other children now as well) was intolerable and frightening to Betty, so she kept at the fruitless task of trying to please her mother.

The point I am making here is that Betty could not win over her agoraphobia without confronting and working through her deep-seated fears of abandonment and low self-esteem. She needed to face her feelings without suppressing them and to change her beliefs about why people love her so that she could stop trying to please them at all costs.

Fortunately, Betty had a close group of caring friends, a wonderful family, and all the prospects of a happy life. As she came to value herself and trust these other people more, her agoraphobia subsided.

(2) *"Everything has to be just so."* This is another theme one hears often from agoraphobics. They tend to be perfectionistic. Everything must be in its place, agoraphobics can't tolerate any untidiness.

This perfectionism comes from the fact that agoraphobics cannot tolerate even low levels of anxiety. They become unusually anxious if they can't find what they are looking for, if something is moved from its regular resting place, or if their environment is cluttered so they cannot keep track of everything. The perfectionistic traits develop as a way of keeping this anxiety at a minimum.

Sue's story illustrates this—and again shows how the origin of the trait often precedes the onset of agoraphobia.

Sue's mother was a perfectionist. Sue's father was a bit of a slob; he liked to just abandon things where he used them. Her mother tidied up while her father messed up. As Sue described her home life, I couldn't help but laugh. Just picture the scene: Sue's mother crouches behind the door, waiting for her husband to put down the newspaper when he's finished reading it. Immediately she jumps up, retrieves the paper, and places it neatly in the trash can. Or imagine that dinner is almost over, and Sue's father is sipping the last of his coffee. As he puts down the cup, waiting hands whisk it away to the already-loaded dishwasher.

Fortunately, Sue can also laugh at the imagined scene now that she's beginning to gain mastery over her own perfectionism. She developed her traits at an early age also, to avoid her mother's criticism. She sees now how a low tolerance for anxiety can be a nightmare. You can't leave work undone; you can't leave a book unread; you can't leave the dishes until a favorite TV program is over. You can't delay anything—it must be done right away so as to get relief from the *anxiety of incompleteness,* a form of obsessive-compulsive disorder. Shortly after Sue married, she began to suffer the first bouts of agoraphobia. With two sons to raise, her perfectionism became a problem that fed her agoraphobic problem. She could not leave the house for fear that the boys would mess something up there. To reduce clutter, she demanded that only one toy could be out of the toy cupboard at any one time. The whole house had to be scrupulously dusted every day to prevent dust buildup, which would create too much anxiety for Sue.

Since this is an unrealistic way of living, Sue had to gradually learn how to tolerate anxiety and how to delay doing things without feeling uncomfortable. It is a slow and sometimes painful process, but there is no other way to overcome agoraphobia.

We devised some strategies for doing this. Sue went from one toy out on the floor at any one time to two toys, then three, four, and so on, with two or three days between each "step" for Sue to feel comfortable. From dusting every day, we moved to every second day, and so forth. By very gradually increasing the anxiety and then teaching her how to relax, we were able to raise her tolerance for the anxiety.

Sue reports that my "giving her permission," with the support of her husband, to leave things be helped tremendously to reduce her anxiety. She was pleasing someone by *not* doing things, which was the reverse of what she had been taught as a child. Slowly Sue learned how to balance the "dos" and "don'ts" of her life so that she could be free of the underlying anxiety of perfectionism, and her agoraphobia diminished dramatically. There are still a number of other issues to be worked on, but Sue has made significant progress.

(3) *"I go crazy when I make a mistake."* This is perfectionism of a different sort. Here, the agoraphobic sufferer cannot tolerate personal imperfections and becomes extremely self-critical. Even very small mistakes are received with great anxiety. This is how one agoraphobic describes the experience:

> Either I do it properly, or I don't do it at all. I can't stand being halfhearted. I don't expect other people to be perfect. My kids, my wife, my neighbors —they can all get things messed up, and it doesn't bother me. But if I put the wrong date on a check, or if I make a mistake adding up figures, or if I cut a piece of wood wrong—it drives me up the wall. It used to be murder when I still worked. I couldn't finish any task. I'd go back over the figures or redo a letter over and over again. I never felt comfortable that a job was done. The boss had to just take it away from me; I could never give it up for fear that there were still mistakes.

People like this develop often compulsive habits of not completing projects. They will work at something until it is *almost* finished, then either trash it or pack it away. Reason? They don't want to finish it for fear that it may have flaws. "Perfect or nothing" is their motto.

The solution, of course, is to learn how to tolerate imperfection— both in one's self and in one's work. Strong self-esteem is important for resolving agoraphobia, and strong self-esteem does *not* come from being a perfect specimen of humanity, but from *accepting the imperfection of your humanness.* For this reason, group therapy is the treatment of choice. Agoraphobic sufferers who cannot tolerate their own mistakes need a place where they can listen to honest feedback about their imperfections but continue to receive unconditional love—and thus learn to love themselves, too.

Personal Inventory 6
ANXIETY AND SELF-ESTEEM: THOUGHTS FOR REFLECTION

Problems with agoraphobia—and anxiety problems in general—are closely related to issues of perfectionism and self-esteem. The following questions are designed to help you reflect on your own feelings about yourself and your basic worth as a human being. Write down your responses in a journal or a separate sheet of paper so that at a later time you can reflect back on your growth in maturity.

- What must I do to be loved?
- Am I a lovable person?
- What has God done for me to make me more lovable?
- What strengths do my friends see in me?
- What weaknesses do my friends see in me?
- What imperfections in myself bother me the most?
- Can I accept these imperfections as they are and come to see them as strengths?
- Do I really believe people when they compliment me?
- Do I play games in order to get people to compliment me more?
- Can I make a mistake and accept forgiveness without letting my mistake devastate me?
- What more must I do to win God's favor?
- Do I fear taking risks because I cannot tolerate making mistakes?
- Do I call myself names or put myself down when I am not perfect?
- Do I humiliate others in order to make myself feel better?
- Do I continue to set unrealistic goals even though I know I can't attain them?
- Do I set goals too low because I fear failure?
- Are there things about myself that I dislike intensely?
- Are there things I dislike about myself I can change?
- Can I accept that which I cannot change and come to like myself anyway?
- Do self-doubts plague my thoughts?
- Do I really have reason to doubt myself, or is it that I ignore the evidence that I can do better?
- How central is God in my life?
- Are there places I go I would never take Him, or do I have friends I would not want Him to meet?
- Do I have my priorities straight?
- Have I sorted out whether something bothering me is essential or nonessential in my life?
- Do I regularly commit my anxieties to God in prayer?

The agoraphobic's problem with personal perfectionism, of course, is an exaggerated version of concerns most of us have about ourselves and our flaws. Our spiritual life ought to be moving us all the time toward a greater acceptance of our imperfections. We can face them courageously because we know that *God forgives us.* We can live with them because we know that *He gives us power* to live with imperfection. If God wanted a creation without mistakes, He would have populated the world with angels. Instead, He created humans so that He could demonstrate the greatness of His mercy and the unlimited extent of His forgiveness. Our humanness, rightly understood and lived out according to God's plan, is His pleasure. Taking hold of this assurance can help free agoraphobics from their prison of anxiety—and help all of us in our struggle to live according to God's plan. Paul writes with great authority:

> Not that I have already obtained it, or have already become perfect, but I press on in order that I may lay hold of that for which also I was laid hold of by Christ Jesus. (Phil. 3:12, NASB)

(4) *"If I stop worrying, something bad will happen."* Agoraphobics are not the only ones who believe this—it is a very common theme among all anxiety sufferers.

What happens is this: Early in childhood, something causes you anxiety. You put your worry or concern out of your mind in childlike trust that the thing you fear won't come to pass. But it does, and you wonder: *If I had kept worrying about it, maybe it wouldn't have happened.* So the next time you fear something, you hang on to the concern "just in case." You worry about it all day, lie awake all night. And the next day it doesn't happen! So—this proves that if you worry about something it doesn't happen. You have just created a thought monster!

Actually, what happens is your worry builds up a state of anxiety. When the feared event doesn't materialize, you feel a sense of relief— the anxiety balloon loses air so rapidly that it shoots away like a jet plane. This relief is so pleasurable that it reinforces the buildup of the next anxiety; unconsciously you build your anxiety so that you can experience relief again. Worry then becomes a bad habit!

Many Christians continue this habit into their prayer life. They use praying as a way of worrying without feeling guilty! I am sure you know the experience. Something bothers you, so you think, *I'll pray about it*—perhaps it won't happen. Five minutes later, you're worried again, so you pray again. Before you know it, you've prayed a hundred times—feeding the worry by building up your anxiety. Then when the feared event doesn't materialize, there is a great sense of relief and the tendency to worry and pray, worry and pray, is reinforced.

Now, don't misunderstand me. We should pray about the things that bother us. But God is *not deaf.* God *does* care. Shouting at Him or nagging Him does not increase our chances of being heard—and may develop into a "spiritual" version of an anxious worry habit. There must come a moment in the cycle of worrying and praying when the focus of your prayer must change from "Lord, take this problem in my life away" to "Lord, help me not to worry about something I have already committed to You." God knows, better than we do, how obsessional thoughts and worrying can be fed by repeatedly praying for something. We can trust Him to be faithful to His word and to understand if we shift the focus of our prayer.

It is important not to misinterpret Paul's advice to "pray without ceasing" (1 Thess. 5:17, NASB), or the injunction of Jesus that "at all times [we] ought to pray," (Luke 18:1, NASB). These verses are often cited by a person who is high in anxiety to support a compulsive need to keep the worry-prayer cycle going. But this is taking the verses out of context. The command to "pray without ceasing, for instance," comes between "rejoice always," and "in everything give thanks" (NASB). Clearly, the meaning of these verses is *not* "keep praying about the same thing over and over again because, if you don't, something bad is likely to happen to you." No, the biblical mandate is simply to "be prayerful all the time." All of us—anxious people especially—should pray often, but our prayer must focus on all of life, not just on obsessional worry.

Similarly, Jesus' injunction in Luke 18:1 is followed by a parable designed to show, as the remainder of verse 1 indicates, that we ought not to "faint" or "lose heart." The context of the parable, in which the widow persisted in pestering the judge to protect her from an opponent, was justice. Jesus' message is, "God knows the injustices of life. Those who are hurt cry out to Him daily for relief. But God is not an unjust judge. In due time He will bring justice, so don't give up hope." Here again, Jesus is not encouraging a neurotic worry-pray-worry-pray perpetual cycle, but simply saying "don't give up hope."

Clearly, the child of God must be constantly ready for prayer. We must pray "in the Spirit" and remain alert with all perseverance praying for ourselves and others (Eph. 6:18). This is our birthright. Let it not become a handicap, but the doorway to a glorious freedom from unnecessary anxiety.

FINDING FREEDOM FROM IRRATIONAL FEAR

If agoraphobia is a problem for you or someone close to you, take heart! Conquering agoraphobia, or any other unreasonable fear, may require hard work and courage—but it *can* be done. Clearly, mastering your fears means more than mastering the moment of panic. It requires paying careful attention to stress factors in relationships, understanding how you feel about frightening situations, and learning how to handle thoughts and feelings. Because of the complexity of the problems involved, any fear that approaches the phobic level is best treated with the help of a qualified therapist.

While panic attacks (including the panic component of agoraphobia) can be controlled with appropriate medication, most phobias require a much more intensive focus on the psychological factors that cause and sustain the disorder. This is especially true in the case of agoraphobia. The more you know about yourself and the more accurate your self-perception, the more equipped you will be to master your problem.

An important part of this self-knowledge is an understanding and acceptance of your human limitations. Expectations that are too high and unrealistic will only intensify your problem, not relieve it. Mastering only a few little steps at first will help you gain strength and build the confidence you need that you can beat your problem. Even if the most you can do at this stage is read this book or turn to God in prayer and trust Him for your daily strength, then you have made a start!

7
ANXIETY IN CHILDHOOD

Nancy is only eleven years old, but in some ways her childhood is already over. Her schoolmates gather together often, sleep at each other's homes, giggle and talk about boys a lot. But the only time Nancy ever seems happy and relaxed is when she's settled in her beanbag chair and planted in front of the TV, lost in a fantasy world of flat screen people. And there's a reason for this escapism: Nancy is the victim of childhood anxiety.

Monday mornings are Nancy's darkest days. She is tense, her stomach aches acutely, she yawns and trembles, and even the slightest change in her schedule and routine of life throws her into a dither. Mislaid homework, a spot on her jeans, being late for school, or any disappointment throws her into a tense frenzy. Her head aches, her stomach churns, she becomes nauseous and runs for the bathroom.

Very few extracurricular activities are appealing to Nancy, even though at her mother's urging she has tried many. Piano lessons, Little League baseball, ballet, junior church choir—all have come and gone with the same result: Nancy became too nervous and tense, and worried too much about how things were going. Finally it just seemed easier to let her do her own thing. The beanbag and TV did not threaten her, so they became her escape from the real world.

A conversation with Nancy revealed an interesting phenomenon: She did not seem to recognize what it was that bothered her. She knows she dreads things and that her problems seem bigger to her than similar-sized problems do to her peers, but why this is so or what she can do about it are questions for which she has no answer. Her anxiety is a mystery to her. And since the more she worries about it, the more anxious she feels, she just tries not to think about it.

Nancy's story is a common one. Childhood anxiety problems are showing a dramatic increase in incidence. Many children in every school across the nation feel out of control; their thought processes are disorganized and their ability to concentrate and to learn are drastically reduced. We need to recognize and understand these early manifestations of anxiety because childhood anxiety, if left uncorrected, will almost certainly develop into a full-blown adult form of anxiety disorder. One never outgrows this type of anxiety problem—it only becomes bigger with time. Fortunately there is hope, and effective help can be provided by a caring parent.

While this chapter may be of interest mainly to parents, it may also help others to develop a better understanding of the origins of their own anxieties.

WHY CHILDREN ARE VULNERABLE TO ANXIETY

Childhood ought to be a period of relative tranquility and security so that the personality can develop to its normal potential. Contrary to what some would have us think, a child does *not* need rough waters to learn how to navigate through life. True, children should not—and cannot—be protected from all discomfort; they ought to be able to observe the cycle of life and death and everything in between that is natural and normal.

But is it normal for a girl of six to be sexually molested by her natural father, as was the case with Nancy (although she repressed this memory)? Is this experience necessary to develop a strong character and prepare one for the rough and tumble of the real world? Certainly not. Such experiences, especially when they come at the fragile and vulnerable stage of early childhood, create intense fear, and this fear in turn creates an exaggerated anxious reaction to *all* of life.

As I have shown in earlier chapters, anxiety is part of the God-given "alarm system" designed to help us recognize and respond to danger. But when the threat that confronts us is something we are not prepared to handle, our basically healthy alarm system can go haywire, resulting in unhealthy or neurotic anxiety.

Figure 5 illustrates how this can happen. All threats represent a "danger" of some sort. And real danger should lead to a "true" alarm of anxiety or fear that in turn should lead to action that can remove the danger and restore calmness. But false alarms, conditioned by real danger and then fed by imagination, become "learned alarms" from which there is no escape—only the hell of anxiety.

Now, as I have shown in earlier chapters, this can happen to adults as well as to children. But children, who by their very nature are limited in their ability to distinguish what real danger is and to cope with that danger, are especially vulnerable to having their healthy alarm system short-circuited.

After all, a child without experience and with very limited skills is not well equipped to handle threats. Add to this a vivid imagination which can make shadows into draculas, and the wind into howling demons—and how can anxiety fail to result.

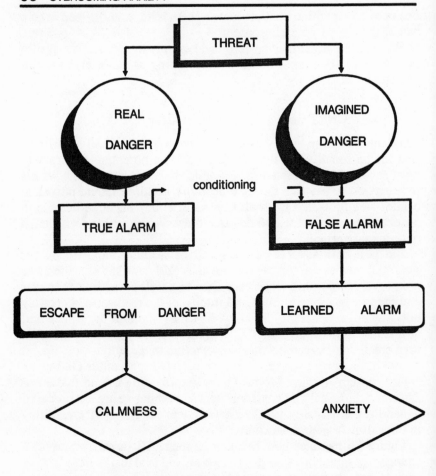

Figure 5: How Threats Develop into Anxiety

Even in the best of circumstances, children have to work to *learn the difference* between real danger and imagined danger—to dismiss the imagined threats and deal adequately with the real ones. This is part of growing up. But if a child is subjected to frequent or intense threats, this learning process never has a chance to take place. Instead, these threats "condition" false alarms to the extent that *everything* creates anxiety.

The heart-wrenching stories of many children bear out this sequence of events. A woman whose father had sexually abused her when she was a child once described to me how she used to lie awake night after night, fearing the sound of footsteps at her bedroom door—her father coming to molest her. "Every time I hear footsteps now I am overcome with a crippling panic feeling, even though it has been thirty years since I was abused," she relates.

"My father's persistent coughing still sounds in my head now, forty-two years after he used to beat me," relates a man—now an agoraphobic who hasn't worked for fifteen years.

My point here is basic and obvious: Children are very vulnerable to threats and do not have the protections that adults have to ward off anxiety. *Most* (some would say *all*) anxiety problems, therefore, have their origins during this fragile period. Anxiety starts as a legitimate signal with a real danger to be avoided, but conditioning can turn it into a false signal that destroys peace and happiness and cripples the emotions.

SOME REASONS FOR CHILDHOOD ANXIETY

But it's not just dramatic abuse experiences that fuel childhood anxiety —although abuse is clearly a major source. There are many circumstances in a child's life today that can lead to or aggravate anxiety problems. The fact that many of these circumstances are on the increase in today's society helps explain why anxiety is such a spiraling problem for children. Allow me to mention a few of the common factors behind childhood anxiety problems:

(1) *Competitiveness.* Children are under tremendous pressure to perform, and competitiveness is deeply ingrained in our culture. Children who do not please parents by delivering good grades or achieving a high level of excellence in extracurricular activities are subtly rejected. Failure represents a threat that is feared almost as much as physical abuse.

Even at a very tender age (beginning in preschool) there is evidence of this competitiveness, as any teacher will tell you. By adolescence, many children have developed the habit of compulsive overwork and a corresponding problem with anxiety.

(2) *Conflict.* Home conflicts, especially when parents don't get along, is a major source of anxiety in many children. With the increase in family breakups has come a corresponding increase in child tension. I know from personal experience the kind of anxiety that can arise from conflict at home.[1] When I was twelve, my parents divorced, after many years of intense conflict. At age twelve and under, one doesn't have much in the way of understanding and only meager resources for adjusting to the disintegration of the home. I remember

[1] See my book, *Children and Divorce* (Waco, TX: Word, 1982).

lying awake at night worrying about the future, reliving the past, and fearing the present.

As a boy I determined to control my pain, but as I discovered many years later, this didn't solve any problems; it only raised my anxiety level. Anxiety has a spiraling effect. One worry leads to two, then to four, and eight . . . it feeds on itself and multiplies geometrically. To push your worries under the surface, as I did, just makes your anxiety a faster-growing emotional cancer. Only the gentle intrusion of loving grandparents saved me from an emotional catastrophe—but that's another story!

Other conflicts such as those with peers, teachers, family members, the law, or with internalized values can also be the cause of heightened anxiety.

(3) *Burnout*. The notion of "burnout" typically conjures up images of air-traffic controllers, nurses, teachers, and ministers—all adult roles. But today's children are prone to burnout as well. Many are "overprogrammed" and rush from one activity to another. Under tremendous pressure, they eventually develop a chronic state of uncontrolled stress. Because their bodies are resilient and their minds somewhat flexible, they appear to be coping with the strain imposed on their young lives. But the stress gives way to anxiety sooner or later, and relief is sought through drugs, alcohol, and other forms of escape. Physical and emotional illness can follow the exhaustion of burnout.

To illustrate, I have a friend whose teenaged daughter maintained a sixteen-hour-a-day routine that tires me just thinking about it. Up at 5 A.M., she gulped down a light breakfast, rushed to early morning swim practice, then to school, home to a music lesson (or drama group), back for late-afternoon swim practice, home to supper, out to a church activity for her youth group, and then finally a couple of hours on homework or other assignments. She hardly had time to breathe, let alone reflect or be quiet.

All through high school, my friend's daughter kept up this pace. It was when she went off to college that the roof came crashing down. Six weeks into the second semester, she woke up early one morning with her chest tight—unable to breathe. She felt she was going crazy and that some terrible doom was about to occur—a classic panic attack brought on by physical and emotional stress.

It took more than a year to restore this girl's confidence, stabilize her emotions, and teach her to "balance" her life with appropriate amounts of time for leisure and reflection. She was fortunate. Many never recover from such a devastating experience.

(4) *Poor self-image and feelings of inferiority*. Imagined or real

human limitations or disadvantages can play havoc with a child's developing self-image and self-esteem. Anxiety results when children compare themselves with an "ideal" self-image and feel they don't measure up. Feelings of inadequacy, often exaggerated by a competitive environment, cause these children to develop an "inferiority complex." They become preoccupied with their shortcomings in appearance, intelligence, friendships, and coping ability—all significant sources of anxiety.

This anxiety is fed further by a heightened tendency toward "impression-monitoring." This is the behavior of always checking up on how you are coming across to others—the impression you make on them.

In our culture, the "impression" we make is considered very important. We always want to make a "good" impression so we can achieve greater prestige, acceptance, or power with others. Because of this, we tend to modify our actions to fit what we think others want of us. This robs us of the freedom to be who we really are; we become puppets with our strings placed in the hands of others. They pull, we jump. They command, we obey. They reject, we feel bad. They accept, we feel relief. What a game!

And the price (or penalty!) we pay for this is anxiety over whether we are doing the right thing, feeling the right emotions, or obeying the right subtle expectations. And, of course, we will *always* fall short. People are too fickle; they change the rules as soon as we have learned to play their game—it's their way of maintaining the balance of power. Impression monitoring—basing our self-esteem on what others think of us—can never be anything but a losing battle.

(5) *Life changes.* Major life changes occur with regularity in all our lives. The impact of life change, however, is not always clearly understood. For children, life change can be even more devastating than for adults because they don't yet have the resources to cope with the change.

It is inevitable, therefore, that changes such as divorce, moving, leaving established friendships, starting new relationships, going to a new school, adjusting to a stepparent, death of a friend or family member, the birth of a new baby, or serious illness—to name just a few—will create states of increased anxiety in children. The greater the changes and the more of them that must be contended with, the greater degree of anxiety. This is a simple law—but not all parents understand it.

More than fifteen years ago two researchers, Drs. T. H. Holmes and R. H. Rahe, discovered that many life changes over a certain period of time could produce a significant increase in susceptibility to illness; in other words, people who went through a period of life change became sick more easily. The greater the change, the greater was the risk of sickness and the more serious the sickness.

Today we understand this to be the consequence of depleted immune system functions. When there is a lot of life change going on, the effectiveness of our immune system, that fantastic complex of white blood cells, T-cells, and killer cells, is decreased. The body and mind throw their energies into coping with the impact of the change instead of attacking bacteria and viruses.

Now the most fascinating aspect of Holmes and Rahe's discovery was that the body cannot seem to tell the difference between good life change and bad. According to their research, birthdays and Christmas have pretty much the same effect as death and divorce—the impact differs only in degree.

For a child, life change requires adjustment, and adjustment produces emotional upheaval. Parents should make allowance for those adjustments and, if possible, reduce the number to a minimum at any one time. Most important of all, change should come as *slowly as possible*. All of us adjust better to slow change than to rapid or sudden change, and this is especially true for children.

(6) *Overexposure to threatening events.* Because of increasingly efficient networks of communication throughout the world—and especially because of TV—today's children tend to be much more aware of threatening events in the world around them. A child cannot even watch the evening news without being acutely aware that planes can crash, people can be murdered senselessly in their homes, children can be abducted and molested, and the world can be blown up in less than an hour.

Even so-called "children's programming" is full of violence, and responsible parents feel it necessary to warn their children about the looming dangers of drugs, kidnapping, and abuse. How can children help but be anxious—especially when their understanding of these events is incomplete?

CHILDHOOD WORRY

The habit of worry often begins in childhood. Children may learn it from a parent or friend, or they may discover it for themselves. But once the pattern of constant worry begins, it can become a millstone around a child's neck.

Worry begins when two unconscious and irrational beliefs take hold:

- The belief that worrying about something keeps it from happening,
- The belief that worrying keeps us in a state of alert.

When these erroneous beliefs take hold, worry begins perpetuating itself. Because children readily accept erroneous beliefs, they are particularly susceptible to developing a worry problem. Helping a child to challenge such beliefs, even proving to them that worrying doesn't change or help anything, can be helpful in avoiding or breaking the worry habit. In part 2, I will devote more time to stopping worry in both children and adults.

DIAGNOSING YOUR CHILD'S ANXIETY PROBLEM

The traditional diagnostic manual used by psychologists and other helping professionals basically divides childhood anxiety disorders into three categories: *separation anxiety disorder, avoidant disorder,* and *overanxious disorder.* The varieties of problems can be much greater than these three categories imply, however, since children share all the adult characteristics of anxiety, including oversensitivity, unrealistic fears, shyness and timidity, pervasive feelings of inadequacy, sleep disturbances, and fear of public places (such as school). Panic attacks have also been known to afflict children.

Interestingly enough, anxiety problems tend to be more common in boys than in girls, quite the reverse of the adult pattern. One reason for this may be that since the mother is usually the primary caregiver, there may be a closer (and more secure) bond between the mother and her daughter, whereas father-son bondings are more precarious and unreliable. Males are not always good models for how to deal with emotional pain, and fathers tend not to encourage a child's expression of hurting.

(1) *Separation anxiety disorder.* The essential feature of this variety of childhood anxiety is excessive anxiety about separating from and overdependence on a major attachment figure, such as a parent. Removal from familiar surroundings can also be a problem.

In most cases, a separation anxiety disorder has a clear cause, such as a home conflict, the death of a relative or pet, a divorce, or another situation that causes the child to fear abandonment. Among the symptoms that characterize this disorder are unrealistic fears, oversensitivity, extreme self-consciousness, nightmares, chronic anxiety, and lack of self-confidence. The child is usually immature for his or her age and is often described as nervous, submissive, easily discouraged, and frequently moved to tears. He or she clings helplessly to the parent and becomes excessively demanding.

Billy's case clearly illustrates how separation anxiety can develop and how it manifests itself. Billy was almost six years old when he

Personal Inventory 7
IS YOUR CHILD OVERLY ANXIOUS?

Over a period of six months or longer, has your child suffered frequently from any of the following tendencies? Answer each question by checking the "Yes" or "No" column.

	Yes	No
1. Does your child worry excessively about future events, such as examinations or visits to the doctor; possible injuries; or inclusion in peer group activities?		
2. Does your child spend an inordinate amount of time inquiring about the discomforts or dangers of sporting, outdoor, or other activities?		
3. Does your child need a lot of reassurance before starting something new or even resuming some activity that has been stopped for a while?		
4. Does your child often complain of a lump in the throat, stomach problems, headaches, nausea, dizziness, or shortness of breath?		
5. Does your child worry about past behavior or other activities?		
6. Is your child much more self-conscious than other children you know?		
7. Does your child worry a lot about not being competent as an athlete, a student, a friend, or other social role?		
8. Is it difficult for your child to relax and have fun?		
TOTALS		

If you answered yes to at least four questions on this list, it is very probable that your child is overly anxious. Remember, however, that these behaviors must have lasted longer than six months and occur quite frequently. If you are in doubt, seek a professional evaluation.

---

began waking up in the early hours of the morning, screaming his little head off. He had always been a sensitive child and prone to cry at the slightest provocation. But these nightmares were new, and his mother realized that something was happening to Billy that needed attention.

As I explored Billy's history, his mother reported that he was terrified of being separated from her, even for a brief period. Two years earlier, she had enrolled him in a beginners' class in Sunday school, but he had become so upset when she left the room she had no option but to return and spend the whole class period with him, hoping he would settle down. This never happened, so she withdrew him from Sunday school.

Later, when Billy's mother tried to enroll him in kindergarten, he became so upset that he went on a temper rampage, kicking and biting everyone he could reach. She persisted in keeping him in school, but after a week of impossible behavior she discontinued the struggle and went to see a counselor recommended by the school. Finally, after three months of little progress, the mother gave up trying to get Billy to go to kindergarten. Aware that soon she would need to enroll him in first grade, however, she tried to prepare him by talking to him regularly about school. It was shortly after this that Billy started the nightmares and early-morning screaming bouts, and the mother sought further help for the problem.

As we explored Billy's problem, it became. clear that the home environment was contributing significantly to his not wanting to be separated from his mother. Since before his birth the parents had been engaged in deep conflict, mainly over where they would live. The father's job took him away from home for periods of up to three months, and the mother had refused to accompany him, even though all expenses were paid. When Billy was born, the mother used this as her excuse not to go, but the father's frequent absences created in Billy a deep-seated fear that his mother would go away also. It was very clear that until the home situation was addressed and stabilized, Billy's anxiety would be out of control, fed partly by the reality that at least one of his parents was abandoning him on a periodic basis. The conflict between the parents over the absences only made his anxiety worse.

In the months that followed I worked intensively with the parents to resolve the problems between them, and some improvements were made. Billy was finally able to start going to school regularly. The sad side to this story is that Billy's tendency toward anxiety will probably be a problem for the rest of his life—such is the power of anxiety when children are introduced to it at an early age.

(2) *Avoidant disorder.* The essential feature of this problem is an excessive pulling away from contact with unfamiliar people that interferes with social functioning with peers. Technically, the problem must exist for longer than six months to qualify for diagnosis as an avoidant disorder, but who is going to wait six months before realizing there is a problem?

Children with avoidant disorder seem socially withdrawn, embarrassed, and timid with people they don't know well; in very severe cases they may even become mute or inarticulate. Relationships with familiar people are quite normal, however—this accentuates why it is a problem.

Because lack of assertiveness is often a consequence of avoidant behavior, therapy focuses on improving assertiveness skills and building self-confidence. Failure to deal with the problem in childhood can sometimes cause the avoidant behavior to carry over into adolescence, and social functioning appropriate for a teenager may not develop.

Some caution is necessary here in diagnosing this form of anxiety. Socially reticent children who are quite free of severe anxiety may be slow to warm up to strangers. This is hardly a serious problem, especially if after a brief period of contact the child relates warmly and in a friendly manner. The excessive shrinking from strangers must be sufficiently severe to interfere with social functioning in order for there to be a problem.

Socially avoidant behavior may also be a sign of depression in children. Depression should be suspected if a child who has had normal social reactions to unfamiliar faces suddenly develops anxious or shrinking behavior. In such a case, the child may need professional help.

(3) *Overanxious disorder.* This species of anxiety is characterized by excessive worry and persistent fears of a general nature. There is usually no stressful life event that can account for the problem.

Symptoms include:

- Excessive worry about future events;
- Preoccupation with trivial matters;
- Physical symptoms, including stomach distress and nausea, headaches, dizziness, shortness of breath, or abdominal pain;
- Difficulty falling asleep;
- Obsessional self-doubt;
- Perfectionistic traits.

But the chief characteristic of children with overanxious disorder is worry. These children worry about everything in their lives—their chief characteristic is worry about such things as taking examinations, going to the doctor, keeping appointments, and meeting deadlines.

Many children who suffer from this disorder are considered very "good" children. They tend to be compliant (almost overly compliant), and often they seem very mature because their concerns seem so plausible and adult. They worry about the things adults worry about and give the impression that they are insightful or have good planning skills. On the other hand, they usually lack self-confidence and may have a history of health problems.

Often the onset of this disorder is sudden and follows severe stress, such as a death in the family or divorce of the parents. This form of anxiety often afflicts eldest children in well-to-do families where there is strong pressure to achieve, even when the child is already above average.

PHYSICAL AND SEXUAL ABUSE —AND ANXIETY

In closing this chapter, I want to add a final word on child abuse, which I have already cited as a major factor in childhood anxiety. Almost any mental health professional can tell you that physical and sexual abuse looms large in the histories of countless people with mental or emotional problems—including excessive anxiety.

The experience of being violently mistreated by adults you trust and on whom you depend must be the most threatening a little child can undergo. And even in our supposedly advanced culture, the statistics on these forms of violation are staggering. Over 200,000 cases of child abuse are reported each year and many more go unreported.[2] Of the reported cases, 20 to 60 percent of the children have been seriously injured.

The impact of physical abuse on children is very significant— cognitive impairment, problems in social adjustment, depressive tendencies, and reduced interpersonal sensitivities. When the abuse involves sexual molestation, such as incest, the long-range consequences and depth of anxiety disturbance are profound.

Why do adults abuse children? There are many contributing factors, including immaturity ("children raising children"), drug and alcohol abuse, chaotic lifestyle, financial difficulties, disrupted relationships, low frustration level, and lack of impulse control. But by far the most significant factor in becoming an abuser is having been abused! There is evidence that 70 percent of abusing mothers were themselves abused as children. Attention to breaking the "cycle of abuse" is therefore extremely important. If you know someone who has a problem in this area—or if you yourself struggle for control because of an abusive background—please know that there is help available. Many communities now offer support groups for abusers who are trying to stop, and many specialists now offer effective help for this problem.

[2] *President's Commission on Mental Health, 1978.*

Personal Inventory 8
ARE YOU HARD ON YOUR CHILD?

Some parents impose tremendous pressures on their children—pressures that can cause severe anxiety reactions. Are you the sort of parent who is hard on a child? Do you make unreasonable demands or impose unrealistic expectations? The following questionnaire will help you decide. Answer each question by checking the "Yes" or "No" column.

	Yes	No
1. Do you consistently refuse your child's requests, even when you know they are reasonable, because you believe that children are easily spoiled?		
2. Does your spouse regularly accuse you of being too hard on your child or of using excessive discipline?		
3. Do you reject your child's excuses when he or she is trying to get out of doing some assigned chore?		
4. Do you believe that most children "have it easy" and need to learn how to fend for themselves?		
5. Do you make your child earn all his or her pocket money?		
6. Do you find yourself being impatient with your child when he or she is emotional?		
7. Do you sometimes find yourself embarrassing your child by forcing him or her to wear clothes he or she doesn't like?		
8. Are you intolerant of your child's fears and tend to "play it tough" so that your child can learn to live in the real world?		
9. Do you find that you use terms like "stupid," "dumb," "never amount to anything" in order to motivate your child?		
10. Do you believe that if you don't punish every infringement of family rules or misbehavior your child will grow up as a "ne'er-do-well" with no respect for authority?		
TOTALS		

If you answered any of these questions with a "yes," you may have a tendency to be too hard on your child or children. Three or more yes answers mean you are probably causing unnecessary tension in your home and running the risk of inculcating anxiety problems.

HELPING CHILDREN COPE WITH ANXIETY

If childhood is where much adult anxiety begins, childhood is also where anxiety can be most effectively treated and prevented. Adults can help by protecting children from situations they can't handle, by keeping communication open so that erroneous information can be corrected, and by modeling healthy ways of coping with stress. In part 2 I will address myself to how we can prevent anxiety in our children and provide help in healing the anxiety problems I have discussed here. I will also show how other practical problems such as bed-wetting, school phobias, fear of the dark, and nail-biting can be dealt with.

8

UNHEALTHY WAYS OF COPING WITH ANXIETY

For most of us, the experience of anxiety is so intolerable that we build defenses against it. From our earliest years, we search for and create ways to avoid anxiety. This search for "defenses" against anxiety shapes our personalities in the same way that a prevailing wind bends the trunks of tall trees, so that the trees continue to bend even when no wind is blowing. We literally "become" our defenses—they define who we are and how we act.

Our defenses against anxiety are mostly *unconscious;* we are oblivious to them and seldom recognize when they are operating. When these defenses are very strong and deeply rooted in our personality, they keep us from feeling any anxiety. But this is not a healthy state, even though it saves us some discomfort, because these defenses also demand a penalty! The suppression or repression of the anxiety creates other tensions within our minds and bodies that break out in the form of neurotic behaviors and psychosomatic diseases. While the anxiety is prevented from reaching our consciousness, it eats away at us until we finally collapse with a bleeding ulcer or excruciating headaches or compulsive behavior. It is far better to have anxiety out in the open where you can listen and respond to it than behind a screen where you can't see what it is doing!

Unfortunately, not many psychologists or psychiatrists pay much attention these days to the operation of unhealthy defense mechanisms against anxiety. Many are trained primarily in behaviorally oriented treatment techniques. And while these techniques can be important weapons in the arsenal of the professional counselor, their use can easily cause the powerful effects of the more dynamic and deeply rooted defenses to be overlooked.

Another line of resistance toward the study of defense mechanisms comes from Christian pastors and leaders. Many reject the notion of these hidden defenses because they originated in Freudian psychoanalysis and are tied to a secular school of psychology that has been antagonistic toward Christianity. In so doing, I believe, they rob themselves of an important tool for studying how the human personality works.

While I certainly do not subscribe to all of Freud's theories, I do have a great respect for his masterful skills of observation and description of the human condition. And I believe he was remarkably accurate in defining and describing the "defense mechanisms" and showing how we use them to defend against unacceptable impulses. I am also convinced that understanding these defense mechanisms is important to understanding how anxiety affects our lives.

HOW DEFENSE MECHANISMS WORK

Almost all the defense mechanisms that the human mind can concoct have three characteristics in common:

- They are ways of trying to reduce anxiety.
- They involve the denial or distorting of reality.
- They operate below the level of awareness, or at the "unconscious" level.

A simple example will illustrate how a defense mechanism operates to reduce anxiety. A patient with whom I was working had suffered significant abuse from his father during childhood. From my patient's earliest years, the father had expressed nothing but intense dislike for his son and punished him severely for every infraction. In addition, the boy was often caught in the crossfire between his father and mother, between whom there were also bouts of intense conflict.

The anxiety this childhood situation created for my patient was intolerable. How can a father, who is supposed to be loving and caring toward his children, behave this way? The father's rejection was so unacceptable to my patient—he could not tolerate the anxiety of it—that he began to rationalize his father's behavior. "He doesn't really hate me. He really hates his own father and is taking it out on me." "He just says what he says because he is much older than other fathers of boys my age. I really think he loves me deep down." By repeating these statements to himself over many years, my client had protected himself from the stark reality of the truth: his father didn't love him. The only way he could live with this truth was to deny it and rationalize his father's behaviors.

THE MAJOR DEFENSE MECHANISMS

What are the major defense mechanisms? A great many have been identified over the years since Freud first described them but because of space limitations, I will confine my discussion to only four. As I review them, remember that to some extent we all use them from time to time and that they are not always harmful. What is at issue here is whether or not we are "aware" of our using them and whether they end up producing more damage than the anxiety from which they are supposed to protect us.

(1) *Repression.* Foremost among the defense mechanisms is undoubtedly repression. Here, in order to avoid the mental pain associated with a thought or a memory, we "split off" the thought or memory from consciousness and put it out of awareness. The threatening thoughts are pressed down and out of the way so that they just do not come into our consciousness.

This defense often occurs in children who have been sexually abused by someone close to them and who simply cannot tolerate the anxiety of that event. (Just imagine what such a memory means!) In such cases, the recall of the event with its associated anxiety is so painful that the patient totally represses any memory of it. Many months and even years of psychotherapy are needed to uncover the memory and to prepare the sufferer to tolerate the associated anxiety.

We have no understanding of what this process of repression represents in neurological terms. Where does the memory go? Is it just the recall that is inhibited, or is there a much more profound mechanism at work? We just don't know.

What we do know, however, is that it takes a constant expenditure of mental energy to keep the offending thoughts out of consciousness, and therefore that exposing them is necessary to mental healing. We also know, however, that exposure of repressed thoughts can be extremely painful; it often takes the presence of a therapist, pastor, or friend—someone deeply trusted—to help the recall and to comfort such a person as he or she peels away the repression and exposes the feared memory.

(2) *Denial.* Denial is the process of avoiding anxiety by minimizing reality or by blocking a threatening awareness from consciousness. Whereas in repression the threat has already "gotten inside" the consciousness and is pushed down, in denial the individual cuts off the threat before it even gains a foothold. In denial, a mental shield is used to deflect the threat. It never, or hardly ever, gets close enough to be seen for what it really is.

Denial is a very common defense mechanism. It can range in severity from a simple refusal to admit anger to the most bizarre forms of "conversion hysteria," in which people actually convince themselves they are blind or lame to avoid confronting a threatening situation.

I encountered an example of this extreme form of denial when I lived in South Africa. A missionary friend who worked among the Indian population of our city called one Saturday morning to ask me for an opinion. He reported that an eighteen-year-old Indian girl, the daughter of a Hindu couple who had recently converted to Christianity, was to be married that day to a young man she had never seen before. As is the custom with Hindus, this marriage had been arranged by the parents when the girl was only a child. Although the parents were now Christians, and their daughter was in love with a Christian young man, they felt they should honor their promise and go ahead with the wedding.

That morning, only five or six hours before the wedding, the daughter had suddenly become paralyzed from the waist down—unable to walk or even sit up. The family was illiterate and had little knowledge of physiology or psychology. But they suspected something was fishy, so they called my friend the missionary for help and advice. I offered to go with him to visit the family. What I found was that indeed the girl was suffering from "hysterical paralysis." The unacceptable and intense fear of marrying a total stranger when she was already in love with somebody else had literally rendered her unable to move.

I assured the parents that their daughter was not faking. This type of defense is triggered by severe denial and refusal to accept reality. It occurs during wartime, for instance, when young soldiers, fearful of battle, become paralyzed in the right arm so that they cannot shoot a rifle. It is not malingering, but a defense of the mind.

We prayed with the girl and her family, called off the wedding, and within twenty-four hours the paralysis vanished. There was nothing mysterious in the situation—just evidence of a brilliantly created mind that provides wonderful protection when needed.

For most of us, however, denial is used not to protect us from a major threat, but from more insignificant and petty conflicts. We refuse to face up to our weaknesses or to see any flaws in our kids. We deny our hatred or excuse our sinfulness as mere "human nature." Addicts (whether to alcohol or drugs), notoriously deny their problem and refuse to admit they are hooked. Denial is all around us, and a little of it helps to keep us sane. But a lot of denial is an unhealthy way of dealing with reality and its associated anxiety.

Reality is not a dirty word; it is God's gift to us. Living in reality is the only way the gospel's power can be released so that we can be ourselves. Reality is a boundary set for us by God, and we only court disaster when we ignore these limits. Thomas Merton wrote in his book, *Thoughts in Solitude*, "There is no greater disaster in the spiritual life than to be immersed in unreality." All around us—in the movies, TV, novels, and even in some preaching—we are presented with a distorted view of life. We tend to like this distortion because it relieves our anxieties, but we pay for it in increased neuroticism and a missing of God's plan for our growth and sanctification.

(3) *Obsessions.* Obsession means filling the mind with one idea—one thought that haunts and dominates all thinking. An obsessive notion becomes fixed or stuck in our minds very much the way a needle on a scratched phonograph record plays the one snatch of tune over and over again. And the more we try to ignore an obsessive thought, the stronger it becomes.

What causes this type of thinking? Partly it is a desire to solve some riddle or dilemma of life, but mostly it the need to control anxiety by flooding the mind with something utterly irrational or irrelevant.

Excessive guilt feelings often underlie obsession. Suppose, for instance, that a woman—call her Diane, is raised to believe that sexual feelings are evil, that they ought to be resisted because they are all part of Satan's "pleasure temptations" to trap us into sin. This belief serves her parents' purpose of keeping Diane from having sex before marriage. But when Diane marries, she discovers (to her own discomfort and her husband's dismay) that she feels guilty about her natural sexual feelings, even in marriage.

The anxiety caused by conflict between her urges and her childhood beliefs becomes so strong that Diane is unable to face the issues. Instead, she becomes obsessed with the color of the house into which she and her husband have moved. She ruminates all day on how the color bothers her and clashes with the new furniture. Why won't the landlord repaint the house? When can they move somewhere else? What will her mother think when she sees how bad the color is? Why doesn't her husband care enough to deal with the issue?

Diane floods her mind with these less important concerns so as to avoid facing the real source of her anxiety. Slowly this distraction by petty issues becomes entrenched and starts to form the basis for an emotional disorder called "obsessive-compulsive neurosis." (As we will see in the next section, compulsions are often linked to obsessions.)

But even if obsessional tendencies don't cause someone like Diane to become a full-blown neurotic, they can shape the personality in a number of ways. For instance, obsessional tendencies can cause a person to become:

- *Overly rigid and inflexible;*
- *Perfectionistic,* always insisting on perfect tidiness;
- *Overly conscientious,* being unable to let a task remain uncompleted or take a coffee break in the middle of a project;

- *Exclusive,* both in terms of social contacts and religious beliefs (things are "good/bad" and people are "nice/horrible," with no room for anything in between);
- *Possessive,* holding on to people and belongings and not being good at sharing; and
- *Superstitious,* seeing danger in pavement cracks and open ladders and developing little rituals (like touching a door handle twice) to avoid a suspected calamity.

As you can see, obsessing can become a time-consuming and debilitating habit.

(4) *Compulsions.* The last of the defense mechanisms I will discuss here is the group of irresistible and compelling urges that are called "compulsions." While compulsions and obsessions go together as a full-blown neurotic disorder, minor forms of these problems can occur separately.

In the severe obsessive-compulsive disorders, persistent, recurring ideas combine with repetitive and seemingly purposeless behaviors to create havoc in a person's life. The thoughts are involuntary and uncontrollable, senseless and often repugnant (for instance, a pastor about to preach a sermon may suddenly be invaded by vile ideas or sexual thoughts he cannot get rid of). And the behaviors of a compulsive disorder are performed according to certain "rules" and cannot be resisted.

I recently heard of a case in which a salesman with an obsessive-compulsive disorder could not drive past children in the street without becoming obsessed about whether or not he had injured one of them. He would drive around the block to see the children again, and even though everything looked normal, he would continue to circle the block, trapped by his obsession. This happened so often that his work was suffering, so he hired a chauffeur to drive him. Unfortunately, he simply told the chauffeur to drive around the block each time he passed children, so this didn't solve his problem.

The most common obsessions are repetitive thoughts of violence (for example, killing one's child), contamination (by germs, disease, or so on), and doubt. This last obsession is seen quite often in Christian groups; a person may become obsessed with having committed the "unpardonable sin."

The most common compulsions involve frequent hand-washing, counting objects, and checking and repetitively touching objects such as door knobs in a kind of ritual to ward off danger.

There are many "normal" compulsions in everyday life. Pacing the floor when we anxiously await a visitor or drumming a pencil on the table as we listen to an aggravating speech by a disliked colleague are both minor forms of compulsion. These may be unconscious behaviors, but they can easily be stopped when someone draws our attention to them. The more serious compulsions are not so easy to stop; the more they are resisted, the more the tension and the urge to do them builds.

Compulsive masturbation is like this. Feeling guilty immediately after the act, the sufferer pledges never to do it again. But the more he tries to avoid thinking about it and the more he confesses it and pleads for forgiveness, the more driven he becomes to perform the act again. Here, again, the inability to face anxiety is usually the underlying cause of the compulsive behavior. The compulsive act, with its guilt consequences, serves as temporary relief (and even distraction) from the real anxiety problem.

Lust and sexual distortions predominate as the source of anxiety for many compulsives, especially in our Christian subculture where we often try to control our urges in unhealthy ways or impose severe sanctions on the expression of sexual urges.

Severe obsessive-compulsive disorders have always been difficult to treat. Until very recently, there has been no effective medication to stop obsessive thinking or compulsive behavior. There is good news on this front, however. A new medication called Anafranil is pending release by the Federal Drug Administration and should be available by the time this book is published. Research reports point to its being very effective in breaking the chain of ideas or behaviors so characteristic of this disorder. While Anafranil doesn't treat anxiety, it will help to relieve many from the thoughts and behaviors that trap them.

The defense mechanisms I have described are not all bad. In moderation, they have their place; they keep us free of unnecessary anxiety and prevent us from suffering worry or emotional pain over issues we cannot control.

In the area of California where I live, for example, we are living on top of a virtual time bomb—an earthquake zone. Experts tell us that sooner or later the "big one" is going to occur, and the minor earthquakes we experience from time to time are reminders of our vulnerability. But we would all go crazy if we worried all the time about the danger of a major earthquake. So we engage in a certain amount of denial. We "prepare" for a major earthquake by storing water and other supplies, thus reassuring ourselves that we will be safe. We avoid confronting the full danger by thinking that when the earthquake strikes, it will strike in some other part of the city. And then—we just stop thinking about earthquakes. We can't avoid this sort of denial if we continue to live in Los Angeles. Reality is too frightening and the consequences too far-reaching for us to do anything else.

Inappropriate or excessive use of the defense mechanisms is clearly unhealthy, however. While they provide temporary relief from the immediate pain of anxiety, they eventually take their toll in more serious emotional disturbances or physical illnesses.

The first step toward freeing oneself from the clutches of an inappropriate defense mechanism is to develop a clear understanding of how and when you use these defenses. In severe cases, of course, professional therapy will be necessary to bring this about. In other cases, the honest opinion of a friend, pastor, or spouse may help you be aware of your unconscious behaviors. Increased awareness helps to increase the options for bringing about change and healing.

The second step, of course, is to develop healthier ways of coping with anxiety more directly. This will be discussed further in part 2.

FOOD AS A DEFENSE MECHANISM

There are many behaviors we could examine (if space would permit) as examples of defense mechanisms, including many that are considered to be "addicting." Many "hidden" addictions such as workaholism, compulsive exercise, and excessive TV watching are ways of coping with anxiety. Since disorders of eating are so common, I will focus on these problems. In doing so, however, I would like to stress that the other disorders are equally as unhealthy as those connected with eating.

Eating disorders (either undereating or overeating) are a major clinical problem today, and many millions of people use food as a type of tranquilizer to avoid or reduce feelings of anxiety. A recent newspaper report about the unfortunate life story of Christina Onassis illustrates this point well. The daughter of wealth (she was reputed to be worth five hundred million dollars herself), with fantastic opportunities and power, this poor woman literally threw her life away because she was the victim of an anxiety-driven eating problem. She died 19 November 1988, at age thirty-seven, as the result of a life of extremes—too many food binges followed by too many diets. Her heart finally gave out.

Christina's personal life, of course, was a mess. Her life was one of excesses—too many romances, too many marriages followed by too many divorces (four in all), too many disappointments in relationships—but no real love. Even though she realized early in life that her weight problem was an emotional and not a physical one, she was never able to gain control of it. Constant medical care, the best that money could buy, could not give her what she needed most: the feeling that she was loved for her own sake. Not to be loved this way is to live in a constant state of anxiety.

There is no doubt in my mind that food is a pacifier of panic and that eating can help to calm anxious tendencies. I am also convinced that problems with undereating (anorexia nervosa) or eating and then getting rid of what has been eaten through laxatives or self-induced vomiting (bulimia nervosa) serve the same purpose. The problem, of course, is that excessive use of food (or food avoidance) to calm anxiety only brings more anxiety—in the form of guilt, social rejection, and loss of control—not to mention physical hazards.

Problems with food are not a modern phenomenon. The Bible, for instance, sees food as one of the essentials of life (Prov. 31:15) and as one of the great gifts of God (Rom. 14:14), but it also makes it clear that our appetites can be misused (Phil. 3:19) and that food is not something that brings us nearer to God (1 Cor. 8:8). The Bible makes it clear that the problem is not with the food itself, but with *eating*—or more specifically, with looking for security and fulfillment in anything other than God. This was a problem from the beginning, when Adam and Eve ate from the forbidden tree (Gen. 2:17).

Apart from the Bible, there are frequent references in ancient literature to eating and being overweight. Leonardo da Vinci, among his many inventions, created a body-weight scale, although it is only in recent times that the use of scales to weigh people has become widespread. Today the body-weight scale is a part of every bathroom, and this is not surprising, since between forty and eighty million Americans are obese. Furthermore, obesity is six times more common for lower socioeconomic groups than for higher. This is true for both children and adults, and it may well be related to the fact that food serves as an effective tranquilizer for coping with life problems.

It is important to understand that in many ways obesity, anorexia, and bulimia are manifestations of the same problem—a dependence on food (or refusing food) to relieve anxiety.

The typical pattern goes something like this. Let us suppose I develop a high level of anxiety. At an early age I find that food calms me, and that food with a high fat or sugar content does the trick better than lettuce. So every time I get anxious I reach for the cookie jar, chocolate bar, or other delicacy! It does the trick, and I feel less anxious—but I have to eat again when anxiety strikes, and soon I grow obese.

But what if I have internalized the cultural norm that only thin people are beautiful and acceptable? In this case, no sooner have I started to reach for the food than another anxiety is created—guilt—

which I now add to my original anxiety. I become obsessed, therefore, with not eating because obsessions are psychological pacifiers for guilt-type anxieties. This would be anorexia. Or I might eat first and then induce vomiting as a way of getting rid of both the food I've eaten and my anxiety. Bulimia can quickly become my obsession.

It's a fact: Food is therapeutic. Food heals our hearts. Calories are tranquilizing. And cutting off the food supply is like pinching the oxygen line for a diver; it threatens the very essence of security and survival. It seems quite clear, therefore, that the problem of undereating or overeating is not just a problem of habit. For many, it is an expression of deep-seated anxiety, and healing requires more than a change in eating habits.

As we proceed to explore our understanding of anxiety in all its forms and develop ways for coping with it, hopefully the reader will find practical help for dealing with this problem.

Part 2

POSITIVE HELP FOR ANXIETY

In part 1 of this book, I examined the complexity of anxiety. I also sought to develop a better understanding of its nature and to show how it inflicts pain and discomfort. In part 2, I will apply this understanding to the task of overcoming anxiety problems.

Many who have struggled for years with a variety of anxiety disorders have watched their lives fall apart, their careers thwarted, and their happiness disintegrating. They have had to carry the burden of their own guilt about their failures and tolerate the condemnation of friends and loved ones. They have reasoned that scores of people face anxieties every day and survive, so why can't they? Many have found that the psychotherapy or medical treatment they have sought has not always been successful. They feel hopeless and trapped by the belief that they will never recover from their problem.

If this is the case for you or someone you care about, take heart. Your condition can be treated, and in many cases cured. Anxiety does not need to cripple. Attention to the basic principles I will describe can both prevent the onset of an anxiety problem and reverse one that is already established. While there are no easy answers, and it will take work to master the techniques I will describe, with God's help the problem can be mastered.

PINPOINTING THE SOURCE OF ANXIETY — 9

In the first part of this book, I reviewed how anxiety symptoms develop and described the various diagnostic categories of anxiety disorders; I also provided some general advice on how to deal with anxiety. In the chapters to come, I want to focus more specifically on ways to bring anxiety under control—both by dealing with the symptoms and by developing a less anxious lifestyle. I will begin by pinpointing the general life issues that cause anxiety and suggesting ways of approaching these issues that will help you avoid destructive anxiety.

LIFE ISSUES THAT CAUSE ANXIETY

The fact that our bodies and minds react to life circumstances the way they do is only one side of the anxiety story. The other side is that anxiety comes from the problems and uncertainties of life itself! Accordingly, the way we approach the basic issues of life largely determines how much anxiety we experience. It is certainly possible to reduce anxiety symptoms and to strengthen the body and the mind to withstand the onslaught of life's turmoils, and in the chapters to come I will show some ways to do this. More basically, however, we must come to terms with—and, if necessary, make changes in—the way we address important life issues.

Figure 6 presents five major life issues that create anxiety, along with five corresponding strategies for overcoming and preventing the anxiety these issues cause. These five strategies are the "building blocks" for constructing a healthy defense against unhealthy anxiety.

INSECURITY

Earlier I discussed the experience of childhood separation and showed how it can cause an anxiety problem we call "separation anxiety." This can be a very debilitating problem for a child, causing unrealistic fears, oversensitivity, self-consciousness, and chronic anxiety. But the effects of early separation are not confined to childhood; they can carry over into the adolescent years and on into adulthood. The problems of one stage of life have an unavoidable impact on the next stage.

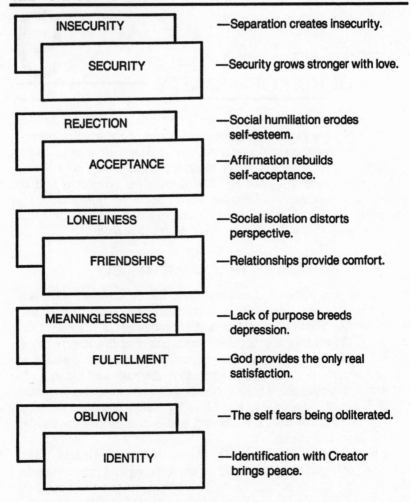

INSECURITY —Separation creates insecurity.

SECURITY —Security grows stronger with love.

REJECTION —Social humiliation erodes self-esteem.

ACCEPTANCE —Affirmation rebuilds self-acceptance.

LONELINESS —Social isolation distorts perspective.

FRIENDSHIPS —Relationships provide comfort.

MEANINGLESSNESS —Lack of purpose breeds depression.

FULFILLMENT —God provides the only real satisfaction.

OBLIVION —The self fears being obliterated.

IDENTITY —Identification with Creator brings peace.

Figure 6: Building Blocks for a Defense against Anxiety

One of the major consequences of separation anxiety is that it sets up a state of heightened *insecurity* that permeates every aspect of life. This insecurity affects relationships, work performance, and self-confidence and often creates a fear of failure.

Insecurity in adult life can cause a great deal of emotional discomfort and be the source of unexplainable anxiety. Failure to pinpoint it as a source means not only that the anxiety will continue unabated, but that it will probably get worse. Insecurities are like hidden cancers.

Uncorrected, they continue to grow in influence, devouring all that is in their way. They should be dealt with, therefore, at the earliest possible opportunity.

I recall a patient whose life was a graphic illustration of how pervasive the influence of insecurity can be. This man was an extremely talented and productive musician—a masterful performer and creator of good music. His gift could have made him a major performer, composer, or orchestra leader, if it were not for a pervasive and acute insecurity that had begun in his childhood.

During his growing up years, this man had never been praised for any success, but always pushed to do better: "Next time you'll get it right." As a result, he came to believe that no matter how well he performed—no matter how much applause or affirmation he received—he was never good enough. This failure to measure up to his own expectations did not become a motivating force, an encouragement to become even better. Instead, it demoralized him and made him feel so anxious and insecure that he frequently wanted just to give up. He steadily became more morose, and finally a severe depression ended his career.

My patient was racked by anxiety because his insecurity kept him from accepting his own limitations. Because we live in an imperfect world, his failure to accept his own imperfections could not help but make him anxious.

In what other ways does insecurity create anxiety in our lives? Here are a few:

- *Insecurity keeps us from loving fully.* We fear that we will be rejected or that our love will not be reciprocated, so we hold back on loving others.
- *Insecurity keeps us from risking.* We lack the courage to take life on with gusto. We don't try new adventures because uncharted waters represent risk. But the person who risks nothing does nothing, and the person who does nothing *is nothing*.
- *Insecurity keeps us from making commitments.* We refuse to commit to any obligation or responsibility because we are unsure of ourselves and our abilities—the boat we are standing in is so shaky that we feel it will capsize at any moment. We don't want to become involved or take on any project because we're not sure we can follow through.
- *Insecurity keeps us from being spontaneous.* We won't laugh because we fear looking like a fool. We won't cry because we fear someone will think we're sentimental. We won't share our ideas

because we're not sure they will be appreciated. Lacking spontaneity, we also lack freedom to be ourselves.

• *Insecurity keeps us from fully becoming God's people.* If we cannot trust people, what makes us think we can trust God? If we cannot give ourselves in commitment to others, how will it be easier to give our all to God? Have you ever considered that your insecurity could perhaps be a barrier to your spiritual growth?

How can we overcome insecurity? The only satisfactory answer is:

BUILD A MORE SOLID SOURCE OF SECURITY.

This is the first building block in building a defense against anxiety.

Understanding the source of one's insecurity can help a little, but this understanding—something we psychologists call "insight"—is actually of limited value in bringing about healing. *Sometimes* insight helps to free someone from the bondage of early childhood training. Knowing why you become insecure may help to reconstruct your understanding of what you are doing in the present and it may free you from self-blame. But most times, insight is just academic. The behaviors still continue unchanged, even though you know why you do them. Now, re-experiencing childhood trauma is quite a different matter and involves more than mere insight; it actually recreates deep feelings and allows for the release of these feelings. But this technique requires a professional therapist; it takes much skill and experience to lead someone through a painful early experience, facilitating the recovery of deep feelings associated with early life traumas, without making the problem worse. It certainly should not be attempted by any reader without professional help.

I once had a client who used to become deeply upset if his wife wasn't waiting for him when he returned from work. He would often climb back into his car and drive around for half an hour until he thought she had come home. If she still wasn't there, he would go into the bedroom, flop on the bed and pout for the rest of the evening. He could not understand why he did this, but he realized his insecurity was ruining his marriage, so he decided to seek help. His request was, "Help me pinpoint the source of these feelings."

Well, it didn't take us long to discover the source of the problem. His early school years had been a painful period of his life. Other children often teased him, and at the end of the school day he would run home to the security and comfort of his mother. But she had many social engagements and often wasn't there when he came home. He would come home to an empty house, aching for comfort. In order to punish her (and to manipulate her into staying home for him), he would go to his room and pout. Mother would come home, try to placate him by explaining why she was delayed, but to no avail; he remained miserable. Slowly this man had developed an affinity for pouting, which offered him a strange comfort in the form of self-pity.

Having identified the source of my client's insecurity I waited to see if he got better. He didn't; if anything, his pouting got worse. We had to shift our therapy focus to another strategy and used a paradoxical approach which often works in cases like this. In effect, we gave his wife permission to stay away when he was expected to return from work and forced the husband to accept this, gradually desensitizing him to his insecurities.

The reason insight alone did not help my client to change is very simple: His pouting had become a habit far removed from its original source; it had taken on a life all its own! No matter how well he understood the cause, his understanding alone would not have stopped the behavior. He had to learn new behaviors more appropriate to his adult status.

If you feel the need to identify the origin of your insecurity, then explore your past and try to pinpoint it. You will probably need someone else to talk to about it, since this sort of exploration is seldom successful when carried on within the confines of your head. Actually talking about your past seems to open up parts of the memory that are difficult to access merely by thinking. Remember, however, that just uncovering the origins of your insecurity won't in itself make you more secure.

If understanding our insecurity won't necessarily make us more secure, what will? Scripture very clearly addresses this issue and stresses that true security must have a spiritual foundation or "grounding." The only safe buildings are those with secure foundations. Similarly, the only truly secure people are those who are "rooted and grounded" (Eph. 3:17) in the security of a relationship with the Source of their being.

Jesus Himself claimed that "whosoever heareth these sayings of mine and doeth them, I will liken him unto a wise man, which built his house upon a rock" (Matt. 7:24, KJV). This is the best foundation anyone can have.

When I was growing up in a small gold-mining community of South Africa, we often sang a hymn by Edward Mote (1797–1894) called "The Solid Rock." Its theology is not very profound, but its spiritual value was enormous to me, especially after I became a Christian at the insecure age of eighteen. It goes:

> My hope is built on nothing less
> Than Jesus' blood and righteousness,
> I dare not trust the sweetest frame,
> but wholly lean on Jesus name.
>
> On Christ the solid rock I stand,
> All other ground is sinking sand,
> All other ground is sinking sand.

That term "solid rock" was very comforting to me as an adolescent. Not much else in my life felt very secure at that time; my home was shaky and my future uncertain. But when I found Christ, I also found a new security deep within my being. I had become "grounded" in eternal security.

Even with this new security, however, I found it took a lot of courage to "come out" for Christ. I had to face up to my buddies' ridicule and tell them I wasn't going to make it on my own anymore. And this points to another essential element in building our security: We have to admit our insecurities to ourselves and others. True, this means the risk of encouraging others to hurt us more, but unless we admit our weakness, we will not cast ourselves upon the "Rock" of Christ. Christ cannot become our security unless we admit to ourselves and others our insecurities.

We all want to appear strong. We don't like to let others see our weak side or to give the slightest impression of inadequacy. We fear that people will not like us or will lose respect for our abilities if we appear insecure. This need to appear strong is perhaps the greatest obstacle to building a solid base of security. Because we cannot show our insecurities, we also forfeit the help and support that others can give us. So if you want to build more security, you must be willing to be vulnerable. And, quite surprisingly, when you show your weakness, most other people can identify with it and become your allies, not your enemies. It's a risk you've got to take.

REJECTION

The second life issue that creates anxiety is the fear of rejection. Let me state my main point here quite clearly: You cannot build an anxiety-free life by avoiding rejection; instead, you must create for yourself a system of acceptance that is *not* dependent on the approval of others.

The fear of rejection—and I am speaking about social rejection—affects us too much in our culture. We give other people far too much power over us. Their view of us sometimes becomes more important than our own view or even God's view. We often come to assume that God sees us as our fellow believers do—that their eyes are His eyes. Not only is this untrue; it is also a source of much anxiety.

Rejection by our parents is, of course, the origin of this fear. We begin life craving their acceptance and then carry this need into our adult lives, generalizing it to other people. This often results in many compromised behaviors and many sleepless nights. And when our need to please others violates our responsibility to do what God wants us to do, we also violate our relationship with Him. After all, our primary obligation is to be approved by God (2 Tim. 2:15)—not by other people. Now, I am not trying to say we must never take others into consideration nor be guided by the wisdom of others. There is a sense in which we are obligated to consider others so as not to cause offense or be a stumbling block. And there are certain friends whose opinions we *should* respect; they see us more objectively than we see ourselves and really care about our welfare.

What I am talking about is the strong tendency I see in so many, myself included, to always do that which pleases others so as to be considered "nice" or to obtain the greatest praise. "People pleasing" of this kind breeds a fear of rejection that causes too much anxiety for our own good.

Some approval, when it is well deserved, is necessary for the development of a healthy self-esteem. Approval which is sought at any cost is neurotic and creates a climate of anxiety, because this need cannot be met continuously. You cannot please some people even some of the time—and you certainly will not be able to please all people all of the time!

Excessive fear of rejection creates anxiety because of two basic facts:

- You cannot go through life without some rejection—so it is *unavoidable.*
- You cannot be too sensitive to rejection without undermining your faith—so you run the risk of being *disobedient.*

What are some of the *unhealthy* ways in which we avoid the anxiety of rejection?

- We say things we don't mean.
- We avoid doing things we ought to do.
- We become a "head nodder," always approving others for fear that they will think we don't agree.
- We become intimidated by stronger people.
- We are always "sweet," even "sugary," no matter what others do to us.
- We end up doing things for others we really don't want to do.
- We buy things we don't need to buy.
- We apologize for things we didn't do.

How does this make us feel?

- We often feel like hypocrites.
- We often feel that we are dishonest.
- We mostly feel angry and resentful at those we must please to avoid rejection.
- We seldom feel in control of ourselves.
- We hardly ever feel self-respect.

The strategy for countering rejection is the second building block in the defense against anxiety:

BUILD A SYSTEM OF ACCEPTANCE
FOR YOURSELF.

It is impossible to withstand the pressure to please others without having a stable and honest method of affirming yourself. When you want to resist being controlled by others, you must be able to do this without any anxiety. Take saying no, for example. Suppose someone has asked to borrow your best piece of jewelry for a date or made some other reasonable or unreasonable request. How do you typically feel when you refuse the request? A little guilty? Very guilty? A little unsure of yourself? Perhaps a little selfish?

Why do you have such feelings? Is it not your prerogative to withhold lending your own property, especially when it is something you prize? Do you not have a right to refuse other people's requests without feeling guilty, even if the request is reasonable? Of course you do! And you must claim this right occasionally or risk becoming an anxiety-ridden person.

How can you affirm yourself and accept what are your reasonable rights? Here are some suggestions:

(1) *Get in touch with your own approval-seeking behaviors and fears of rejection.* I don't just mean find out what their origins are, but try to increase your awareness of them when you actually feel them.

(2) *It helps to pull back and be very clinical or therapeutic with yourself at these times.* See each new demand as a challenge, not as a threat. Ask yourself, "Am I merely wanting to please someone so as to avoid being rejected?" If your answer is yes, don't do it!

(3) *Remind yourself that you cannot be controlled by the fear of rejection.* Try to focus on understanding what is going on as a way of freeing yourself to do what you really believe needs to be done, not what you think someone else wants you to do.

(4) *Claim the freedom God gives you to please only Him*—and then *do* it by faith!

(5) *After you act, don't engage in a lengthy analysis of whether or not you did the right thing.* Acting in faith will always leave a residual question or two about your action—if you were 100 percent sure, you wouldn't need faith! When you've acted as you see fit—then *trust* your action. Even if it turns out wrong, God will take care of the situation.

(6) *Don't let other people's problems become yours.* Keep a clear line of differentiation between your problems and theirs. Be aware when someone else is "putting a monkey on your back" and remind yourself that it is not your "monkey." Politely return it to its rightful owner!

(7) *Throughout, maintain an attitude of love.* Never respond with anger to any request for a favor. Anger indicates that you don't feel in control. Remind yourself that the reason you want to break the cycle of rejection and anxiety is that you want to become God's person more completely. You are not doing it out of a spirit of revenge or to be "ornery." Love may have to be tough, but "tough love" is a far cry from anger and aggressiveness.

LONELINESS

Loneliness is a frequent cause of anxiety, and a difficult one to resolve in some situations. Actually, loneliness in itself does not cause anxiety. But because it serves as a catalyst to other life issues, loneliness easily becomes a significant *amplifier* of anxiety. It does this in two ways:

(1) *Loneliness robs the sufferer of a system of support, which is essential in preventing anxiety.* For many of us our families are a major, if not the primary, support system. We rely on our spouses, children, parents, siblings, aunts, uncles—and even the cat—to provide support, comfort, and a listening ear (and occasionally serve as a scapegoat) and thus to relieve our anxieties. Friends, co-workers, and fellow church members also can be part of this circle of support.

But many in our society have no support system—no immediate family, and not even a single friend! They live by themselves, cut-off from any intimate or caring relationships.

Others may have people around them, but the relationships are cold and uncaring—like the husband and wife I heard of recently who haven't spoken to each other for more than five years. They live together, eat together, watch TV together, and even go to the movies together, but they only grunt yes or no at each other. They never share a laugh, enjoy a sunset or even poke fun at each other. Together—yes. Lonely—absolutely! And the wife, at least, is eaten up daily with anxiety. How does the husband manage? No one knows. He won't talk to anyone about it!

The lack of a support system can be a significant problem, but it is also one that is easily rectified by reaching out to others. In every neighborhood there are scores of other lonely people; it is really not hard to find a friend by being a friend. Church is also an important resource in building a support system; supporting one another in the Christian life is part of what the Body of Christ is all about.

(2) *Loneliness can also be a catalyst for anxiety in its own right: it becomes a source of concern to the one who is lonely.* In our society we believe strongly in community, even though we may not practice it much! This causes many who are lonely to feel more lonely than they ought to because they become so acutely aware of their loneliness and grow anxious over it. They erroneously believe that others are not as lonely as they are.

Even though support systems are important, it *is* possible to be alone without being crippled by anxiety. There are people who can manage quite satisfactorily without much support from anyone else. We call them "anomic persons" to describe their being released from the restraints of traditional, conventional social settings. They just don't need people that much. They may have a sense of being lonely, but they don't feel as if they don't belong or that anything is wrong with this. They survive quite well despite their relative isolation.

What this says to me is that we should not become so preoccupied with and fearful of loneliness that we do not see the value of being alone. We should not be so afraid of it and become so concerned about not having a lot of social contacts that the fear of loneliness becomes a source of anxiety. When this happens, lonely people can become so desperate for relationships that they becomes possessive, almost smothering. They frighten the other person away with their excessive need for company, thus destroying the very thing they want so desperately.

The topic of loneliness is a large one, deserving of many books and not just the brief reference I am giving it here. My primary purpose in discussing it is to point up a third building block in a defense against anxiety:

BUILD LASTING AND MEANINGFUL RELATIONSHIPS.

But relationship is a vast topic in itself! For reasons of space, I will limit my discussion to only one important aspect of relationships— how we *sabotage* them.

There is a considerable body of research that shows that positive social and family relationships can lessen the impact of stress and alleviate anxiety. Why, then, do we set up barriers to intimacy and closeness and make it so difficult for people to love us?

Here are some possible reasons, together with suggestions for remedying the sabotage. As you review them, ask yourself whether you engage in this sort of sabotage. If you're not sure, ask the person who is emotionally the closest to you to review the list with you and give you honest feedback.

(1) *We sabotage our relationships because we are more interested in manipulating people than we are in loving them.* Insecure people have a great need to manipulate their friendships in order to increase their security. Power-hungry and dominating people manipulate to meet their need for domination. But manipulation destroys the very basis of all meaningful relationships: that there be an equal giving and receiving of respect, love, and care. Meaningful relationships are a matter of "give and take," and taking more than you give destroys the balance of the relationship.

(2) *We sabotage our relationships because we don't nourish them.* I must confess to something: I am a terrible gardener. I love beautiful gardens; I can enjoy them for hours and appreciate their beauty. But I cannot keep a garden going without lots of help. My problem is that I forget to water the plants, protect them, and feed them—consequently they die. This is a good analogy for relationships. They also need loving care and lots of nourishing. They require time, attention, openness, and a willingness to be a source of comfort and support.

(3) *We sabotage our relationships because we allow our needs to dominate over the needs of others.* If we go anywhere, we go to the place *we* have chosen. If we do anything—it is the activity of *our* choosing. *We* decide when we meet and how often. As a spouse, perhaps, we don't even ask what it is our partner would prefer; we feel we know the other person so well that we can choose for him or her. Philippians 2:4 suggests an antidote to this kind of relationship sabotage. I particularly like the Living Bible translation, which reads, "Don't just think about your own affairs, but be interested in others, too, and in what they are doing." This is sound advice if you want to build healthy relationships.

(4) *We sabotage our relationships because we force others into becoming what we want them to be.* I call this "coercive molding." We decide what we need in someone else and then, in effect, we construct a mold and then ask the other person to conform to it.

Why do we want others to be a certain way? Perhaps it's because we feel we can then relate more easily to them. Perhaps it's because the way they are doesn't meet enough of our needs. Who knows? But true friendship gives others the freedom to remain as they are; it doesn't demand that they change in order to meet our needs. People are always changing and growing, but they must change and grow at their own pace, not ours. We cannot force them into a pattern of our design and then expect them to continue being our friend.

Only one mold should govern anyone's life, and that is the mold that God imposes on us. His mold perfectly fits His plan for us. By giving others the freedom not to change to meet *our* needs, we free them to become what God intends for them to be.

MEANINGLESSNESS

Meaninglessness is a life issue that can cause very intense anxiety because it strikes at the very core of our existence. Many people today are deeply concerned about the predicament of humankind, the breakdown of traditional faith, the alienation and depersonalization of the individual, the domination of drug abuse, and the inability of the superpowers to create a peaceful world. Many others, however, are more concerned about their humdrum, purposeless routine of boring work that translates into a life of meaninglessness. The really "big" issues of human existence never touch them because they feel they have enough to contend with just getting through each day.

With increasing frequency, I am encountering business executives and professionals (including Christians) who feel their lives are meaningless and who experience intense anxiety as a consequence. They come to therapy because they feel that life has lost its purpose. They have no idea where they are headed; they are not sure why they exist! Some contemplate having an affair or giving in to a midlife crisis just to introduce some excitement into their lives—others have already launched their actions in this direction. They feel that family matters are no longer important and are quite ready to dump all their responsibilities. "Let my kids fend for themselves," I hear them say, "I had to put myself through college, so they can too."

Often these individuals have been extremely successful in their work, earning both financial security and respect, but these successes no longer mean anything to them. Days at work are viewed as "wasted," "going nowhere," and "worthless." "What's the point of it all?" one said to me recently. "I make good money, but I don't seem to be any happier. I've got all I want, but I'm not satisfied." These are typical statements one hears again and again.

And there is also a lot of anxiety pain for these people. They are panicked *and* bored at the same time. They fear that life is passing too fast, that they are missing out on the action. At the same time, they feel stale and listless, and dread hangs over them like smog over a city, choking out any remaining shreds of meaning or purpose.

What can one say to such a person? What building block in the bulwark of defense against anxiety offers an answer to this life issue? Meaninglessness can only be avoided if we:

DEVELOP A SENSE OF DIRECTION AND FULFILLMENT.

Now, I am not just talking about self-fulfillment. Our preoccupation with self, in fact, is the source of the problem. In our success-driven society, too many see fulfillment only in terms of satisfying selfish needs. Such a person almost inevitably experiences a "life crisis" at some point, because sooner or later the hollowness of such a pursuit becomes obvious.

The fulfillment which serves as an antidote for meaninglessness is the fulfillment that comes from feeling and believing that you are being successful in accomplishing the purposes of God. It is succeeding in the totality of your life, not just in your career or business.

In addition, real, deep fulfillment comes not so much from achieving some level of material or personal success as from *resting* from the need to do a great work. *Being* is more fulfilling than *doing*. And we can achieve more in God's name if we get this order straight, because then we will be striving to be successful for the right reasons and in the right areas of life.

In support of this idea, let me refer you to an important passage of Scripture. In Hebrews 3 and 4, we encounter several references to "rest." The first three verses of chapter 4 make clear that this is a spiritual "rest" into which we enter into by faith. Later, verse 9 points to the eternal rest that awaits us in the future: "There remaineth therefore a rest to the people of God" (KJV).

Between these two great "rests," we have to live out our lives to the best of our ability. We must make the most of every opportunity (as the parable of the talents suggests) and fulfill God's plan for our lives. And even in the period between these two great "rests" we are to "labour together to enter that rest" (Heb. 4:11, KJV).

I suggest that all of our life in Christ is to be a "resting." We rest from our selfish motives to succeed. We rest from our need to appease God or anyone else we may have put in His place. And we rest from our need to "do it our way." We rest every moment of every day in the Christ who sustains and gives us life. This is the only way to a meaningful and fulfilling life.

OBLIVION

We come finally to the ultimate life issue—a source of deep anxiety. It is the realization that life is limited and that, when all is said and done, we are but a speck of dust on this earth. Most of our anxiety can ultimately be traced back to fears related to this life issue—fears like the fear of death and of oblivion. In addition, this issue finds expression in lesser forms of anxiety, including fear of heights, flying, earthquakes, pain, and of dentists!

Most of the time, of course, we move about and conduct our lives without actually believing in our own death. We know in the back of our minds that we will die someday, but we don't let the fact consciously bother us. We continue to live in the shadow of volcanoes, in the path of tornadoes, and on the ridge of earthquake-prone faults. Denial helps us to go about our lives more or less normally; perhaps we even fool ourselves into believing, irrationally, that we'll beat death and attain immortality. When we live in denial of our own human finitude, our most fundamental fear, the fear of dying, finds expression in other anxieties.

It is surprising how few of my patients come to therapy for the express purpose of resolving their fear of death. Usually this fear is expressed in more mundane complaints. A few come in when a terminal illness forces them to confront the reality of death, but most only discover this fear in the process of their therapy. By and large, this fundamental and largely biological fear has to be discovered through the exploration of other forms of anxiety.

If we live in denial of this basic fear, what happens to it? Mostly we push it out of our awareness by becoming preoccupied with our quest for successful living and enjoying our pleasures. These repressions are then only jarred loose when some life-threatening experience—a car accident, a near-fatal heart attack, an earthquake—brings us to the brink of death. Our repressions are then momentarily set aside, and the stark anxiety of oblivion strikes terror deep inside us.

Now, this ever-present fear of extinction, whether openly acknowledged or pushed out of our awareness, can take one of two courses:

- It can be absorbed into the fabric of everyday life and used to give zest and provide perspective for effective living. This is clearly the healthy option.
- It can force us into distractions such as alcohol, anxiety, neuroses, and workaholism. This is clearly destructive.

I have suggested that the anxieties caused by the fear of flying, heights, snakes, knives, and other dangerous activities are essentially variations of the fundamental fear of dying. Let me elaborate on this point.

It is essential to the survival of the human organism that it be afraid of everything that threatens its survival. Some fears, such as the fear of falling, are therefore instinctive to ensure this survival; you can see these clearly even in a baby. Other fears, such as the fear of fire, have to be learned. Just as pain alerts us to organic destruction, so fear alerts us to threat and danger.

Flying is obviously a dangerous activity. Those of us who fly regularly very quickly lose our anxiety over being six or seven miles up in the air, at the mercy of a crate of aluminum, and with a total stranger at the controls. But it only takes one frightening personal experience to remind us of how precious life is and how easily we can associate anxiety with anything that threatens it.

Flying back from Hawaii a short time ago, I was relaxed and engrossed in a book. My wife was by my side. We had enjoyed a restful few days following a busy speaking schedule. Everything was safe and cozy, and I settled back in my seat after dinner for a comfortable read.

Then I smelled it. Something was burning. I knew the smell well. It was like burning plastic—just the sort of smell you get when you have a short in an electrical appliance. But we were flying at thirty-five hundred feet over the ocean, with two hours to go before we reached Los Angeles. What was burning?

I called a steward, who was also alarmed by the smell. He called the pilot. Together we began to search for the cause. The movie projector had not worked earlier, so there had been no entertainment on the flight. Perhaps the short was in the projector? We did a quick check, but the smell wasn't coming from the projector. For eight or ten anxiety-filled minutes, we searched all around for the cause. We all had the same thought—could this be a fire that could cause us to crash?

Twenty years of indifference toward the hazards of flying began to dissipate for me on that plane. I realized that my fear of flying—and of death—was still very much alive. If I allowed it to take hold, I could easily become extremely anxious.

Fortunately, we finally found the source of the problem—an overheated lighting ballast. We turned out the lights and flew the remainder of the way in darkness to prevent any further problems, but we all arrived safely in Los Angeles. That plane flight was a powerful reminder to me that we desperately cling to life and that any threat to take life away causes us intense anxiety.

What can counter this basic source of anxiety?

BECOME AWARE OF YOUR IDENTITY.

But the label *identity* doesn't do full justice to what I want to say. If the state we fear is oblivion or extinction, then what God gives us to hold on to is the peace of knowing that we will always exist for Him. He gives us an *eternal* identity. And with this identity, this realization that life is only a part of a broader, more glorious existence, we can begin to accept and face the real dilemma of existence: that we are mortal creatures who have full consciousness of our mortality.

How hard it is for us to really grasp this truth without being threatened by it! Knowing we are destined for death ought to affect us in such a way that we live every precious moment to the fullest and that we redeem every mistake or moment of bitterness. My cat doesn't know she is going to die; her brain lacks the capacity for this knowledge. But because I know it, I am capable of living a more satisfying and complete life than my cat. This then becomes the challenge: How can I live my life more satisfyingly, more completely, knowing that my earthly life is limited?

The fear of death and oblivion can be an incentive to living a fuller life, especially when I realize that God gives me an eternal identity. I can surrender to His will and achieve the highest personal development because I can know my life has purpose. My eyes are opened to the reality of eternity, and this gift of seeing the whole and glorious plan of God engenders hope and comfort.

As a result I can begin to quell the voice of anxiety that would seek to scare me. I can gracefully.embrace aging and one day look forward to being released from this pain-bearing and decaying body to take on a new one, "fashioned like unto his glorious body . . . " (Phil. 3:21, KJV). In this life I have been lent a natural body, but it is to be raised as a spiritual one (1 Cor. 15:44), and *because* of this I am called to be "stedfast, unmoveable, always abounding in the work of the Lord . . . " (v. 58).

We can't help thinking of death as a terror. But in reality, life is the terror, the real source of all our anxieties. And there is only one solution to the terror of life—to be healed by embracing the Source of all life. God, in Christ, waits to give us that healing.

10 CONTROLLING ANXIETY THROUGH CORRECT THINKING

Whatever form your anxiety takes, whether it is a biological reaction to depleted brain tranquilizers or a psychological reaction to impending threat, you can be certain of one thing: Your thinking—the activities of your mind—are always involved to some extent.

In some cases of anxiety, the source of the problem lies entirely in the realm of the mind. In other forms, the mind is recruited by hormonal deficiencies or oversensitive adrenalin receptors to do battle with itself. So whatever approach you take to overcoming anxiety, sooner or later you must confront the contribution of your thinking—what you believe, how you perceive, and the way you do logic. We are creatures (some would say victims) of the mind, which is why it desperately needs to be renewed.

The process of thinking is very complex. Some thoughts we can control; others control us. Some beliefs are easy to change, others are indelibly imprinted and remain throughout our lives. Some thinking takes place consciously; we know what we are thinking and how we are reasoning. Other thinking is unconscious and needs to be brought into the light of our awareness and controlled if we are to reduce anxiety.

One very important component of our thinking is *imagination.* It is important because when uncontrolled it both creates and feeds *all* anxiety. This God-given creative power also has the negative potential to entice us away from reality, to exaggerate little fears and turn them into monsters, to rob us of our strength by convincing us we are beaten. Above all else, then, the anxiety-ridden person must learn how to take control of his or her imagination, to challenge and contain it.

This chapter will address the problem of thinking and show ways in which it can be challenged to reduce anxiety. Those who suffer from anxiety must be willing to confront old, learned habits of thinking and exercise self-discipline in the realm of the mind. Without these changes in thinking patterns, no amount of tranquilizer or psychotherapy is going to bring about healing! Because anxiety is ultimately a problem of the mind, aided and abetted by the body, it is in the mind that we must effect change if there is to be a cure for pathological anxiety.

Fortunately, the resources made available to us through the gospel

138

can help us cope with our sometimes unreasonable and often irrational minds. Paul reminds us that Christ came to transform us "by the renewing of [our] mind[s]" (Rom. 12:2), and that we have "the mind of Christ" (1 Cor. 2:16).

I take this not only to mean that I must be Christlike in my thinking, but also that I do not have to rely entirely on my own mental resources. I do not have to be perfectly logical nor have a high IQ to live a Christlike life. I need *only* to let His mind take full charge of me as I surrender to His will. In this way, I can begin to turn my thinking around and to lay a healthier foundation for the way I view my world.

But I also take the "mind of Christ" to mean that I have a responsibility to "order" my thoughts and pay careful attention to how I think. There is a part I must play in bringing my thoughts under control. I am neither a puppet nor a programmed computer. What and how I think is *my* responsibility. Second Corinthians 10:5 makes this very clear, exhorting us to "Cast . . . down imaginations . . . and bring . . . into captivity every thought to the obedience of Christ" (KJV). This is both a spiritual *and* a psychological exercise.

WHAT MAKES UP OUR THOUGHTS?

We all know that we think. But we seldom stop and consider what makes up our thoughts and how we do our thinking. For instance, have you ever thought about how susceptible you are to all sorts of sincere but erroneous beliefs, how gullible your attitudes are and how deceptive your rationalizations?

Basically, there are five *components* to our thoughts: beliefs, attitudes, expectations, assumptions, and perceptions. Singly or in combination, these components determine how we feel about things, what sort of car we buy, how we dress, what we eat, and so forth.

(1) *Beliefs.* Beliefs are the foundations of our thoughts. The human mind is designed to be able to *believe* things. Ultimately this capacity is to be used in relating to God. Animal minds don't really believe—they just accept. But we are capable of discriminating between a thing's being true or false, real or unreal. We can be firmly persuaded that Christ has died for our sins—and this then becomes a belief.

Beliefs determine much of what we do and especially what we feel. If I believe that being anesthetized is very dangerous and that having surgery is likely to harm me, for instance, I am likely to be very anxious when undergoing surgery, even for an impacted tooth. Unfortunately, therefore, beliefs can become somewhat distorted and then become "false." We call beliefs "irrational" when they do not have a basis in reality or when they are destructive, but that doesn't make them any less powerful in controlling our thoughts.

(2) *Attitudes.* A further complication to thought processes is the fact that people do not always know what it is they believe, nor why. When beliefs operate without conscious reflection, we refer to them as *attitudes.* For instance, I may have a negative "attitude" toward guns or alcohol—I don't like them and may even avoid them—and this attitude operates the moment I see a gun or a bottle of booze. I don't have to think about my beliefs regarding guns or alcohol. They are hidden below my consciousness, and they do their work before I consciously react to these objects.

Attitudes are ready at all times to tell me how to feel about something. Attitudes are therefore very important to the experience of anxiety, and anxious people must examine their attitudes closely. The beliefs underlying an attitude toward snakes or high places may have specific origins in experience, or they may be totally irrational and without basis in reality. Until these hidden beliefs are uncovered and understood, however, anxiety over these things will continue to destroy tranquillity.

(3) *Expectations.* Expectations are set up by our beliefs, and they can make or break our happiness. We all have expectations. At the end of the month, I expect to get paid. When I come home in the evening, I expect my wife to kiss me and welcome me with a smile and a cheerful greeting. When I eat a meal, I expect it to be free of harmful ingredients and to satisfy my appetite.

Expectations like this are basically reasonable, although of course there are situations in which those expectations might not be fulfilled. But not all expectations are reasonable. When I expect all people to love me, no matter how I treat them, my expectation is irrational, even unreasonable. When I expect always to succeed at everything I do, I am being unreasonable. If I expect that life must only deliver pleasure and never pain or hardship, I am thinking unreasonably.

So many of our expectations for ourselves and others are irrational and unrealistic. This is the cause of much anxiety, since we cannot control our world or predict how people will behave. We begin to worry when our expectations are not met or when others do not "deliver the goods." This anxiety robs us of tranquillity.

Expectations need to be constantly monitored so that unreasonable ones can be challenged. When we become aware of an expectation, it's a good idea to ask ourselves, *What causes me to think this is a reasonable expectation?*

(4) *Assumptions.* Assumptions are ideas we take for granted. When I drive on the freeway, I assume that other drivers will stay in their lanes

and give me warning if they want to change. This is basically a reasonable assumption, even in Los Angeles traffic! When a husband invites his wife to go to dinner and then assumes that she will make the restaurant reservation without his asking her to, and when he usually does this, the assumption is unreasonable.

We make assumptions, both reasonable and unreasonable, all the time. No exchange of ideas or communication is so complete that it removes the need for assumptive thinking. Let us suppose the husband did make the reservation, told his wife he would fetch her from home at 6:30 P.M., and reminds her to get a babysitter. He still may be surprised to find her dressed in blue jeans and a sweater when he plans on taking her to an exclusive and expensive "top of the town" revolving restaurant!

So many assumptions are necessary in our lives. It would take too long and be too expensive to have to spell out every plan and idea. But assumptions, especially unfounded ones, can also be sources of anxiety. These assumptions become activated when we run into problems or encounter stress.

All of us make assumptions about subjects like religion, health, relationships, and success, and many of these assumptions are framed in an "all-or-nothing" way with no room for gray areas. Here are some examples of assumptions we may make that can make us anxious. Try to identify the assumption underlying each statement and decide whether it is reasonable or unreasonable:

- I am only valuable as a person if everyone loves me.
- If others are to like me, I must never get angry.
- I must at all costs avoid being criticized, because criticism means personal rejection.
- Failure always means that I am useless.
- I must always be at my best and never make a mistake.
- To be competent, I must never let others tell me what to do.
- I must be in control at all times; otherwise, my world will crumble.
- God is always on my side and will punish those who are against me.
- I don't have to take responsibility for what I do because God always acts through me.

Where do we draw the line? How much do we assume and how much should we insist on making clear? When must we challenge our assumptions and when can we ignore them?

Obviously, there are no absolute rules. Every situation is different. Some of us, however, tend to operate out of a greater pool of assumptions than others; we tend to take more for granted than we should and not to communicate our intentions fully. We are always being embroiled in some misunderstanding and thus end up with more anxiety than is necessary. It's a good idea, therefore, to pay attention to our *assumptive* style and make changes where appropriate, to avoid the stress of operating under false assumptions.

(5) *Perceptions.* Perceptions are important because they involve the way we experience the world around us. The world exists for us only because we can see it, touch it, hear it, smell it—and so forth.

But perception involves more than just the operation of our physical senses; it is also a matter of how our minds interpret this sensory data. This means that what we experience through our senses is distorted— or at least colored—by the way our minds work. What we perceive, therefore, may be different from what someone else perceives.

When we say, for instance, that we see "a beautiful tree with green leaves, red apples, and a brown trunk," this is *only our perception* of the tree. A horse would see the colors and even shapes differently because it has a different sensing system. A person who is color-blind would probably also have a completely different perception. And a person who feels differently about apples might have still another perception.

It is a common human trait to confuse "seeing" with "perceiving." Perception is *always* subject to distortion; one never "sees" things perfectly. This has important implications for social relationships, because it reminds us that two different people may have entirely different perceptions of the same object or event. When your wife says to you, "You are only nice to me in front of our friends," you could probably argue with her until you are blue in the face that she's wrong. She sees (perceives) the situation differently. Who is correct? In many social situations, probably no one. But we have to accept perception as legitimate and give the other people credit for perceiving situations differently from the way we do. In addition, knowing the world is not always how we see it, we must make allowances for our own misunderstandings and misperceptions, as well as differences in perception.

In a previous book, now out of print, I told a story that is worth repeating here, because it makes the point that even though we trust what *we* see, we must make allowances for how others perceive situations.

One day early in our marriage, my wife came home and said, "I saw the strangest thing today. I was coming out of the supermarket, and a car turned the corner in front me. It only had three wheels."

"You mean it was a three-wheeler?"

"No," she replied, "it was a regular car. But it was riding on only three wheels."

Well you can imagine how I responded to such an idea! "Come on, now—no ordinary car can stand just on three wheels. Why do you think we use a jack to change a tire?"

And so I argued, but she was adamant: "The car only had three wheels; one wheel was missing."

Very soon my disbelief in her perception caused a full-blown argument, and for many months afterward that three-wheeled car was a source of disagreement between us. I thought, *Why does she not understand the laws of nature?* She probably thought, *Why does he not believe me when I tell him what I saw?*

Well, what eventually resolved the matter for me was the realization that things are not always what they seem—and that even if we are only "perceiving" something, the perception is still *very* real to us. We may never know what my wife really saw that day. Did a shadow cover the fourth wheel? Was her glance too quick to take in the full facts? I don't know. Since telling that story I have received numerous accounts of how people have been able to adapt a car in an emergency to ride on only three wheels.

What my wife was asking me to do that day was to believe her perception. She saw a car with three wheels. If I could have just accepted that, I could have avoided an argument. And if we can only accept the legitimacy of other people's perceptions, true or false, we can begin to build a more harmonious world for ourselves.

Our memories, which are largely reconstructions of our perceptions, are also subject to distortion. If our perceptions can be distorted so as to disagree with someone else's, how much more can our memory of the perceptions be wrong or fuzzy? Unconsciously we select the details we want to remember, reinterpret the facts, and reconstruct pictures that don't always match reality—then we get upset when others don't agree with our version of "the facts." Anyone who has ever tried to solicit eyewitness accounts of an accident or a crime will understand just how much differences in perception and memory can alter reality.

This leads to two important rules for low-anxiety living:

- Always entertain the possibility that the way you perceive things may be wrong.
- Always give other people credit that whether their perception matches reality or not, the perception is real for them.

Since we are all prone to these foibles of human thinking—erroneous beliefs, unreasonable expectations, irrational attitudes, careless assumptions, and faulty perceptions—it's a wonder we are not all trembling with anxiety! Fortunately there is hope. And as we will see, there are ways we can bring ourselves to a healthier and more disciplined way of thinking.

SELF-TALK: GOOD AND BAD

In addition to these components of our thoughts, there are also a number of different ways in which we think; for instance, we can reason, imagine, or evaluate. The way we think is mostly determined by what we say to ourselves—the conversations we carry on within our minds. In beginning to explore the principles of disciplined thinking, we must start at the point of this "self-talk."

We talk to ourselves all the time—not necessarily out loud, but mentally. This self-talk generates ideas and reactions that ultimately become translated into emotions. Often, however, we are totally oblivious to the inner conversations that precede our emotional states. Unless we attend to our self-talk, we can be controlled by an unconscious force that often works to sabotage our tranquillity.

Self-talk is usually more irrational and illogical than conversations we have with others. Anyone who has ever had the experience of "talking out" a problem with a friend knows that we usually think more clearly when we talk to someone else than when we talk to ourselves. Often, sharing our feelings and thinking with another gives us a better understanding of what is happening to us. Suddenly everything makes sense, and we realize how ridiculous our reasoning has been—or perhaps we validate our thinking and realize we are on the right track after all. It is difficult to achieve this when we just talk to ourselves.

Let us suppose you have just had a telephone conversation with a girlfriend. She tells you that she cannot go to dinner with you next week. She is sorry she has had to cancel this engagement, but something else has come up. As you go back to your office desk you begin to converse with yourself. The conversation may go something like this:

> *I wonder why she doesn't want to go to dinner with me? She knows I planned this weeks ago. She knows how much I have looked forward to it. I wonder if her mother has been talking to her? I know her mother doesn't like me. What could her mother have said? Perhaps I didn't show enough enthusiasm over her garden when she showed it to me. But why would she hold this against me? Maybe I shouldn't have called so late the other evening. Nothing ever goes right for me. Ever since I can remember, things have gone wrong. I must be jinxed or something. . . .*

Very soon you are deeply depressed or anxious, although quite possibly *none* of your thoughts are true; they are all products of your imagination.

Does the previous self-conversation sound ridiculous as you read it? Why don't you try writing down every conversation you have with yourself over your spouse, kids, boss, employees, pastor, or friends? You might be surprised at the sort of things you say to yourself when you see them on paper. It isn't until we see it written down that the irrationality of our self-talk becomes obvious.

Self-talk that produces anxiety tends to have the following characteristics:

- It tends to be emotionally charged because it comes from hurts (real or supposed) and is fed by other feelings.
- It is fed by a vivid imagination. Rather than keeping in touch with reality, it tends to exaggerate and be oversensitive.
- It overgeneralizes, taking one little event and trying to prove that every other event is like it.
- It is irrational and illogical most of the time. It feeds off doubts and uncertainties and is seldom satisfied with reality.
- It usually tends to "catastrophize" everything—finishing up, as my fictitious example does, with statements like "I am jinxed," "I am terrible," or "Nobody cares for me."
- It is usually self-pitying and selfish. "I" am the center of the conversation and the focus of all offense, and "I" just want to wallow in the mire and lick my wounds.

To be free of the anxiety induced by self-talk, we must be able to recognize and stop our negative self-talk. The way to do this is to keep a record of typical self-conversations and then honestly and courageously challenge them when they are ridiculous, untruthful, and destructive.

Here is an exercise that can improve your recognition of negative self-talk:

(1) *Set an alarm or use some event to signal you at least once every hour.* You can use class breaks, coffee breaks, or any other natural break in your day to signal the time for the exercise.

(2) *At the moment you are signaled, stop what you are doing and carefully review the conversation you have been having with yourself during the previous five minutes.* Write it down as sentences, trying to recall as many ideas or self-statements as possible. Pay particular attention to the conversation you were having with yourself at the moment the signal occurred.

(3) *Review your list of self-talk sentences.* Ask yourself the following questions about each one:

- Is it true?
- How do I know it is true?
- Is it realistic—am I being realistic?
- Am I overreacting or catastrophizing?
- Will it be different tomorrow or is it going to be the same?
- Am I being sensible and mature?
- What is the real issue behind this self-statement?
- Am I facing up to the real issue?
- Where will this idea take me?

(4) *Share your responses with someone (a friend or spouse).* Irrational self-talk is best challenged in open conversation with another person who can help you remain objective. If no one is immediately available, share your responses with God. After all, this is part of the purpose of prayer.

STRESS INOCULATION

Although self-talk can be the source of negative, anxiety-producing, and destructive ideas, it can also be a source of strength in resisting anxiety. Psychologists call the technique of using self-talk to counter anxiety "stress inoculation," and it is often taught to patients whose emotions are out of control. (Anger and anxiety respond well to the technique.)

The idea behind stress inoculation is that people can be trained to make self-statements routinely that focus on altering how they approach stressful situations. Just as giving a small dose of a mild virus or disease organism can help to protect patients against the disease, so small doses of self-talk can "inoculate" us against anxiety or stress.

The technique of stress inoculation is only suited to those problems that result from faulty beliefs or ideas that persistently erode confidence. Since much anxiety falls into this category, however, it can be a very helpful technique to learn and practice.

There are usually three steps in stress inoculation:

(1) *Cognitive preparation.* First, the client and therapist or counselor explore the beliefs and attitudes that give rise to the anxiety or problem. Destructive self-statements are identified and then examined for truthfulness. If they are untrue or irrational, a new set of self-statements are identified that are healthier, more honest, and more positive.

(2) *Skill rehearsal.* In the second stage, the new self-statements are practiced and reinforced. Let us suppose, for instance, that you have discovered your job gets you down. You feel overwhelmed in your work situation, and you feel incompetent most of the time. You've become aware of your negative self-talk and realize that you keep talking yourself into unnecessary anxiety.

Here is a list of healthier statements that can be practiced:

- *I must focus on what I must do—not on what I feel.*
- *I am as capable as others, so I can expect to do my job as well as anyone else.*
- *I must focus on the present and not imagine what might happen tomorrow.*
- *I need not be afraid of what might happen to me—because God is in control.*

(3) *Application and practice.* The third step is to apply and practice the stress-relieving self-talk. It should be used first in "safe" situations and then gradually extended to more difficult ones.

Incidentally, regarding the last self-statement listed above—that God is in control—I am reminded of a story told by Thomas Hora, a Christian psychiatrist, about a woman referred to him for treatment who for years had had an incapacitating fear of traveling on the city subway.[1] In the course of their initial interview, Dr. Hora happened to remark to the woman that "God is in control of the subway." She looked at him incredulously, but evidently the remark stuck in her mind, because after a few days she was able to travel on the subway without any fear.

In explaining this dramatic reversal of a fear, Dr. Hora states that it is possible to become so aware of God's sustaining and harmonizing presence under all circumstances that fears can dramatically be relieved in many circumstances. God is in charge of all our affairs. What more do we need to overcome anxiety?

THE STREAM OF THOUGHT

Another way to understand your thinking is to imagine that it is like a stream that flows through your mind. It starts somewhere out of consciousness, passes the "window of your awareness" for a brief moment, then moves on again out of consciousness, possibly to influence some other part of your being. Sometimes your thought is a small stream; your mind is quiet and there is little activity. At such times, your whole being is peaceful and nonaroused.

At other times, the stream of your thought can become a raging torrent or multiple streams that disturb your tranquillity. Thoughts flood into your head, tumbling over each other, eroding everything in their path, and making you feel very unsettled. It seems that even in sleep this

---

[1] Thomas Hora, *Existential Meta-Psychiatry* (New York: Seabury/Crossroad, 1977) 157.

stream or streams continue to flow, feeding dreams and sometimes robbing one of much-needed rest.

A significant key to controlling anxiety lies in being able to control and influence these streams of thought. But how? There is much about thought that you can't control. It is involuntary; its tributaries start by themselves, deep within the mind, and it continues to flow whether you like it or not. You do have control, however, at the point where the stream passes your "window of awareness." At this point you can reach in and remove what you don't want. Although you can't stop thoughts from springing up at their source, you do not need to dwell on all the thoughts that flow by. You can set aside certain thoughts and even ignore them. If you do this, the source of that particular stream will begin to dry up.

You can also *choose* to inject pleasant thoughts into your mind. For instance, if I choose, I can begin to think about a happy childhood event. Let's say I want to think about the first time I ever went to the beach. I can recall it clearly. I was four or five years old. My parents gave me a small brightly colored tin bucket and a wooden spade (they use plastic buckets and spades these days). I remember filling my bucket with wet sand, then turning it over to deposit a neatly shaped cone of sand on the beach. I repeated this many times all over until it seemed as though the whole beach was covered with my sand castles.

What am I feeling as I think about this period of my childhood? Happiness! I love this memory. I can even recall the smells of the salt water, of canvas chairs, milkshakes, and seashells.

Deliberately choosing to think about this event brought me pleasant feelings. But I can also stop this stream of thought at any point and intentionally start another. If this is true of pleasant thoughts, it is also true of unpleasant ones.

Does this sound simple? Yes, it certainly is, but this truth is so liberating that it needs to be sounded again and again: *I can choose to change my thoughts and therefore determine what I am feeling.*

The importance of all of this is that we can control much of what causes us anxiety by deliberately changing the stream of our thought any time we choose. We simply have to *begin* thinking about another pleasant or happy event. We have the power to originate thought. Most unhappy people neglect to do it.

THOUGHT STOPPING, THOUGHT REDIRECTING, AND THOUGHT INITIATION

These are three important strategies that follow from my comments in the previous section. I believe I have strong biblical support for the value of intentionally determining what we think about. Paul, in the closing chapter of his Epistle to the Philippians, reminds us that we are to think on things that are true, honest, just, pure, lovely and of good report (Phil. 4:8, KJV). His point is clear: If we think on these things, we will both protect ourselves from unhealthy thoughts and develop the habit of right thinking.

But what happens when thoughts are overwhelming you like a raging torrent and you cannot control what you are thinking? Two strategies are valuable: "thought stopping" and "thought redirecting." These two techniques can be used together or separately or combined with a third technique—"thought initiation"—in reducing anxiety levels:

(1) *Thought stopping.* This technique has been in clinical use for many years. It is learned first with minor and only mildly bothersome thoughts. After the technique is mastered, it can be tried on more troublesome thoughts.

To practice thought stopping, lie on your bed in a comfortable position. Select a thought that sometimes bothers you. Take a deep breath and let the air out slowly, relaxing every part of your body.

Think for a moment about the troublesome thought. Then take the flat of one hand, hit it against your thigh with a sharp and quick slap (but don't hurt yourself), and either shout out loud or think, "stop." Immediately change the thought.

Relax again. Concentrate on your breathing and the tension in your body. Try to relax every part of the body that feels tense. If the thought comes back again, repeat the slap and shout the word *stop.*

Later, when you have conditioned the word *stop* to the thigh slap, just thinking the word will have the same effect. You may find it helpful to tape-record these instructions, along with appropriate additional suggestions to yourself. You can then play the tape while relaxing and learn the technique more effectively.

Having practiced the slap-and-stop method on minor troublesome thoughts, make a list of more bothersome thoughts that you find frightening. Practice the technique with each of these thoughts in turn. Then try the technique while going about your regular daily routine. You can do it while driving, counting change, or changing diapers. No one else need be aware that you are doing it. Every time a thought bothers you, say *stop* to yourself and change your thought.

While you may have to repeat the exercise eight or ten times on each thought before it goes away, with practice you will find that thoughts actually do stop when you tell them to. Later you should be able to catch troublesome thoughts the moment they occur and nip them in the bud.

You may say to yourself, *This thought is not going to be helpful. I choose not to let it remain,* and then proceed to stop the thought.

(2) *Thought redirecting.* This is a variation of the thought-stopping method and can be a useful follow-up. Its purpose is to help you rechannel your stream of thought. After you have discovered a thought you don't want and told yourself to stop it, you may find that the thought returns after awhile because nothing else has taken its place. This technique helps to fill the empty stream bed with an alternative pleasant thought.

For instance, let us suppose a colleague at work says something that hurts you. An hour later, you catch yourself dwelling on your colleague's words; you can't stop them from playing in your head.

When this happens, relax wherever you are, standing or sitting, and think for a moment about the words that are bothering you. Say *stop* silently to yourself as in the previous exercise, then immediately begin to think positive things about your colleague. Envision his office, his desk; recall the good things you know about him. Think about the nice things he has said to you in the past. Think about his wife and children. Think of your friendship. Think about how human he is—no better than you, but also no worse. And so on, and so on . . .

The idea here is to *immediately* substitute a chain of thoughts that originates with the bothersome one but which slowly takes you away from it to something more positive and pleasant. You don't have to force yourself to think nice things about someone you dislike. You can move on to other thoughts.

With practice, this technique can become a habit so that you need never allow troublesome thoughts to dominate you again. By redirecting your thinking away from the original negative thought, you occupy your mind with wholesome, healthy, and healing thoughts. The Christian can focus this redirection ultimately on Christ, His love for us, and His glorious salvation. There is always a lot to think about here!

(3) *Thought initiation.* Keeping unwanted thoughts out of your mind is only part of the battle against anxiety. One further step is needed: learning to initiate pleasant thoughts whenever you choose. Not only do these help to displace unpleasant thoughts; they also help to reduce anxiety by building a more tranquil atmosphere in your mind.

Here is an exercise to help you initiate pleasant thoughts: First, take a card and write down five or six events you know will give you pleasure. These can be events from your past (memories of happy childhood outings) or present (your last visit to a friend), or they may be events you anticipate with pleasure in the near future (such as an upcoming vacation).

Next to each pleasant event, write down two or three specific ideas or aspects of the event that interest or captivate you. For instance, if you are planning a vacation you may wish to write down "planning vacation wardrobe" or "examining travel brochure for places to visit," as specific ideas. If you are recalling games you used to play with your grandfather, write down the names of the games or recall the rules. (I have many such memories of my own grandfather.)

Keep this card with you at all times. Every hour or two, take it out, select one of the pleasant events you specified, and deliberately begin to think about one of the specific ideas associated with it. Take a moment to savor the pleasant feelings it generates. Try to think about the pleasant idea for four or five minutes. Then return the card to its place and go about your business.

In time, learning to initiate pleasant thoughts will become a habit that can dramatically turn your anxiety around.

CORRECTING ERRORS IN YOUR THINKING

Even when you are able to capture your irrational or negative thoughts and either stop them or redirect them to more tranquil and positive ideas, you may still have a tendency to engage in illogical thinking or be susceptible to certain "thinking errors." These thinking errors need to be recognized so they can be corrected at the earliest possible moment.

Here are some major thinking errors to examine and avoid:

(1) *Catastrophizing.* This is a tendency, often learned in early childhood, to react to every danger or difficulty with an exaggerated response and to perceive total disaster as the outcome.

Say, for instance, that your child comes home from school with a report card that says he is not concentrating in class and is easily distracted by other children. This has never happened before, and you have no real reason to suspect a serious problem, but immediately you start thinking panicky thoughts: *What does this mean? Is Johnny going to pieces? Perhaps there's something wrong with his brain. I better take him to the doctor.* When you finally have a conference with the teacher, you discover it is not a big issue. Johnny is merely "testing the limits" of the system and is basically a good student. You feel stupid because you overreacted.

Or perhaps you are due for an annual physical checkup. You've felt a little under the weather lately, so you start wondering, *Could I have something seriously wrong with me? Perhaps I've got cancer!* Before you know it, your anxiety is through the roof and you are catastrophizing every ache and pain.

Now, we all catastrophize to some extent. But the more anxiety-prone we are, the more we will tend to do it—and catastrophizing in turn feeds our anxiety. Often we are not aware of this tendency, so we may have to depend on feedback from others to alert us to it. Careful analysis of our self-talk can also help.

(2) *Exaggeration.* Exaggerating is a little different from catastrophizing. When you exaggerate, you don't necessarily imagine the worst, but you do emphasize the negative. You look in the mirror, see a few gray hairs, and begin to think of yourself as old. (I suppose for some this could be a catastrophe!) A colleague gets a promotion; you realize other people are as good, if not better than you; and you begin to see yourself as a failure.

Because exaggeration is not as dramatic as catastrophizing, it is more elusive. You don't know you're doing it, but it slowly shapes your beliefs and attitudes and raises your anxiety when you least expect it.

(3) *Overgeneralizing.* I remember vividly the first time I ever failed significantly at anything. I was twenty-six years of age, a young civil engineer doing well in my job. I had taken an advanced mathematics class at our university to help me in my work. After a year of study (I did not try too hard because I felt fairly confident), I took the examination and totally "bombed out."

I was devastated. First I did some catastrophizing: *This is the end of my life!* Then I did some exaggerating: *If I can't master this math, my friends will think I'm stupid.* Then I began to overgeneralize: *Since I've failed this examination in mathematics, perhaps I am just a failure at everything. I'll never get anywhere in life because of this failure. It will haunt me the rest of my life.* Overgeneralizing is, therefore, a tendency to think that everything is a disaster when only one thing is.

It was this failure that caused me to rethink whether I wanted to go on being an engineer. The next year I began my studies in psychology, so the failure turned out to be God's gentle nudge redirecting me to another form of service. In retrospect my experience with that examination was hardly a failure at all, and God meant it "for my good."

The failures and other negative experiences in our lives can bring us wisdom or direct us to better pathways. Too often, however, that doesn't happen. Through generalization, we let our failures immobilize us—we just give up and stop trying.

CHANGING YOUR THINKING

How does one avoid making these errors of thinking? I have several suggestions:

(1) *First, work at increasing your awareness of when these thinking errors tend to occur in you.* Anxiety always increases when you think incorrectly, so a feeling of anxiety is often the best clue.

(2) *Question your thinking.* For example, if you are catastrophizing a failure, ask yourself: *Does it really mean that this is the end? Does it really mean I am incompetent? Will there be other opportunities? Am I catastrophizing?* You'll discover that you can live through just about every life crisis. Try to avoid increasing your anxiety by distorting your thinking.

(3) *Gather whatever facts you can to counter the negative beliefs at the root of your thinking pattern.* Knowledge is the best antidote for irrational fears. If you fear trains, gather as much information about them as possible. If you are afraid of snakes, then study them and become an expert on them. By increasing your interest in these sources of fear, you will gradually feel more in control, and this will help you to lower your anxiety.

(4) *Constantly try to avoid taking the "worm's eye view" of your situation.* Pull back and enlarge your perspective. Soar high and try to see the larger picture of your life—try to see it from God's perspective. This will help keep you from exaggerating your misfortunes.

(5) *Develop clear and specific plans for coping.* Every problem in life, no matter how small, should be countered with a plan of action for coping. Such a plan helps to avoid the feeling of helplessness that only feeds anxiety. The plan should emphasize *coping* in your circumstances, not mastering them. It is enough to ask yourself, *How can I get through this day? What can I do right now just to cope with this problem?* Emphasize to yourself the value of dealing with each problem *one at a time.* Don't try to solve all your problems at once. Take each one singly and forget about the others.

LIVING WITH REALITY

When all is said and done, correct thinking has to do with our being able to live with reality. Anxiety is the consequence of not being able to engage reality fully. But when we live in full harmony with the real world, the world as God presents it to us, we can be at peace. Unreality is a mirage; fantasy is a delusion. And our world tends to create much unreality in the hope that it will ease our anxious thoughts or distract our worried minds. But sooner or later we must return from the make-believe world of movies, TV, or novels and face our pains and problems.

Well-adjusted people have a reasonably accurate view of themselves and their world. They know their limitations and those of their environment. Maladjusted people, on the other hand, tend to be unrealistic—to set goals that are too high or too low, or to pursue unrewarding goals. Needless to say, they are also prone to higher levels of anxiety. They seem unable to formulate meaningful life plans, and they drift through life with little or no sense of direction. The result is that they experience feelings of dissatisfaction and aimlessness—they feel lost.

The greatest gift you can give yourself is the courage to face your real world. Life has many "givens." We can't all be superstars; we all grow old; sooner or later we die. But these givens of life can take on new meaning when we live in full acceptance of their reality. Every minute becomes precious. We don't waste time wishing things were different, wallowing in self-pity, or regretting failure. When life knocks us down, we rise quickly and get back into the race as soon as we can. This is the only way to live! And it is for the *real* problems of life that God provides us strength to carry on.

It is quite remarkable how courage rises in the face of *real* danger or *real* catastrophe. I've known many people who have lived fear-ridden and anxiety-dominated lives, anticipating problems that never happened or expecting the worst. For years they have worried about everything. Then one day a real problem comes along—a son is killed in an automobile accident, a husband has a stroke, a business fails. And in every instance, God has given these unfortunate people tremendous inner strength to rise above their catastrophes.

What happened to their anxieties? How can they cope with the real issues of life but almost go to pieces worrying about something that may never happen? This is the paradox of the human spirit: We can deal with real dangers or threats; we cannot cope with unreal ones.

A patient of some years back—let's call him Randy—illustrates this truth very well. When I first met Randy, he was on the verge of suicide. At forty-six years of age, he was always miserable and depressed. All his life he had anticipated the worst and had often been overcome with intense anxiety. Now he had reached the point that his troubles felt too burdensome; he no longer wanted to live.

For many years, Randy had done the rounds of psychologists and psychiatrists, but no one had been able to help him. He was intelligent and had accumulated a few degrees, but no vocation attracted him, so he worked at odd jobs here and there. He wished he were like other people, and he spent hours brooding over his misfortunes and catastrophizing the future.

Randy blamed his mother for his problems. She had conceived him when she was only sixteen and never married the father. "Perhaps I'd be a happier person if I'd had a father," he frequently moaned.

Then one day, out of the blue, Randy discovered he had leukemia. His life was on the line. And I found myself wondering how he would react, I thought long and hard about how I would deal with this new situation in therapy. All along he had only hung to life by a thread. Now that he was facing a real danger, how would he take it?

I was amazed at Randy's response. He was transformed! He took control of his illness, set up all the right appointments to start treatment, and all of a sudden his life fell into place. Faced with a real threat, he discovered that he had tremendous inner strength. He was no longer anxious—afraid, yes, but not anxious. No longer was he confused about life. For the first time, he wanted to live, really live. He was willing to take responsibility for making his life work, and he stopped blaming his aged mother for his problems.

I lost contact with Randy a few weeks later because he moved away to be nearer his mother. Whether he recovered from his illness I don't know. I do know that he taught me the value of facing reality square on and that my encounter with him equipped me as a psychologist to help others face the reality of their own lives with courage.

When we confront reality, we put God in control. We discover anew that God has resources He is willing to make available to us. Avoiding reality may reduce some of our anxiety, but will almost always introduce new sources of anxiety. When we accept reality, we always have the comfort of knowing that no matter how bad our circumstances are, God has gone before us and has prepared the path we should follow. He will lead us through the valley of those circumstances no matter how dark it is. This is what Paul so clearly tells us in 1 Corinthians 10:13: "God is faithful; he will not let you be tempted [or tried] beyond what you can bear. But when you are tempted, he will also provide a way out so that you can stand up under it" (NIV).

11

TAKING CONTROL OF PANIC

Taking control of panic is not something that can be confined to the few minutes of an anxiety attack. The moment of an attack is not the time to begin asking, "What should I do now?" Fighting panic is something like fighting a battle. You have to plan ahead and prepare—rehearsing maneuvers, equipping the soldiers, working out strategy. After the attack, you have to review your effectiveness and plan new strategies. The purpose of this chapter is to provide specific help for every stage of your campaign against panic.

In chapter 5 I described the nature of the disorder we call panic attack or anxiety attack. In this chapter, then, I will assume that the reader is clear about the particular form of anxiety disorder he or she is experiencing. I will also assume that in the more severe cases of panic the reader has obtained appropriate professional help, including medication if necessary, to deal with the major symptoms. (The use of anti-anxiety medication is described in chapter 14.)

The next step, then, in gaining control over your panic attacks is to learn how to change the manner in which you *anticipate* the moment of attack.

FIRST THINGS FIRST:
BOOSTING YOUR SELF-CONFIDENCE

Panic's most powerful weapon is that it undermines your confidence. You begin to doubt yourself. You come to believe you can't fight your anxiety.

That first encounter with panic loosens the very foundations of your self-confidence and self-trust, just like a major earthquake shakes and loosens the foundation of a house. If this process is allowed to continue, it can quickly gain a foothold in your life and topple every accomplishment.

Most panic sufferers, by the time they get around to taking control, feel confused about their problem. Often they have done the rounds of many physicians, psychologists, or what have you, and have become frustrated and angry both at the professional world and themselves. They have begun to think they are "crazy." They feel alone, weak,

156

vulnerable, and hopeless. And these feelings easily feed into a "fear-of-fear" response and set up the conditions for the next attack.

It is this *self-doubt,* therefore, that must be attacked first. Every exercise and technique I will describe for controlling panic will be ineffective if you do not work at *restoring your self-confidence.*

In approaching your problem of self-doubt you can take one of two approaches. You can entirely spiritualize it and trust that God will move in and instantly restore your confidence. Or you can realize that you have your part to play in rebuilding self-confidence and then use the resources of God to help you overcome it.

I have no doubt that God *can* miraculously restore your self-confidence—but He may not choose to do it. While some have been dramatically relieved of their panic disorder, many others have not. Perhaps God is too loving to relieve us of all responsibility for how we live our lives! Who knows why He does not always heal? We must trust God's great wisdom in this matter and begin to work on the problem ourselves, depending on Him for the strength and courage we need to face our fears.

There is yet another possibility, though. You can "go it alone," leaving God out of the picture entirely. If it were me, however, I doubt if I could gather the strength entirely within myself to restore my confidence and heal my panic attacks. (Talk about trying to pull yourself up by your own bootstraps!) As you proceed, I believe you will find that you need all the assistance you can get and that your faith in God is vital to successfully overcoming your problem.

ANTICIPATING THE MOMENT OF PANIC

After an initial panic attack, the sufferer usually assumes a physical cause (often it is a suspected heart attack) and seeks medical attention. When no cause is discovered, the individual goes home somewhat perplexed and returns to his or her normal life pattern. After a second or third episode, however, the person's attitude changes dramatically, and a state of *anticipatory dread* is created. He begins to avoid places associated with attacks and constricts activities drastically. It is this *anticipation* of an attack that greatly increases the fear associated with the attack.

There is no medication that can remove this anticipatory anxiety. How can one then alleviate it? The basic approach involves changing a negative, defeatist, doubting attitude to one of confidence and control.

Remember, a lot of anxiety stems from inaccurate beliefs. If one has come to *believe* that a particular place (theater, bus, train, room, or so forth) is a trap, being in such a place can start an attack. The solution, therefore, is to reverse the belief. Until you can do this, however, it may be wise to avoid the situation that triggers a panic attack. Forcing yourself to get on an airplane, for instance, may not always help you overcome the fear of flying. Professionals have highly developed techniques for helping people overcome such fears; these include gradually approaching the feared situation, beginning with the imagination (systematic desensitization), or going cold turkey (implosion therapy). But the haphazard approach of the average lay person seldom works and can make panic worse.

Unfamiliar situations can provoke a panic attack because strange people, places, and projects can heighten anxiety and because in such a situation one does not know the rules nor the way of escape. Until your panic is under control, then, try to avoid these situations and stick with the familiar. Once control is established, you will be able to explore new territory!

Stressful situations are also provokers of panic and should be avoided where possible. When you are going through a period of heightened panic-proneness, you should avoid making major life decisions or embarking on new projects. Now is not the time to be buying a new home, initiating a divorce, changing your job, painting the house, or starting a new business. Hold off on all unnecessary and extraordinary demands, both on your physical and psychological being.

This *is* the time to be strengthening your spiritual legs, disciplining your prayer life, and reading Scripture. You will need to draw on God's power to see you through the tough months or even years ahead, so do your best to draw on the resources He provides.

Here are some useful steps to relieve anticipatory anxiety:

(1) *Plant the right thoughts in your mind.* As I indicated in chapter 5, perhaps the most important belief that you can implant is that *panic attacks never kill anyone.* They may embarrass and inconvenience you, but they will not kill you. Remind yourself of this fact all the time. If you feel an attack coming on, say it to yourself over and over—and affirm it to yourself after the attack is over.

The very worst that can happen in a panic attack is that you will pass out. The hyperventilation that causes the sensory disturbances is self-limiting. If you faint, your breathing will return to normal, so don't aggravate your fear by thinking you might die.

(2) *Increase your awareness that you are free to choose whether or not you are going to have an attack.* I believe very strongly that *you* have a choice in most panic situations. I have known cases in which a person on the edge of panic felt the attack subside at the sight of a

spouse or friend. What changed? Nothing, really, except that the patient felt reassured by the presence of someone he or she trusted. Now, if all it takes is some reassurance to abort a panic attack, why not train yourself to give that reassurance *to yourself* whenever you need it? Increase your freedom to choose by claiming your power to choose. In your mind, create a haven of safety, where only you and God are, and *believe* it is your choice as to whether you will panic or not.

(3) *Build your confidence to control an attack.* You can do this by practicing the techniques I will describe later in this chapter and implementing them during times when you are *not* panicking. This is very important. Rehearse control techniques over and over again until you can do them without thinking.

If you are on medication for your panic disorder, *don't* resist taking the medication. It is a part of your overall treatment—and part of its role is to restore your confidence that you are in control of your panic, not vice versa. Medication is also essential in controlling the biological factors that contribute to panic. Trust the medication to do this; you have enough to cope with on the spiritual and psychological fronts!

(4) *Forget about your attacks.* Once you have prepared yourself by building your confidence and practicing control techniques, the next best thing you can do about anticipating your attacks is forget about them! Don't feed your fear by wondering, *When am I going to have my next attack?* Instead, remind yourself that whenever it does come—*if it comes*—you'll be ready for it. Don't listen to your "worry center." Redirect your thinking elsewhere, if necessary, and go about your normal duties. (The techniques for changing your thinking described in chapter 10 may help you do this.)

CONTROLLING THE MOMENT OF PANIC

With all the prevention in the world and the most careful planning in avoiding specific triggers, panic attacks can still happen—and when you least expect them. Here is what to do when you become aware of the onset of a panic attack:

(1) *First, move yourself to a safe place.* Doing this is absolutely essential because you *may* faint. (Don't be afraid of fainting—it is the body's natural way of limiting an attack. As soon as the oxygen level in your blood gets above a certain level, you pass out and the body restores its normal breathing.)

Here are some examples of "safe" places: If you are driving a car, pull over and park. If you are in a meeting, excuse yourself and find a comfortable chair. If you are at home, lie down on your bed. The "safe" place should prevent any physical harm but, more importantly, it should also give you a feeling of security.

(2) *Test for hyperventilation.* Remember, a few panic sufferers may have low instead of high oxygen, and treatment for hyperventilation will only make the panic worse, so it's important to do the following test before proceeding.

The hyperventilation "test" involves trying to hold your breath for eight to ten seconds. Normally, this is neither difficult nor uncomfortable. If you are hyperventilating, however, holding your breath will create an *urgent* need to breathe; you'll want to open windows and gulp in great globs of air.

Now, this seems strange, because the problem is that you are getting *too* much oxygen. But remember, your panic attack means your system has gone haywire. The pH of your blood has changed, and the respiratory reflex center is confused, forcing you to breathe more than you should.

Now here is the clincher. Unless you do this test, you won't know if you are hyperventilating. Most sufferers don't recognize it—they think they are breathing normally. So don't trust your subjective feeling—try to hold your breath.

Doing this test can also help you recognize the early signs of panic. Long before you feel the onset of panic or fear, you will have started to increase your oxygen level. The test is also useful for mild cases of hyperventilation. Periodically, after a bout with high demand and too much work, I wake up in the early hours of the morning feeling awful and full of doom. I do the "breathing test" and, sure enough, I can sense the air hunger and the compulsion to resist holding my breath. I perform the breathing technique I will next describe and the sensations go away. It appears that dreaming can trigger a hyperventilation bout (even though you can't recall the dream), which is why many panic attacks occur in the early hours of the morning.

(3) *Bring your hyperventilation under control.* The way to do this is to capture and rebreathe the carbon dioxide that you are exhaling; this will lower the oxygen level in your blood.

There are two ways to rebreathe your carbon dioxide. The surest way is to keep a small brown paper bag handy. (Do not use plastic!) Blow it up and place it over *both* your nose and mouth. Continue breathing to recycle the carbon dioxide and cut down the oxygen. After a minute or so you should feel less panicky. Continue the process as long as necessary. You may have to repeat it every five minutes for a while.

Don't be afraid of breathing in too much carbon dioxide; the worst that can happen is that you will feel faint. Usually there is enough leakage in the bag to maintain an adequate oxygen supply (which is why you should not use a plastic bag).

A less conspicuous method is to cup your hands over your nose and mouth and rebreathe your carbon dioxide as you breathe in through your nose and out through the mouth. This technique is always with you —so learn to master it and don't delay in implementing it. It can abort a panic attack in many cases.

There is a third technique that can be used either during a panic attack or to improve breathing habits and improve your sense of control after an attack. Take in a breath through your nose, but do it *very slowly.* The idea is to slow down the frequency of your breathing. When the breath is in, very slowly start to let it out. Concentrate on how *slowly* you can let the air out (preferably through the mouth). You may feel the urge to breathe rapidly, but resist it. When all the air is gone, inhale and exhale again *very slowly.*

Slow breathing like this lowers the oxygen level in the blood by reducing the number of breaths you take over given period time. It can be performed in the middle of a committee meeting or in any public place —and people won't even know you are controlling your hyperventilation tendency.

If you do not suffer from hyperventilation during a panic attack, you may be suffering from one of the other variants, such as lactate sensitivity or too much carbon dioxide. If you are exercising at the time of the attack, you are almost certainly bringing it on by increasing your lactate level. Stop the exertion and rest. Follow whatever prescription your physician has given you for tranquilizer or other deficiency replacement.

(4) *Remain quiet and distract yourself.* After you have gotten your hyperventilation under control through rebreathing, remain quietly in your place and concentrate on some immediate task to get your mind off the attack. Do something repetitive, such as paging through a magazine or counting pencils in a box.

The goal is to *distract* your thinking away from the panic and to avoid feeding your panic with negative self-talk. If, for example you are at a concert or in church, concentrate on the program or the church bulletin—study it intensely. If you are in a restaurant, look around and see how many people you can recognize, or pray for each one you see, even if you do not know them. Any significant distraction at this point can keep the attack at bay.

Next, talk to yourself in a calming, reassuring voice: *I am in control, even here. Nothing can destroy me because God is in control. This is not an emergency, and I can care for myself. As soon as the hyperventilation subsides, I will be back to normal feelings again.*

If you find it helpful, pray, but don't feed the panic with catastrophizing prayers. If praying increases your anxiety (because it means focusing on the discomfort of the panic), don't pray—God understands. After all, He does not hear us just because we form words in our mind. He hears our hearts and understands our deepest needs, even when we don't go through the motions of prayer.

Relax for a few more minutes, breathing slowly and regularly. Do *not* try to resume your normal activities right away. Continue relaxing and distracting yourself until you feel confident that the attack is over. Then, and then only, resume your duties.

One last thought: Don't be ashamed to tell those around you what is happening to you. Be open about your panic problem with family members, fellow workers, friends, or even chance acquaintances. Not only will this mobilize help; it will also defuse the fear of embarrassment, which can make the attack worse. It will help to reduce your tendency to panic because it removes the fear of embarrassment. If your friends your can't handle your problem, remind yourself that it's their problem, not yours.

WHAT TO DO AFTER AN ATTACK

Most sufferers of panic attacks never think about what they should do immediately following an attack. They are usually so relieved that it is over that they want to run away from it as fast as their legs can carry them. But careful follow-up can reduce the possibility of future attacks. Here are some things to do:

(1) *Write down all the details of the attack.* This will help whoever is treating you and will give you further insight into the nature of your unique form of panic attack. You may find a brief questionnaire or checklist such as that in personal inventory 9 helpful. Make several photocopies of the blank form and fill one in as soon after an attack as possible. Do this *every* time you have an attack and present it to your psychologist, psychiatrist, or physician for review.

(2) *Inventory your life for any complicating factors.* (Your panic inventory can help you do this.) Did you exercise immediately before the attack. Check your diet: Have you been consuming too much caffeine or sugar? Do you have any food allergies that may be contributing to your panic responses? If you are a woman, could PMS be pushing you closer to panic? What about hypoglycemia or depression? Talk to your psychologist or physician if you suspect any of these conditions are complicating your panic problem.

(3) *Increase your attention to managing the stress in your life.* If

Personal Inventory 9
RECORD OF PANIC ATTACK

Name: _____ Date of attack: _____

Time attack started: _____ Time attack ended: _____

Where were you at the time? _____

_____

What were you doing? _____

_____

Was there any precipitating event (e.g., exercising/conflict, etc.)? _____

_____

_____

Were you hyperventilating? Yes _____ No _____ Don't Know _____

Did you confirm with a breathing test? Yes _____ No _____

Which of the following symptoms did you experience? (circle those applicable):
Dizziness, faintness, fear of dying, heart palpitations, difficulty breathing, rapid
breathing, urge to urinate, sweating, flushing, confusion, feeling of unreality, sense
of being detached from body, difficulty speaking, shakiness, trembling, nausea,
vomiting, choking sensations, heart racing, numb or tingling sensations, chills,
chest pain, fear of going crazy.

Do you: drink alcohol? drink coffee, tea, or caffeinated soft drinks? smoke? take
drugs?

Known physical disorders: _____

_____

Describe feelings during attack: _____

_____

Did anything help to stop the attack? _____

_____

What medications are you taking? _____

necessary, seek some stress-management therapy. At the very least, survey the stress in your own life and see what you can eliminate or what changes you can make to simplify your lifestyle. (Remember to count "good" or "pleasant" stress as well as the unpleasant kind.)

It is not my intention here to give a crash course in stress management. I have done this in another book (*The Hidden Link between Adrenalin and Stress*), and other helpful guidelines to stress management have been published both by secular and Christian publishers. I would prefer the reader to focus on one of the Christian approaches, because I have become increasingly convinced that underlying much of our stress, and certainly our problem with anxiety, are issues of values and the final purpose of life.

Again and again, as I work in therapy with panic victims, I am impressed with how our life in Christ ought to impact how we live, and with the penalty we pay for not having our spiritual priorities in order. If our sole goal is material gain or power to influence others, then our stress will eventually be out of control. It is the person who can balance his or her life between work and play, the spiritual and the physical, family and company, challenge and rest, essentials and nonessentials, who is healthy and stress-free. In the final analysis, only that which is important to God ought to be important to us. When it is—we're on the way to wholeness, health, and a distress-free life.

RELEASING YOUR TENSIONS

Very often the period before a panic episode is characterized by an increase of tension. Some, but not all attacks can be avoided if you increase your recognition of when this tension is building up and use a relaxation technique to lower it.

Deliberately quieting the mind and relaxing the body are good for almost any physical or mental distress. Relaxation helps the body heal when we are sick. It helps restore the brain's natural tranquilizers when we are anxious, and it prepares the body for high demand.

Relaxation also helps to lower the level of the stress hormone adrenaline in the blood. Adrenaline is part of the body's natural emergency response system; when we encounter threat or challenge, our adrenaline rises to prepare the body and mind for "fight or flight." It is this elevated adrenaline that can trigger a panic attack. Deliberate muscle relaxation can lower the emergency arousal and thus prevent an attack.

Now, since there has been a strong reaction in many Christian circles against techniques such as yoga or transcendental meditation, let me hasten to add that *I am not advocating these practices*. I think it is most unfortunate that Eastern religions and the New Age movement have cottoned on to the tremendous benefits that conscious relaxation can provide. This has caused many to pull away from relaxation techniques of any sort, because they inappropriately associate them with some non-Christian religious practice.

But Eastern religions and New Age practitioners do *not* have an exclusive right to relaxation! God has provided it for all of us, and Christians ought to claim the right to relax as much as anyone else. We need to advocate a Christian-based meditation practice, encouraging "quiet times" and the discipline of thoughtful reflection on God's Word. This is not New Age; it is every believer's birthright. If we fail to do this from a Christian perspective, we only encourage people to turn to Eastern religious practices to obtain the relief from tension that their bodies so desperately need.

For Christians, a twenty-minute "quiet time" that combines relaxation with prayer or reflection on God's Word can be a powerful restorer of energy and balance. It can serve as a time of devotion or simply as an opportunity to relax the muscles and lower adrenaline.

To practice conscious relaxation, find a comfortable couch or lie on your bed and make sure you are not going to be interrupted. Take the phone off the hook and hang out a "do not disturb" sign if necessary. Then proceed with your relaxation in three stages:

(1) *Consciously tense and then relax your muscles.* Starting at your feet, hold each muscle group tense for a count of five, then relax the muscles and allow them to loosen. Repeat this process from toes to head.

(2) *Lie still.* When you have tensed and relaxed each muscle system in turn, including arms, neck and face, try to lie motionless for the remainder of the twenty minutes. It is the lack of motion that encourages relaxation.

(3) *Meditate.* While relaxing, think of a favorite verse of Scripture or recount some experience from the life of Christ. This will help to keep your mind from wandering off into anxious thoughts. Breathe slowly and evenly, allowing your stomach to rise and fall on each breath.

At first you will find it very hard to lie still for as little as twenty minutes. Relaxing will feel uncomfortable because your body is used to tension. If you must move, do so, and then go through the tensing/relaxing process once again. After five or six sessions, this relaxation process will become easier and more enjoyable. You will get up feeling refreshed.

After you've mastered relaxing on your bed or couch, try the same exercise while sitting in a chair or driving your car. Remember that tension is the result of excess effort—trying too hard to do things that can be done with less effort, with the result that our muscles jam and work against each other. Making a conscious effort to relax your muscles when sitting at your desk, driving your car, walking, or just sitting still can reduce this excess effort. Try to speak more slowly, move easily, and especially relax the jaw (a tight jaw means that you grit and grind your teeth) and your forehead muscles. Try to sense where the tension is in your body and focus your relaxation at these sites.

One main cause of tension is "hurry." People who hurry are always stressed, so whenever you sense you are hurrying, deliberately slow yourself down. Find an even pace at which to work, walk, or talk—*the slower the better if you are prone to anxiety attacks.*

Whenever you feel tense or sense a panic attack beginning, find a safe place and do your relaxation exercise. If you are sitting on an airplane, then your seat is your "safe" place; relax right there in your seat. If you are working in a crowded room, you can relax right there also. In fact, there is really no place you cannot relax once you have mastered the technique. If you really must find a less threatening place, then you can either go to a restroom or ask to be excused and find a garden bench or even just lie on the grass.

Some people try to overcome anxious thoughts that lead to panic by replacing them with so-called "positive" thoughts. For instance, if they are thinking *I'm going crazy* or *I'm losing control,* they tell themselves, *No, I'm not going crazy; I am just confronting my human limits,* or *No, I'm not losing control; I am perfectly in control and will calm down soon.*

These positive thoughts can help us up to a point. Sometimes, however, they only create an internal quarrel or debate and the anxiety increases. It is preferable, therefore, as soon as you realize that thinking "positive thoughts" is backfiring, to switch to *neutral* thoughts. Use your imagination or turn your mind to pleasant experiences.

For instance, you can imagine that you are on the beach or lying on a haystack with the sun warming you all over. Take an imaginary walk along a country lane and think of the animals you will meet—rabbits, squirrels, or even a deer. Have an imaginary conversation with each one of them. Ask about their families; inquire about how they gather food and what they do in the winter time. By thinking neutral thoughts you don't have to debate yourself into tranquillity; it will come naturally and more quickly.

PRAYER AND THE CALMING RESPONSE

The relaxation method I have just described leads naturally to what is known as the "calming response," which is the opposite of the adrenaline arousal that can bring on panic attacks. Instead of gearing up for "fight or flight," the body moves to a calmer and more tranquil state. Not only does this calming response help us avoid panic attacks; in a calmer state we also *think* more clearly. This means we can evaluate our situation more honestly, reassure ourselves more easily, and avoid creating more anxiety.

The calming response works by switching off the *sympathetic system,* that part of our body that helps cope with emergencies, and switches on the *parasympathetic system,* which counteracts the sympathetic response and lowers muscle tension, reduces blood pressure, lowers oxygen demand, and returns blood sugar to a normal level. These parasympathetic reactions prevent the occurrence of panic attacks, which is why medication that blocks adrenaline helps reduce panic.

Perhaps the most powerful trigger I know for the *parasympathetic system* is the process of prayer. Prayer invites a calming of the body and mind when it is used properly. Anyone who has successfully turned to prayer during a crisis knows how powerful it can be in bringing a calming response. It invites God to take control, helps us gain perspective on our problems, and puts us in touch with God's power to help us become calm. While relaxation techniques can facilitate this, conscious relaxation is only the first step. To move to a more profound state of calm takes a deep trust in God and an ability to use prayer meaningfully.

Scripture is also a great source of calm. Verses such as "Thou wilt keep him in perfect peace, whose mind is stayed on thee" (Isa. 26:3, KJV) and "The peace of God, which passeth all understanding, shall keep your hearts and minds through Christ Jesus" (Phil. 4:7, KJV) have brought a calming response to people throughout the ages.

FIND A FRIEND

Everyone who suffers from panic attacks should find someone who can be a friend and supporter through the period when the attacks are occurring. We *need* friends and social support. Panic tends to isolate its victims and removes them from this important resource.

A friend needs to be someone who cares about your well-being and values your worth. It must be someone who really understands the problem of panic anxiety and who will not make you feel guilty when you feel as if you have failed. Often a spouse can be this friend—but not always. Spouses can sometimes be too close and personally affected to remain impartial. They are inconvenienced by your attacks and may even be hostile. If this is true, don't feel guilty about this or blame your spouse—just establish a helping relationship with someone else. (Needless to say, the friend should preferably be someone of the same sex to avoid complications.)

This friend can help the problem of panic in a number of ways:

- The friend can be available to talk with you when you are feeling anxious. This provides an outlet for your worries and helps keep them from making you anxious.
- The friend can remind you of your "freedom to choose" and to exercise confidence in overcoming the attacks.
- The friend can help you rehearse positive self-statements and coach you through the exercises I have outlined in this book.
- The friend can serve as an impartial observer, helping you keep your problem in perspective and reminding you of your strengths.
- The friend can aid you in reviewing your strategies and determining where you went wrong in preventing a panic attack. It's hard to do this by yourself because you can't remain objective.
- The friend can simply *be* a friend. In his or her presence you can feel safe. Having someone to listen to you can help you feel understood.
- The friend can be a prayer partner.

A LIFETIME COMMITMENT

To win the war against panic, we must use all the resources we can muster, especially a clear understanding of how God desires us to live our lives. We can then apply the best psychological and medical resources to help us overcome our problem.

Remember that the ultimate goal should be total healing, and this calls not only for relief from the symptoms of panic anxiety, but also for a realignment of our lives so that we live relatively free from destructive anxiety. We must change our values and priorities. Any healing that does not dramatically readjust our lives so that they are more balanced and wholesome is *not* complete healing. We may obtain some relief from our immediate symptoms, but it is only a matter of time before the problem will reappear.

Take Mark, for example. He is a hard-working and self-made businessman who has recently succumbed to anxiety attacks. For years Mark's entire life focused on one goal: making enough money to retire before age fifty-five. Neglecting personal comfort and seldom taking time to relax, he gave every ounce of energy to his business. He left for his office early in the morning and came home late. While he professed to be a Christian, he often skipped church to take care of some paperwork. He occasionally retreated with his family to a beach apartment the family owned, but he always took work with him. While his wife and kids relaxed on the beach, he would pore over some contract or business deal until it was time to pack up and go back home again.

Now, what amazes me about Mark is that he never once complained about his lifestyle. If anything, he was addicted to it. Hard work always excited him and gave him tremendous pleasure—until his panic attack fell on him like a ton of bricks.

It happened early one morning. As usual, he had allowed himself only about six hours of sleep. As he was shaving he became afraid, and suddenly he felt a terrible dread come over him. All the typical panic feelings followed: tightness in the chest, inability to breathe, and a strong urge to run away and keep on running.

After a month of treatment we were able to bring the panic symptoms under control. Mark felt confident that they would not surprise him again. It was at that point I began to stress the need for Mark to make some changes in his life. He needed to relax more, enjoy time with his family, find a better "balance." His values were lopsided—money and material things were all he lived for—and his spiritual life was being entirely neglected. "If you make these adjustments to your life," I promised, "panic will be a thing of the past. If you don't, it will haunt you the rest of your life."

Unfortunately, Mark did not make the changes I suggested; relief from his symptoms was all he wanted. He took the easy road—at least for a while. Only after his fourth bout with panic—each attack worse than the previous one—was he ready to make those fundamental life changes that are necessary for a balanced life.

The point I am making is absolutely vital: Panic anxiety and, for that matter, all anxiety disorders, call for major changes in lifestyle, priorities, values, and commitments. Your anxiety is a warning that you are not living a balanced life. A few anxiety sufferers are handicapped by oversensitive anxiety mechanisms in their bodies, but the majority are being called by their panic or discomfort to make important adjustments.

As you work to reduce panic's power in your life, then, keep in mind the need to evaluate your priorities and rearrange your spiritual values. Ask yourself: *Is what I am searching for or trying to accomplish important in the light of eternity? Is it bringing the most happiness to the greatest number of people or does it only satisfy my needs?* If you really are confused here, I suggest you seek counsel from your pastor or a trusted friend. You may need an outsider's perspective on your value system to help you clarify your life priorities.

12

NAP YOUR WAY TO A TRANQUIL LIFE

Sleep is perhaps the most convenient and effective therapeutic experience available to us today. Right under our noses (or should I say upon our pillows) is a resource for overcoming anxiety that is natural, free, abundantly available (if you make time for it), and extremely effective. And it is so sadly neglected!

I recently examined a large number of handbooks on how to deal with anxiety, including panic attacks and phobias, to see if any mention was made of the value of sleep—and could not find a single reference to it. Yet I know from many years of clinical practice that I can work miracles in a patient's mood simply by prescribing more sleep.

Why is sleep so unrecognized as a source of healing? One reason is widespread belief that we do not need as much sleep as we think we do. There is a myth abroad that sleep robs us of valuable time and that the more we sleep the less we get done. Some even go so far as to equate sleep with slothfulness or laziness.

But nothing is further from the truth! If we rob ourselves of adequate sleep, we become *less* efficient, more prone to making errors, and less productive overall. Fortunately, a significant amount of research in recent years has confirmed this observation and helped reverse the negative bias our culture has held toward sleep.

But my concern for the value of sleep goes further than seeing it as a facilitator of productivity. I also believe sleep deprivation is the most neglected and frequently overlooked *cause of anxiety*. Whatever your particular form of anxiety, when you're not getting enough sleep it gets worse.

Pay attention the next time your sleep is disturbed or you suffer from jet lag. You will notice that you worry more about lesser things than when you are rested and sleeping well. All it takes is some careful self-observation to see the connection.

All of us have times when, for one reason or another, we sleep less than we should. But some people *never* sleep sufficiently, either because they force themselves into a brief sleep cycle (they stay up late and wake up with an alarm) or because their adrenaline flows so strongly that they can only stay asleep for a short period. People like this actually choose their sleep deprivation. And their anxiety levels are likely to be extraordinarily high, although many will deny this until their first panic attack.

There are many questions I want to address in this chapter. How important is sleep in *preventing* anxiety problems? How does anxiety *disturb* our ability to sleep? How might we use sleep to facilitate our *overcoming* of anxiety? But before we look at the relationship between sleep and anxiety, however, let us take a closer look at how sleep functions and what it does for us.

THE NATURE OF SLEEP

Before electricity, light was precious, difficult to produce, and expensive to buy. So most of the world went to sleep when darkness fell and slept until daybreak. Electricity has changed all that and shortened the sleep cycle for most of us. In recent years, more and more researchers are pointing out that we are an *underslept society.* Not only are we more competitive, operating at a higher level of arousal that inhibits the need for sleep, but we have also prolonged the working day beyond its natural light-and-darkness cycle by offering attractive and captivating TV programs, news, movies, and late-night talk shows to make us feel that if we sleep we are missing out on an important part of life.

Our desire to sleep is regulated to a large extent by a cluster of neuronal cells located just above the roof of our mouths called the "hypothalmic suprachiasmatic nuclei" (or SCN). This group of cells is our "biological clock." It regulates just about everything in our body, from sleeping to eating and drinking and sexual behavior, and it is set by the eye's exposure to light on a cycle of approximately twenty-four hours. But this natural clock is very sensitive to drugs, hormones, body temperature, and alertness. Many substances, including our own adrenaline, can upset it.

Shift workers who must change regularly from working days to working nights have a real battle with this clock, because even though they might get sufficient sleep during the total day, their clock confuses them and often tries to put them to sleep while they are working. This can be hazardous. One study of thousands of shift workers found that at least half nodded off at work at least once a week. Many reported near accidents because of sleepiness during the work week. Similarly a study of medical interns on night shifts revealed that one-fourth reported regularly falling asleep while speaking on the phone. And then when they tried to sleep, 35 percent had to use alcohol to fall asleep.

It is a powerful clock, this SCN. And when its controls are violated we pay a penalty.

But why does this clock force us to sleep? What intention of creation does sleep serve? Sleep plays an important role in restoring and reorganizing certain systems and nervous networks. Sleep is *more* than just physical rest. Resting is important, but any insomniac will tell you that just resting does not do the job. A high degree of anxiety and nervousness almost always follows a period of insomnia. And while some of this insomnia anxiety is simply due to concern about not sleeping—to lying there for hours worrying about lack of sleep— a significant portion of it is part of the body's rebellion. It is sending you a very loud message: "We are not getting enough sleep to restore and rejuvenate our systems."

ANXIETY, STRESS, AND SLEEPLESSNESS

Millions and millions of people do not sleep adequately. They toss and turn, have difficulty falling asleep, or wake up early and can't get back to sleep. One estimate is that as many as *fifty million* Americans sleep poorly, if at all.

Some of this sleeplessness is due to *insomnia;* some to a *decreased sleep need.* There is an important difference between these two problems. In *insomnia,* the person *wants* to sleep and feels the *need* for sleep, but can't. In *decreased sleep need,* the body may require sleep, but because of a heightened state of arousal (usually caused by recruiting excessive amounts of adrenaline to carry on ordinary activities), the person feels stimulated and not tired.

It is the latter of these two conditions, the reduced need for sleep, that is a major cause of stress disease and, I believe, of damaging anxiety. The higher level of arousal causes excessive "wear and tear" on the body and mind (like having the idle turned high on an engine), and insufficient time is provided for restoration and rejuvenation of body systems. The result? Disturbed body systems, hormones out of balance, decreased immunity to disease, and general fatigue. These stressful consequences eventually "catch up" with the person who just doesn't feel the need for sleep.

Through the study of how hormones affect brain amines, we are now beginning to understand just how anxiety disturbs sleep and how lack of sleep in turn produces anxiety. Researchers are discovering that the brain operates on and is controlled by a number of chemical "codes."[1] Two of the principle code chemicals (which operate similarly to keys that turn in locks) are acetylcholine and noradrenaline, which are found

[1] See chapter 8 in Alexander Borkely, *Secrets of Sleep* (New York: Basic, 1986).

throughout the nervous system. They help to stabilize activities such as heart rate and stomach digestion.

Researchers are also discovering that these "codes" (especially noradrenaline) also produce *dexedrine,* which is the body's naturally produced psychic energizer. This is the substance that helps us to stay awake and alert when we have to. No doubt you have many times felt the effect of this dexedrine on yourself. Your eyes are wide open, you are alert and able to take in many stimuli. You become "wired," active, and cannot relax.

Now, when the dexedrine level becomes excessive, instead of its just keeping you awake and alert, it makes you feel restless and anxious. More important, you lose the ability to sleep. The chemical "code" forces you to stay awake, presumably because it senses an emergency. The result? Sleeplessness. It only takes a *small* increase in dexedrine to turn average arousal into acute anxiety and to turn off your sleep clock.

Another chemical cause of decreased need for sleep is elevated adrenaline. If you are excited about a project or pick up an exciting book just before you fall asleep, your adrenaline level will be high and will almost certainly keep you awake. You won't feel sleepy any more. You'll feel alert and wide awake, and won't feel the need for any sleep.

This is a deceptive message your body is sending. The reason you are not sleepy is that you are "overcharged," not that your body doesn't need the sleep. You may even feel good at the time, but your systems are being deprived of their much-needed rejuvenation time. You thus begin to create the conditions for increased anxiety and a state of sleeplessness.

It is a vicious cycle, which, once it has taken hold of you, is very difficult to break.

SLEEPING WELL PREVENTS
ANXIETY PROBLEMS

I am thoroughly convinced that a person who sleeps sufficiently to provide adequate recovery time for the body and brain is not as likely to become anxiety-prone as someone who doesn't sleep adequately, all other factors being equal. Good sleep gives you the best protection against the onslaught of anxiety.

Surprisingly, not a lot of research has been done on the topic of how sleep lowers anxiety. My firm belief comes first of all from closely observing my own anxious tendencies and how they track with my sleeping patterns, and then in observing my immediate family and my patients over many years. I doubt if I am living in a body that is different from everyone else's; we're all pretty much subject to the same biological laws. And what I've discovered in myself and others is a direct link between adequate sleep and reduced anxiety.

Perhaps we can best understand the value of sleep by seeing what happens when we are intentionally deprived of it. Many experiments have been conducted, and they all come up with the same results: The first night without sleep is tolerated well. The second is marked by a strong urge to sleep. From the third night on, the person starts to experience illusions and disturbances of perception similar to that seen in schizophrenia. One subject described the floor as being covered with sticky particles that made it difficult to walk and the air as being filled with colored specks. After ten and a half hours of sleep, the disturbances disappeared.

But do extraordinary periods of sleep deprivation prove anything? I think they show how essential sleep is to the human. But just how much sleep is enough sleep?

No study has yet been devised that could finally, and without question, tell us exactly how much sleep we ought to get. It varies from person to person and is controlled by many factors. But I think there is abundant evidence that ours is a sleep-deprived culture. For example, most people sleep longer on weekends, making up for a sleep deficit during the week. Many people wake up to the clamor of an alarm clock, their bodies crying out to stay in bed. Others have to use stimulants such as caffeine to keep themselves awake or even to "get going" in the morning. I would think this was evidence enough! But recent research also confirms that the normal amount of sleep most of us get lies *below* the ideal amount. Mary Carskadon and William Dement were able to show, for example, that most of us live with a *permanent sleep deficit.*[2]

Because it is hard to specify just how much sleep is enough, I have developed a technique to help my clients discover their optimal sleep needs. For what it is worth, I will describe it here:

(1) *On the first day, add a half-hour to your normal sleep period* by either going to bed earlier or waking up later.

(2) *Repeat this longer sleep period for three days.*

(3) *Then add a further half-hour of sleep* and repeat this for the next three days.

(4) *After a week, take stock of your mood, energy, efficiency, and overall feeling of well-being,* comparing how you felt before and after you added the first half-hour, then the second, and so on.

[2] Mary Carskadon and William Dement, "Current Perspectives on Daytime Sleepiness," *Sleep,* 5(1982): 73-81.

(5) *If you feel better at any time after adding sleep, you probably needed the extra sleep,* so make the extra amount a permanent part of your life.

(6) *If you still don't feel better after a week, gradually increase your sleep time* in half-hour increments until you do begin to feel better. Most of my patients have reported dramatic improvements in how they feel generally after adding at least one hour of sleep.

The reason I suggest you continue for at least three days after each increment is that usually after adding extra sleep you will not feel better *immediately.* At first you will probably feel worse, especially when you first wake up the next morning. This is because you are beginning to allow your arousal system more rest, and since it isn't yet rested enough, it craves still more. You are "tantalizing" your body with more sleep, but not yet giving it enough. This is why a single, very long sleep doesn't feel relaxing; it switches off your arousal to such an extent that you feel lousy. One needs three or four such sleeps for sufficient recovery. If you are not aware of this phenomenon, you are likely to believe erroneously that "extra sleep" only makes you feel worse.

IS TOO MUCH SLEEP BAD FOR YOU?

Can one sleep too much? And how can we know whether we are sleeping enough or whether we would feel better if we slept less?

Except for rare sleep disorders, and assuming that you are not depressed or have a tendency toward laziness, I would say you could never really sleep too much; as soon as you are rested enough, your body will come alive again. In depression, there is a tendency to want to sleep a lot as an escape, and this is not helpful to recovery. Otherwise I have yet to be convinced that we can sleep too much.

There is, of course, a way you can test whether you are sleeping too much. You can reverse the sleep-adding experiment and *remove* sleep in half-hour increments, and then see if you feel better. But let me save you the time or trouble—as I have already suggested, the data indicate that except in relatively rare situations we don't sleep more than we should, but less.[3]

Further evidence for my contention that sleeping well helps to prevent anxiety problems is found in a study by Dr. Ernest L. Hartmann comparing short (less than six hours) with long (over nine hours) sleepers. Dr. Hartmann concluded that there may be a relationship between

[3] See Ernest L. Hartmann, *Functions of Sleep* (New Haven, CT: Yale University Press) 55.

personality and sleep time and that the "worrier" kind of person naturally requires more sleep. He found that these worriers especially need more *dream* sleep, a fact that will become clearer later, when I examine the purpose of dreams. In Dr. Hartmann's study, those who slept longer also experienced a greater reduction in anxiety following the sleep. So go ahead, sleep your worries away!

HOW TO SLEEP WHEN YOU ARE ANXIOUS

If sleeping helps reduce anxiety, it would follow that we need sleep most during times when we are anxious. But I think we all find it difficult to go to sleep during those times. Have an argument with your spouse or neighbor, for instance, and see how hard it is to go to sleep. Plan a meeting the next day with someone you dislike or with whom you have a conflict, and notice how your mind keeps you awake, almost forcing you to plan for that meeting and anticipate what you might or might not say.

What is happening in such situations is that your mind is forcing you to try to resolve as many of your anxieties as possible *before* you go to sleep. That's why it will remind you of things you have left undone, of doors you have forgotten to lock, or of people who have hurt you before releasing you to slumberland. I am amazed how often my mind tells me things I need to do just as I am trying to go to sleep. Unless I write these things down (usually on a notepad I keep next to my bed) so that I won't forget them, my mind will give me no peace.

Sleep *is* far more peaceful if you can resolve your anxieties before you nod off. Perhaps this is why Paul advises us to never let the sun go down upon our anger (Eph. 4:26). Not only is it spiritually destructive to allow anger to remain unresolved after the end of the day; that same anger is also going to disturb our much-needed sleep and rob us of the rejuvenation we need.

This leads me to conclude that some of the anxiety we experience before we go to sleep is healthy. Up to a point, the sleeplessness anxiety produces is helpful in that it forces us to resolve our conflicts, disagreements, and fears *before* freeing us from the day, and *before* surrendering us to sleep where we might forget these conflicts and thus do ourselves more harm.

Unfortunately, however, many of our anxieties cannot be resolved by the end of a day; they are either beyond our control or too complex to be set aside. When that happens, our anxiety can then become obsessional and rob us of sleep. The sleeplessness then weakens our thinking, feeds our imaginations, and tires the body further, making us *more* prone to worry.

How can we avoid that cycle? How can we attend to our presleep anxieties so that we can free our minds for rest, while at the same time not create overwhelming fear that will prevent us from sleeping? Let me suggest the following exercise, which I have found to be helpful with a number of my high-anxiety patients:

(1) A little while before you go to bed, take a pen and notebook and find a private, quiet place where you can do some reflecting.

(2) Ask yourself, *What worries have I not resolved this day?* Write down all unfinished tasks, concerns, or activities you did not get around to. Writing them down, even if you can do nothing about them, gets them out of your mind.

(3) Then ask yourself, *What essential tasks must I do tomorrow?* Place an emphasis on *essential* and don't crowd your mind with petty issues.

(4) Continue by asking, *What hurts have I not forgiven today?* Write down a phrase or idea that captures the hurt. Perhaps you were insulted or overlooked. Perhaps you were not promoted, or someone robbed you of something. Whatever the hurt was, write it down, because putting it on paper will help get it off your mind.

(5) Now pray over each hurt. Ask God to give you the strength to forgive the hurt and then let it go. As a symbol of this act of forgiveness, cross each hurt off your list as you forgive it. If there are some hurts that you don't feel ready to forgive, then leave them on this list as a reminder that they are "unfinished business" and remind yourself that you will attend to them the next day.

(6) Now make a list of people *you* may have hurt. If you can put right any of these hurts now, before you go to bed, then do so. If you can't, leave them on the list for action later.

(7) Now, close your notebook and *don't* open it again before you go to sleep. Consciously set aside any thought about your list that might come to you as you try to go to sleep. Focus *only* on the feeling of comfort and relaxation as you lie in your bed. Fold your arms, lean back on the "everlasting arms," and surrender your all to the One who cares for you more than any friend, who has promised to surround you with His protection and deliver you from any harm (Ps. 34:7).

DREAMS AND ANXIETY

Earlier in this chapter I suggested that dreaming plays an important role in helping us cope with anxiety. Evidence for this comes from a number of sources, and it is helpful to understand the critical role dreaming plays in the experience of healing and wholeness. This understanding may also help reduce the fear that some have about their dreams and assist others in not overinterpreting their meaning.

Sigmund Freud concluded that the *interpretation of dreams* was the royal road to a knowledge of the unconscious activities of the mind. While he performed an important service in opening up the strategic significance of dreams, Freud may have put too much emphasis on the *content* of dreams and not enough on the *process* of dreaming. In other words, it is not so much *what* we dream about that is important (we can't always recall dream content), but the fact that we *do* dream. Dreaming is not an accidental occurrence or a nonessential part of human existence. As we will see, it is necessary for emotional health, and it certainly is important in helping us overcome anxiety.

Scripture makes frequent reference to dreams, yet I find many Christian believers to be very afraid of how we interpret dreams, as if dreams were some alien part of the Christian experience. Some notable dreams in the Bible include Jacob's dream when he was traveling to Haran (Gen. 28), the dreams of the chief baker and chief butler of Pharaoh concerning Joseph (Gen. 40), and the dream of Solomon (1 Kings 3). Each of these dreams—and most other dreams recorded in the Old Testament —was a means of communication between God and His people. This is also true for certain New Testament records of dreams, such as God's appearance to Joseph, to announce the conception of Jesus (Matt. 1:20), and to Pilate's wife, to tell her to warn her husband not to have any part in the judgment of Christ (Matt. 27:19).

Now, while we have these recorded instances of God's using dreams to communicate to His people, most of our dreaming has more of a natural function. Our dreams are *not* necessarily God's message to us. Jacob, Joseph, and Pilate's wife doubtless had *many* other dreams that are not recorded for us as God's communications because they were natural happenings and not of any special significance.

I believe that too much emphasis on the strategic or spiritual significance of dreaming can be very misleading. In all of history, and in every recorded culture, the mystery of dreaming has been exaggerated. Dream interpretation has even altered the course of nations. Oracles have dreamed the future, and pagan dream-rites have been used to cure the sick. American Indians enacted their dreams when awake, and scores of people still pay therapists to interpret their dreams in a manner that mimics the superstitions and fortune-telling of the Dark Ages.

From the time of the ancient Egyptians, there have been attempts at spelling out the specific significance of objects and occurrences in dreams. But these culturally determined interpretations simply cannot be taken seriously. There is no central part of the brain that stores these symbolic meanings—no universal language for dreams that is common to all cultures. A snake may mean something to one person and something totally different to another. To a third it simply means a snake! We each learn our symbols differently, and while our culture may provide some similarities, by far the greater influences on these symbols are our own individual experiences. The most significant dreams are those that don't need interpretation; they tell you *exactly* what they mean.

This is *not* to say that dreams don't have significance! The content of some dreams very clearly reflects the conflicts and anxieties of the dreamer. But to suggest that everything we dream is significant is ridiculous. Unleashed from reality and detached from reason, dreams play freely around in the mind; they go where they like and uncover both truth and fantasy. And dreams, furthermore, cannot tell the difference between reality and fantasy.

Many, if not most, of our dreams are not remembered. Those we do remember usually remain in memory only for a brief period of time. As I sit here writing I am trying to recall what I dreamed yesterday—and cannot. It's gone! The only dreams that remain permanently in mind are those that were very frightening or of great significance.

WHAT HAPPENS WHEN WE DREAM?

What actually happens during dreaming? This is the all-important question. If we can understand how dreams work, we will have a better understanding of what purpose they serve.

At this point, however, we are into speculation. Despite centuries of being intrigued by dreams, we do not yet know precisely what happens when we dream. We do know that dream sleep occurs only after a period of regular sleep (sixty to ninety minutes). Nondream sleep prepares us for the dream stage, which makes up about 25 percent of our total sleep. After a short period of dreaming, we then return to the nondream state or even to light wakefulness. Throughout the night, then, we dip in and out of dreaming.

To the best of our understanding, while regular sleep clearly has a restorative function for the body, dream sleep seems to be important for restoring our psychological and emotional health. Systems involving our ability to maintain an optimistic mood, energy, and self-confidence as well as those that involve our emotional adaptation to the world are all helped by dream sleep.

If we deprive people of dream sleep, we rapidly produce emotional disturbances and even psychotic delusions and behaviors. Certain emotional disorders can be relieved by medication that does nothing more than enhance dream sleep. And research has shown that larger quantities of dream sleep are needed after days of stress, worry, intense new learning, or conflict. All of these findings speak to the purpose of dreams.

Dreaming also plays a role in consolidating memory or learning and in reconnecting disconnected memories and disposing of memories no longer needed. In this sense, dreaming is very much like the "cleanup" program used in large computers to sort out the memory used, straighten up temporary work areas, and then rearrange the core of the computer. Dreaming is the mind's cleanup time. We purge away associations, reconstruct and reinterpret the day's activities, and dispose of unnecessary worries. One researcher described the process this way: "We dream in order to forget," and I think that very accurately sums up the function of dreaming.

Dreaming provides us with four Rs. It allows us to *review, revise,* and *rehearse* our worlds. And when life is tough and full of anxiety, it also provides a mechanism for emotional (and perhaps spiritual) *repair.* This then leads us to two questions:

- How does anxiety get relieved in the process?
- What happens to the stuff in our minds that is still unresolved but cannot be forgotten in our dreams?

On the first point, if dreaming is a process of sorting and disposing of unresolved issues, then dreaming plays a very important role in helping us cope with anxiety. Since much, if not all, anxiety, other than that produced by biological factors, is based in our imaginations, dreaming can help us "forget" what we imagine. I know that things always seem gloomier to me *before* I go to sleep than when I wake up. During sleep my mind makes connections and develops insights; I am always better able to put things in perspective *after* I've slept than before.

On the second point, many conflicts remain unresolved at the end of a day and find expression in our dreams. We may actually recall in our dreams an expression of that conflict. In this sense, our dream recall is anxiety's way of informing us: "This issue in your life is not yet settled. Go and take care of it."

Let me illustrate. Perhaps, during a dream, you relive some disagreement you have had with a friend. All night you toss and turn, while your dreams replay the issues over and over again in various forms. Your dreams keep telling you that this is something to worry about, something that needs to be resolved. Such dreams *are* significant.

Now, a particular dream may not always reflect a conflict directly. *Sometimes* our dreams are symbolic, which is the mind's way of presenting the problem indirectly. The more we use denial as a defense mechanism, the more likely we are to dream symbolically, because our conscious awareness won't face the conflict directly.

These symbolic dreams must be understood and the issues resolved if we are going to be freed from their tendency to create anxiety. They need to be talked about (with a friend, for example) and their implications teased out. You may need to consult a professional counselor to help you face the more frightening or unacceptable aspects of such anxiety. Don't hesitate to seek help—unresolved conflicts that keep emerging in your dreams will rob you of peace and create a high anxiety level.

I recall a client who in her mid-thirties had become a severely troubled and anxious person. As we explored the reasons for this, she reported that she had recurring dreams about her father, who had died of a heart attack when she was fifteen years old. The dreams were always erotic—but her father was not the focus of the sexual eroticism. He was always in the background condemning her for doing what she was doing.

Slowly this woman's dreams began to change even as we explored them. Finally she was able to admit that the focus of her erotic feelings was indeed her own father. She began to recall that shortly before her father's death she had had twinges of erotic feelings for him (a common experience of adolescence) · but had dismissed these as "terrible thoughts." When her father died, she somehow felt that her erotic feelings had caused his death.

As my client began to understand the origin of her dreams, they began to diminish. She had finally resolved her conflict, and her mind no longer needed to remind her of it. She discovered a new freedom from anxiety. The fear of going to bed at night that she had developed because of her dreams also dissipated and her sleep improved. This also reduced her anxiety level considerably.

DREAMS AND SEX

Since so many dreams have sexual connotations (this can be frightening to some), perhaps a word about this aspect of dreaming might be appropriate. Freud saw sexual motivation as a strong influence on all our dreams. This is not surprising, given the sexual repressions of his age. But I think there is also a more natural explanation, especially for males. Preceding every dream period, from infancy onward, males have penile erections. These erections also occur on waking in the early hours of the morning due to a reflex response to a full bladder.

This does *not* mean that these erections have overtly sexual content. In fact, what would such a sexual dream signify to an infant? The predream erections are quite natural. There may be some body-brain learning going on. We know that limbs also move, the infant sucks and even smiles during the same stage of sleep. Clearly there is a strong connection between drives, dreams, and physical reactions, but the connection is at a very basic physiological level, not necessarily at a complex psychological or sexual level.

There is another aspect to the connection between dreams and sex. Dreaming is a very private experience. It is also a way the brain expresses living experiences which may or may not signify deep, dark secrets. Since sexual experiences and feelings are strongly controlled in our society, it is natural that our sexual conflicts will also be expressed through our dreams.

Most adults, for example, will begin to have sexually explicit dreams when they have been deprived of sexual expression for a time. Sometimes they feel ashamed of these dreams because they do not reflect waking morals. But there is not necessarily a direct connection between a dream and a waking desire. The fact that you have a dream in which you are sexually involved with someone other than your spouse, or, if you are single, with someone you admire, does *not* mean that you secretly desire such a union!

You cannot control what you dream. If you dream something you don't like or that suggests you are an uncontrolled sex maniac, chances are high that your brain is merely exploring the roots of fantasy or revealing areas in which you have exercised strong control. Since we have to exercise control over our sexual urges in real life, it is normal that in our dreams we may abandon these controls. What is important is that we are in control of our real world. What happens in our dreams does not have to happen in waking life.

Some people, it is true, may have erotic dreams because they have a lot of denial going on in the area of their sexuality. It is far healthier to be honest with yourself about what attracts or excites you sexually than to run away from these feelings or suppress them. Denied feelings will emerge one way or the other—if only in your dreams. If you find this bothersome, seek help from an understanding counselor—and by all means talk to God in prayer. Getting in touch with these denials will free you from such anxiety-producing dreams.

HOW TO IMPROVE YOUR SLEEP

Improving your sleep is good not only for the physical rest it provides, but also because it improves your dreaming. Disturbed sleep also disturbs the quality of your dreaming.

Table 4
DIFFERENCES BETWEEN GOOD AND POOR SLEEPERS

Good Sleepers	Poor Sleepers
Fall asleep quickly	Take twice as long to fall asleep
Awaken less frequently	Awaken twice as often during the night
Suffer less restlessness	Toss and turn more
Have a lower pulse rate	Have a higher pulse rate
Dream more (24 percent of total sleep)	Dream less (16.9 percent of total sleep)
Are emotionally healthy	Have higher incidence of psychiatric help in history
Suffer few psychosomatic complaints	Have high level of psychosomatic complaints

No two people are alike when it comes to sleep habits, and not every night of sleep is the same. One night passes like a brief moment; the next drags on interminably. From one night of sleep we awaken serene and rested, from another we are wrung out. Worry makes sleep difficult, yet many worries may be relieved by sleep. Depression may cause us to awaken in the early hours of the morning, and illness can rob us of all sleep.

So how can we improve our sleep, no matter what our circumstances? First of all, consider the differences between good and poor sleepers as revealed in research at the University of Chicago[4] and shown in table 4. Perhaps the most significant difference discovered between good and poor sleepers is that poor sleepers seem to be in a somewhat heightened physiological state both before *and* during sleep—they have higher heart rates and seem to overproduce neurochemicals that stimulate the arousal system. Clearly, in my opinion, this is indicative of the higher adrenaline levels seen in stress reactions such as anxiety.

All this suggests some important ways in which you can improve the quality of your sleep:

(1) *Resolve all conflicts and dispose of your anger before you try to go to sleep.* I have already provided suggestions for doing this.

(2) *Lower your stress levels by paying attention to the things that cause you to become overaroused.* My book *The Hidden Link Between Adrenalin and Stress* addresses this problem specifically and provides practical help for coping with stress.

(3) *Try to create as quiet a sleeping environment as possible.* While it is possible to adjust to sleep in a noisy environment, quiet is better. I

[4] See chapter 5 of Hartmann, *The Functions of Sleep,* 53-79.

favor the use of ear plugs, especially the soft plastic ones that can be molded to fit the ears. While they don't shut out noise totally, they provide enough muffling to prevent you from being awakened by barking dogs or screeching brakes.

(4) *Get into the habit of going to sleep at the same time.* Regularity helps with sleep onset. The body prefers for us to cooperate with the internal SCN clock.

(5) *Avoid all stimulants such as caffeine or chocolate after about 6 P.M.* Also avoid stimulating activities, books, or TV shows within an hour or two of going to bed. Your adrenal system needs time to wind down before you can go to sleep.

(6) *Try not to become upset if you cannot fall asleep or if you wake up too early.* Doing so will only raise your adrenaline and certainly keep you awake. If you can't sleep, relax and enjoy the time alone. Savor the comfort of your bed and relish the time of relaxation. Resting is just as necessary as sleep.

Mild insomnia is usually caused by strong emotions (anger, fear, joy) or worries that are on the mind, new surroundings (trips or vacations), minor illnesses (colds, influenza), and caffeine or alcohol. Some of these you can treat; some need to run their course. But most will disappear in a short time.

(7) *Don't use sleeping pills unless it is absolutely necessary.* They have undesirable side effects and do *not* bring about natural sleep; they change the natural progression of sleep stages. Furthermore, they affect your work performance and can become habit forming.

(8) *If you cannot sleep and cannot continue to relax, then get up and have a warm nonalcoholic or nonstimulating drink (milk is good).* Do *not* get into any exciting activity or read a novel (unless it's very boring). Do something nonarousing that will make you drowsy and ready for sleep after a short while.

(9) *If you have a few sleepless nights in a row, I recommend that you add some daytime naps.* Mothers of small children often have their night sleep disturbed. If this happens, then sleep when your baby sleeps —even if it is daytime. Sleep does not have to come in one continuous block of time; it can be broken down into different segments and can take place at any time without loss of value.

NAPPING AND TRANQUILLITY

In closing this chapter, allow me to comment on the value of the "forty-wink nap." Recent research is beginning to show how valuable these brief periods of rest or sleep can be.

Most Americans have been brainwashed into regarding napping as wasteful or self-indulgent. We look down upon European or tropical cultures who take "siestas." But napping is not only healthful and beneficial; it can also make the difference between vigor and lethargy, success or failure—according to Dr. David Dinges, a sleep psychologist at the University of Pennsylvania.

Americans typically do not break the day with a rest or nap but interrupt their work with a lunch break (often a substantial meal). The afternoon is thus a time of drowsiness—a period known to be the peak for performance errors and sleep-related accidents. Those who are able to nap at midday or early afternoon, however, find themselves refreshed and energized.

Who ought to take naps? Most of us, says Dr. Dinges. He believes that brainwave studies show the need for sleep twice a day, with the less urgent and shorter sleep period to take place at midday or early afternoon. That's why even people who sleep well at night feel drowsy in the early afternoon. In fact, the lower your stress level, the more likely you are to feel the need for a nap. High arousal blocks out this need—but at the cost of increased "wear and tear" on our systems. Naps also significantly improve our moods and benefit our relationships. And coronary heart disease is lower in siesta countries, so there is that benefit to consider also.

How long should we nap? It varies. Some can feel refreshed in five minutes, while others may need an hour or two. What is clear is that naps are more valuable *before* you feel tired than after. A nap taken only after you are overcome by fatigue is too late to be really beneficial.

So why not try a nap before you get tired? I know that your emotional well-being will be improved.

One last word of caution: Most people feel groggy when they wake from a nap. Researchers call this "sleep inertia." It's just the body's craving for more sleep, so don't fight it, and certainly don't read it as a sign that napping is bad for you! Quite the reverse is true; it's probably a sign that you need even more sleep.

Pleasant dreams!

13

UNDERSTANDING ANTIANXIETY MEDICATIONS

A short time ago, I taught a seminar to a large group of pastors and their spouses on how to manage stress in the ministry. During the discussion time, the question of the appropriate use of medication—especially the use of antidepressants and tranquilizers —came up. Many of the pastors present had difficulty accepting that taking one of these medications is quite normal. There is such a strong antidrug sentiment in the modern church and in society today that the idea of using any "mind-altering" drug filled them with apprehension.

I can well understand this sentiment. Much human misery can be traced to the misuse of tranquilizers—not to mention illegal drugs. There are pastors who grew up during the sixties and may have abused drugs themselves; now they have an aversion to any type of medication that affects the mind.

Yes, I understand these feelings—but in the case of anxiety, I believe that much of this concern is misplaced. I also believe it is both wrong and unnecessary for anyone to suffer from, say, a severe case of panic disorder when there is appropriate and safe treatment for the condition in the form of medication. I see little value in going through life miserable and unhappy. If a problem is clearly caused by a biochemical disturbance, it is only natural that one should correct it with appropriate medication and return the body and mind to normal functioning.

I know of scores of pastors and missionaries, not to mention devout Christian lay people, who go through life suffering unnecessarily from disturbed biochemistry or hormones. Out of misunderstanding, they refuse to avail themselves of the available help that could transform their lives and free them to be more effective in their ministries.

As an example of this dilemma, let me relate one pastor's story. Although it concerns a depression problem, the issues are the same as for anxiety.

For about six years before I met Ralph, he had suffered from a low-grade but persistent depression. It seemed to him that he was always depressed. His work had become a chore. He hated people, the telephone, preaching, counseling; in fact, almost everything about the work of ministry had become a nightmare to him since the onset of his pervasive depression.

The main reason Ralph stayed in the ministry was that he didn't know what else he could do. He felt trapped—too old to think about changing careers. But he also remembered that once he had felt a strong calling to the ministry—and he had enjoyed many happy and effective years in this calling before the onset of the depression. This memory kept him holding on to the hope that someday things would change and he would get better again.

Ralph's depressive pattern was quite interesting and very typical of a certain type of endogenous (biochemical) depression that responds well to antidepressant medication. Two features stood out. The *first* was that his depression was always worse first thing in the morning. No matter how well he slept, he felt absolutely miserable upon waking. Getting up was emotionally extremely painful for him, and many times he prayed that God would just take him home before he had to get up. Often Ralph would lie in bed until noontime, refusing to budge, while his wife coaxed and encouraged him to get up. As the day progressed, however, Ralph felt a little better. By evening, he would feel much better—so much better that he feared going to bed because he knew sleep would make him feel rotten again.

The *second* feature of Ralph's depression, which is quite characteristic of endogenous depression, is that whenever there was an emergency, or whenever he was called upon to use his adrenaline (such as when he had to preach a special sermon) he felt much better. High adrenaline arousal made his depression disappear—until the adrenaline dropped again, when the depression would return with a vengeance.

These two features, plus some other clinical signs, convinced me that Ralph would respond well to antidepressant medication. But Ralph resisted; he didn't like the idea of being on drugs. He wanted to feel better, but was concerned about "what others would say." I assured him that antidepressant medication was *not addictive* and that he could stop it anytime he liked—that the medication would only work if there were a defect in his body's chemistry. Finally he agreed to try the medication.

The first drug we selected brought only minor improvement. After three weeks, the psychiatrist who was consulting with me agreed to switch to another drug, and bingo! Exactly two weeks later (this type of medication needs two weeks to take effect), Ralph's depression lifted. He felt, in his words, as if someone had "turned on the light." Vigor, energy, motivation, and a happy spirit returned. Today Ralph continues to live a happy life and be very effective in his ministry. He may need to take the medication the rest of his life, but he considers that a small price to pay for recovering his interest in living.

WHY CONSIDER MEDICATION?

As I have indicated, major depression is not the only emotional disorder where medication is sometimes appropriate. Many anxiety disorders also have a biochemical component and respond well to medication. Except in relatively minor cases, the effective use of medication is essential for effective treatment of panic and other anxiety disorders.

One reason medication is especially important in treating anxiety is that in anxiety, unlike depression, the symptoms themselves become sources of the problem, so that the disorder literally feeds on itself. The fear of a panic attack, for example, causes anxiety and thus sets up the conditions for further attacks. This is the "fear-of-fear" response I mentioned in an earlier chapter, and it quickly sets up a spiral effect in which the anxiety builds to higher and higher levels. It is imperative, therefore, that this spiral be interrupted and the system stabilized, so that the necessary counseling or therapy can be introduced. If one is running away from the symptoms one hardly has energy to address the life issues that originally give rise to anxiety problems!

The purpose of anxiety medication, then, is to stabilize the various systems, reduce the fear of the symptoms, restore control and confidence, and "buy time" so that the underlying issues can be addressed in therapy. This involves some risk, as every professional therapist knows. Once the symptoms are relieved, there is always the strong possibility that the patient will not be motivated to make the necessary life changes or address the underlying conflict that is causing the anxiety problem.

Some therapists, therefore, may refuse to use any antianxiety medication at first, if at all. Others will allow a modicum of symptom relief, but leave enough anxiety in place to motivate attention to underlying issues. As in any other physical disorder, every case is different; how much medication to use is a matter for the individual therapist or physician to decide.

In the case of all but the most mild panic attacks, however, I believe medication should definitely be used. My experience has been that it is not possible to make progress in therapy while the possibility of a severe attack persists. The potential for an attack undermines all confidence and destroys the results of therapy; months of hard work can be undone by one panic attack!

How can you know if you need medication to control your anxiety? Here are some definite indications, which your therapist will usually take into account when evaluating your condition:

- Is the anxiety so debilitating that no progress can be made in therapy without medication?

- Is progress being made already without medication? If so, it is likely that you can continue without it.
- Can you function adequately at home and/or work without medication? If so, it is unlikely that you need to take it.
- Are you suicidal or demoralized, or does the anxiety present any risk to your life or others? If so, medication is essential.

TYPES OF ANTIANXIETY MEDICATION

It is a miracle of modern medicine that we have a large number of effective medications to reduce the pain of people who suffer from mental and emotional disorders. I never cease to thank God that I live in an age when such suffering can be minimized. Research is continuing to find more effective medication, especially for panic attacks, agoraphobia, and obsessive-compulsive disorders. I believe that the next few years will see some significant progress in these areas.

In the meantime there are *four* kinds of medication that appear to help reduce anxiety symptoms: tricyclic antidepressants, tranquilizers, adrenaline blockers, and antihistamines. Sometimes barbiturates are also prescribed, but their use is now falling into disfavor because of the high risk of addiction and the depressant effect they have on the central nervous system. I will confine my remarks, therefore, to just the four kinds of antianxiety medication I mentioned above:

(1) *Tricyclic antidepressants.* These agents are traditionally used in the treatment of severe depression or depression mixed with anxiety. They have also been found to be effective in lesser depression that is biologically based and in reducing the incidence of panic attacks. They are used in much lower dosages for anxiety than when used for depression.

No one really knows why antidepressants block panic. Perhaps there is a connection between depression and panic through the adrenal system, but we don't know what is going on at this stage.

Almost any of the dozen or more tricyclics will work in reducing anxiety. For instance, a common medication used for panic anxiety is imipramine (Tofranil). Very small dosages are used at first (say 10 to 25 milligrams per day) and then gradually increased so that the side effects can be tolerated. The full dosage is usually taken once a day, at bedtime. Tricyclic antidepressants do not take effect immediately; it may take up to two or three weeks before improvement is noted and the attacks subside.

Side effects are always a consideration in the use of these antidepressants, but they usually subside to a minimum after a few days. Dry mouth and constipation are the most common effects; your physician will also check for any blood-pressure problems. If the side effects are intolerable, another antidepressant may help—this, of course, is a matter for a physician to decide.

In chapter 8, I mentioned a drug called Anafranil. This medication, a tricyclic antidepressant, was used many years ago in the treatment of depression. It is now being brought back to treat obsessions and compulsions because clinical trials show that it is effective in about two-thirds of such cases. (This is good news, because the tranquilizers usually used in treating anxiety disorders have not proved helpful for obsessive-compulsiveness.) At the time of this writing, Anafranil is pending release by the Federal Drug Administration. It should be available by the time this book is published.

The major value of antidepressant therapy in the treatment of anxiety disorders is that it is *nonaddicting;* you can stop taking the medication anytime you wish. This should be done gradually, however, because the body does become accustomed to the medication. The doctor's instructions should be followed closely.

(2) *Tranquilizers.* Unfortunately, antidepressants are only helpful in some anxiety disorders, notably panic attacks, and even then they only help in about one-third of cases. The next important category of medication in treating anxiety, therefore, is the tranquilizer. This category of medication plays a very important role in the treatment of general anxiety.

There are two types of tranquilizers: major and minor. Major tranquilizers are mostly used to treat severe psychotic disorders such as schizophrenia and occasionally are used in severe anxiety disorders. The most common tranquilizers, however, are minor ones. They are called minor not because they are less powerful, but because they are used to treat the lesser problem of anxiety.

Most minor tranquilizers are part of a family called benzodiazepines. The newer agent, Xanax (generic name alprazolam) is a similar chemical but of a different family called triazolobenzodiazepines. The tranquilizers in these two families are the most widely used of all antianxiety agents and have been found to be effective throughout the world. Before they came along, anxiety sufferers had to rely on barbiturates and other sedatives for anxiety, with consequences that were both dangerous (addiction and overdose) and inconvenient (a "doped up" feeling). But modern-day tranquilizers are not so sedating; one can live a very normal life even on high doses.

Among the antianxiety benzodiazepines are the well-known tranquilizers Valium and Librium. These are used less often than they used to be because newer agents such as Xanax are more effective in alleviating acute anxiety, have fewer side effects, retain their efficacy longer, and are not so sedating. The overall safety record of these newer drugs is unparalleled.

As I described in chapter 1, these agents work by interacting with brain chemoceptors specific to them. There is strong evidence that agents like Xanax work by augmenting the brain's own tranquilizers when they become deficient, thus restoring the brain to a tranquil state.

I also indicated earlier there are problems with the long-term use of tranquilizers. However, if withdrawal from the drug is very carefully controlled, there is little danger of dependence. Later in this chapter I will present a technique for weaning oneself off a tranquilizer such as Xanax without causing the symptoms to reoccur.

Unfortunately, tranquilizers are not always used as carefully as they should be. A recent report in *USA Today*[1] indicates that Xanax has become the third most commonly prescribed drug in the United States —up from sixth place a year ago. True, our society is anxiety-prone! But such usage can hardly be ascribed to high anxiety; it must be attributed to these tranquilizers' being overprescribed and misused.

Let me emphasize: When the brain is deficient in natural tranquilizer, it *is* appropriate to use a tranquilizing agent on a short-term basis to restore balance. Prolonged use of tranquilizers or using them for relatively minor states of anxiety is *not appropriate*. When a tranquilizer is used inappropriately, there is a danger of long-term dependency. Tranquilizers should therefore be used only when one is under the care of a competent professional who knows how to treat anxiety.

Specific tranquilizers vary in efficiency, duration, number and duration of side effects, and ease of discontinuation. It is always necessary to trade off the various benefits and drawbacks to match a patient's specific needs.

Xanax, for example, is an extremely effective tranquilizer, but it can be addictive if not handled very carefully. In addition, Xanax can sometimes cause drowsiness and sedation. (Those taking Xanax should not drive when first starting treatment, until they learn how to handle these side effects.)

Dosages of Xanax usually start at 0.25 milligrams, three or four times a day, and go up to as high as 2 milligrams, three or four times a day. In severe cases, the dosage can go as high as 6 milligrams, but side effects become quite severe at such high dosage.

[1] 3 February 1989, "LIFE" section, 1.

Withdrawal symptoms (which hardly ever occur if the medication is tapered off *very slowly*) include rebound anxiety (anxiety returns much intensified), agitation, diarrhea, insomnia, headaches, ringing in the ears, hypotension (low blood pressure), and blurred vision. Stopping Xanax suddenly can precipitate severe panic attacks because the brain has become dependent on an external supply of tranquilizer to block its receptors; the sudden withdrawal of this agent causes many receptors to be left raw and exposed.

Xanax used in combination with an adrenaline blocker such as Inderal has been very effective in the treatment of panic attacks. The adrenaline blocker, which reduces the body's "fight-or-flight" reaction, is used in much lower doses than in treating heart disease and takes about two weeks before it is fully effective. In the meantime, Xanax works to control the anxiety. The Xanax is then gradually reduced until only the adrenaline blocker is in place.

A newer tranquilizer called buspirone (BuSpar) has recently been introduced. It shows great promise; when used skillfully and with the right type of patient it has fewer side effects, is not sedating, and is does not create dependency. This is partially because the medication takes longer (up to four weeks) to begin controlling the symptoms; since the patient doesn't feel immediate relief, he or she is less likely to become conditioned to the use of the drug. In this respect, it is more like an antidepressant and thus safer to use. BuSpar is given together with Xanax initially. It is long-acting and Xanax is short-acting, so the Xanax controls the anxiety in the short term until the BuSpar takes effect. The Xanax is then *slowly* withdrawn, leaving the BuSpar to control the anxiety without the same dependency risks.

Another effective tranquilizer is known as Klonopin (generic name is clonazepam). It has strong antiseizure properties and is preferred for long-duration administration because it is easier to remove.

How long does a tranquilizer work? Table 5 provides details of the duration of effectiveness of the minor tranquilizers. Remember, short-acting tranquilizers provide rapid relief but also wear off more quickly. Long-acting agents do not have rapid onset but provide a longer period of relief.

(3) *Adrenaline blockers.* Adrenaline blockers do not act directly on anxiety, but more on the hormones that activate the body's "fight-or-flight" reaction. (Adrenaline is one of the major hormones in this group.) The adrenaline blocking thus helps to calm the system and reduces the rush of adrenaline often seen in panic. It is also helpful to control speaker's anxiety or stage fright and to reduce general tension. However, ordinary anxiety, or that associated with the phobias, is not helped by an adrenaline blocker.

Table 5
DURATION OF EFFECTIVENESS OF TRANQUILIZERS

Tranquilizer	Daily Dosage
Short Acting	
alprazolam (Xanax)	0.75–4 mg
lorazepam (Ativan)	2–6 mg
oxazepam (Serax)	30–180 mg
Intermediate-Acting	
chlordiazepoxide (Librium)	15–100 mg
diazepam (Valium)	4–40 mg
temazepam (Restoril)[2]	15–30 mg
Long-Acting	
clorazepate (Tranxene)	15–60 mg
flurazepam (Dalmane)[2]	15–30 mg
halazepam (Paxipam)	20–160 mg
prazepam (Centrax)	15–30 mg

As I have already indicated, Xanax is often used in conjunction with an adrenaline blocker such as Inderal (propranolol). This medication blocks certain receptors in the nervous system that primarily control the cardiovascular system, so they are very effective in anxiety disturbances that cause rapid heartbeat and other cardiac reactions. Used at higher doses than usually used for anxiety, Inderal lowers blood pressure. It should be avoided by patients with asthma or diabetes.

Dosages of adrenaline blockers range from 40 to over 120 milligrams per day, divided into three or four doses. Dizziness or light-headedness, slow pulse, and lethargy may be experienced in some cases.

(4) *Antihistamines.* Because of their sedating effects, antihistamines such as hydroxyzine (Atarax and Vistaril) are sometimes used to calm anxiety. Hydroxyzine is more sedating than a minor tranquilizer and in some patients it can cause agitation, so it is not used often. Its value lies in its *rapid onset of sedation,* so it is effective in very severe anxiety reactions where an immediate effect is desired. It also does not cause as much physical dependence or abuse, so it is a useful alternative for patients who are prone to drug dependence.

[2] Note: Dalmane and Restoril are classified as hypnotics and are very likely to induce sleep.

Usual doses range from 200 to 400 milligrams per day in up to four divided doses. Hydroxyzine can be administered intramuscularly as well as orally.

Persons with seizure disorders should *not* take an antihistamine, because antihistamines tend to *lower* the seizure threshold, while other antianxiety medications usually *raise* the seizure threshold.

TREATMENT FAILURE

There are many reasons why the treatment of anxiety with medication may fail. These include:

- Overlooking some other physical cause of the anxiety,
- Taking the wrong medication,
- Failure to take sufficient medication,
- Frequently skipping doses of medication,
- Use of alcohol or other substances that interfere with the effects of the medication,
- Using a generic form of the medication that is not as effective as the original,
- Inadequate support therapy, especially psychotherapy.

This last point is quite important. Not all forms of anxiety respond to medication. And even when medication does help, failure to make the necessary life changes to remove the cause of the anxiety will only perpetuate the problem. In all cases, therefore, supportive counseling or psychotherapy is essential to effective treatment.

Certain phobias and obsessive-compulsive disorders are resistant to traditional medication. For these problems, psychotherapy is the preferred treatment. This usually involves some form of desensitization, or real-life systematic exposure to feared objects; it may also include in-depth exploration of early-life traumatic experiences. Cognitive strategies to address "automatic" and recurring thoughts can help obsessive thinking.

How long should medication be taken? This depends largely on the severity of the anxiety. It is not unusual for medication to continue for at least a year. Thereafter, the medication can be tapered off slowly. If a relapse occurs, the medication is reinstated.

The ultimate goal of all treatment is, of course, a medication-free (and less anxious) life. With cooperation between patient and therapist, this should always be possible. Table 6 sets out the steps to be followed in most effective treatments of anxiety.

Table 6
STEPS TO BE FOLLOWED IN THE TREATMENT OF ANXIETY

(1) Evaluate the specific nature of the anxiety.

- Rule out physical disease.
- Rule out other psychiatric disease.
- Review other medications now being taken that could interfere with treatment.

(2) Explore psychological causes for the anxiety.

- What life issues are causing anxiety?
- Can the patient cope without medication?
- Consider psychotherapy as first course of treatment.
- If panic attacks are severe, don't hesitate to use medication.

(3) If medication is indicated:

- Select physician or psychiatrist for treatment.
- Review pros and cons of various options.

(4) Follow through on treatment prescribed for at least one month.

- If treatment doesn't work, ask for a review.
- Consider combining tranquilizer with either an antidepressant or an adrenaline blocker.
- If you are not satisfied with your physician's expertise, seek a second opinion or change physicians.

(5) If you take a tranquilizer, ask the physician to clearly describe how and when you should stop the medication.

- Never stop tranquilizers suddenly.
- Review the method for stopping tranquilizers described in this chapter and consult your physician for advice.

(6) Every two months, ask your psychotherapist and physician to review your treatment and evaluate your progress.

XANAX—USES AND ABUSES

Given the widespread use of Xanax and its effectiveness in treating a wide variety of anxiety disorders, I want to provide a more complete description of its use and abuse, along with some clear guidelines on how to withdraw from Xanax without triggering severe anxiety. The higher the dosage of Xanax, the more critical it is that the procedures I will outline be followed. (Any such procedure, of course, should be checked with the prescribing physician).

Xanax has properties similar to benzodiazapines such as Valium, although it is chemically a little different. It is specifically helpful in panic anxiety, but also helps other anxieties and depression. It is short-acting, with a half-life of between eight and twelve hours, and therefore must be taken in three or four doses per day so as to "spread out" its effect.

Xanax is also a "controlled substance" in that it is a *hypnotic,* although it is in the lowest category of controlled hypnotics. This means that it produces sedation, and prescriptions must, therefore, be rewritten after six months or five refills.

Now, the most important point of all to bear in mind is that Xanax, when taken on a regular basis, *will* produce physiological dependence when the body reduces its production of natural tranquilizers. *How long* it has been taken is probably more important in setting up a withdrawal problem than *how much* has been taken.

How long does it take to set up dependence? If the dosage is between 2 milligrams and 4 milligrams per day, it could be four to six months before noticeable withdrawal symptoms occur—although this can occur more quickly if the patient has been dependent on a previous tranquilizer. It is clinically apparent that, once dependency is established, the patient has great difficulty tapering it off by him or herself.

Since Xanax is short-acting, withdrawal symptoms can occur very suddenly after the medication is discontinued. The first symptom to appear is a sense of anxiety, fear, and a "trembly" feeling. Often a mild frontal headache occurs. This rapidly progresses to feelings of panic-like anxiety, rapid heartbeat, and an altered sense of reality—and all the senses becoming "amplified." Sounds seem louder and lights brighter. Dizziness then follows, with hot or cold sensations.

More severe withdrawal signs include extreme variations in mood, with sudden outbursts of crying and panic-like anxiety; fears of heart attack or stroke; a feeling of deep grief or bereavement; and, as it progresses, illusions, or hallucinations. Patterns and geometric shapes appear, with delusions of bodily dysfunction. Disorientation can then follow with, in some cases, a risk of seizure.

Please understand that I am not describing these symptoms of withdrawal to frighten anyone from taking Xanax; I often recommend it to my patients. But it is important to be able to identify the withdrawal problems so that a careful withdrawal procedure can be implemented.

WITHDRAWAL FROM XANAX

The seriousness of the symptoms that can attend sudden withdrawal from Xanax highlights the need for competent supervision when using it and also when discontinuing use. *Never lower your medication without medical supervision.* While only prolonged use at high dosages is likely to cause the major withdrawal symptoms, many users have to cope with the lesser symptoms. With proper help, however, even these can be easily avoided.

Severe withdrawal symptoms must be treated with two other agents: *Tegretol,* which can reduce the risk of seizure and help control pain, and *Klonopin,* another tranquilizer that helps to bridge the gap between Xanax and the brain's natural tranquilizers. The process is a fairly lengthy one that must be closely monitored by a physician. Once the withdrawal is complete, BuSpar (with or without an antidepressant) can often be helpful in maintaining improvement and controlling anxiety following treatment with Xanax.

For those who have been on a low dosage of Xanax (say, below 3 milligrams per day) or taken it for a short period of time, there is a very effective and almost foolproof way of withdrawing. (This, or any other method, should of course be approved by the patient's physician.)

The principle is this: Reduce the dosage of Xanax so slowly and imperceptibly that your body adjusts to the change very gradually, almost imperceptibly. This means reducing the dosage in increments far smaller than a tablet at a time.

Let's take, for example, someone who is taking 2 milligrams per day in four tablets of 0.5 milligram. Dropping one of these tablets is equivalent to 25 percent of the total dose, and for Xanax this is just too much of a drop at any one time—such a reduction will cause many to feel the withdrawal through increased tension, anxiety, and general discomfort.

To reduce the reaction, the secret is to reduce the medication by much less than 25 percent or one tablet. Make sure, first of all, that your prescription is for the smallest tablet available—0.25 milligrams. (For example, if you have been taking one .5 milligram tablet, substitute two 0.25 milligrams tablets.) Then, using a clean razor blade, shave off just a little of the tablet, so little that your system will hardly tell the difference. Keep up this slightly reduced dosage for between four days and one week. Then shave a little more off the tablets, and keep this up for four days. Continue to *gradually* reduce the size of the tablet until you are at one-half, then one-fourth, and so forth. When you have shaved away the entire tablet, start on the next one until you are down to almost nothing. The moment you notice an increase in anxiety or withdrawal discomfort, hold the dosage constant until the discomfort disappears, then continue to shave away a little more.

I know the entire procedure I have described sounds tedious, and it *is* time-consuming, but it also reduces the risk of withdrawal problems to almost nothing.

During and after the treatment of Xanax withdrawal, patients need a significant degree of emotional support and constant reassurance. I strongly recommend ongoing counseling or psychotherapy to facilitate this. It is also important that the patient refrain from *all* other stimulants, including coffee and over-the-counter stimulants. Caffeine is a benzodiazepine antagonist and prevents tranquilizers from doing their work. Alcohol should also be avoided.

The key to withdrawing from Xanax without the discomfort of withdrawal is *patience*. In the process, your brain's own chemical factory will be trained to do what it does best: keep you tranquil and at peace. Shalom!

PREVENTING ANXIETY IN CHILDHOOD — 14

In chapter 7 I discussed how anxiety originates in and affects children. I also looked at the variety of anxiety disorders that children can experience, as well as how anxiety manifests itself in the child. In this chapter I will address myself more specifically to how we can prevent anxiety from getting out of control. I will also provide help in dealing with such common problems as bed-wetting, school phobias, fear of the dark, and nail-biting.

I can think of no sadder sight than that of a young child overcome with anxiety. Take separation, for example. Young children become extremely anxious when separated from a parent.

The other morning I agreed to watch my eighteen-month-old granddaughter, Nicole, while my daughter went to a class at the seminary where I teach. My intention was to distract her while Mommy slipped out the front door unnoticed. I set up the breakfast table, made a great show of the fact that she and I would be eating our cereal together, and settled down to eat my cereal with great animation so that she would be amused.

The distraction lasted all of three seconds! Suddenly Nicole turned her head and saw no Mommy around, then terror filled her eyes. She began to scream, jumped off her seat, and ran to the spare bedroom where they had spent the night—but Mommy had gone!

I used all my skill as a psychologist and grandfather to try to calm Nicole down, but to no avail. This was an unscheduled separation, not the routine ones she was accustomed to, and her young mind understood the difference. At that point, my wife rescued me (Nicole loves to hug her grandmother—it distracts her from separation), and peace was quickly restored. But the look in Nicole's eyes when she realized she had been separated from her mother is a look I won't easily forget.

Fortunately, short separations like these, if handled carefully, rarely leave any psychological scars. This is *not* true of all separations, however. Some children are particularly prone to terror, even when separated from a parent for brief periods. Other children, with previously well-functioning behavior and no signs of unusual separation anxiety, can suddenly be overcome by panic at the thought of separation.

Because children lack adaptation skills, they are at greater risk for becoming anxious. The more severe the anxiety and the earlier in life it is invoked, the greater is the risk that the anxiety will become a permanent part of the child's life. However, there is much that adults can do to *prevent* the development of anxiety problems in children. We cannot do much to alter the genes we give our kids, but we can create safe environments and avoid passing on to them our own anxious temperaments.

THE MISUSE OF FEAR AS A CAUSE OF CHILDHOOD ANXIETY

I believe that a major cause of anxiety problems in children is the misuse of the fear-response mechanism by insensitive parents. Because children have a heightened capacity to experience fear, parents quickly learn to use it as a way of controlling their children. The fear-response mechanism of the child is supersensitive. Overuse— one could even say "abuse"—of this fear-response mechanism can lead to significant handicaps later in life. Many homeless men, for instance, blame their lack of interest in life and their wasted existence on the extreme fear and distrust that their fathers instilled in them at an early age.

Parents who rely on excessive threats to get their children to obey them tend to create a fear response that goes way beyond the normal. This kind of parenting inculcates a high level of anxiety in children, with excessive concern about pleasing other people, as well as diminished capacity to rely upon their own resources for affirmation and self-esteem. Since many Christian parents are likely to be stricter than parents who are less concerned with morals or values, they may be more vulnerable to misusing fear and provoking abnormal anxiety.

Let me suggest some important points to be remembered in the parenting of young children:

(1) *Never use fear to teach your child right behavior,* unless *the behavior is life-threatening.* Don't threaten or ridicule a child. Appeal to the child's developing sense of rightness and wrongness of things to guide behavior.

(2) *If a threat is to be used, use the threat of a consequence that adequately matches the undesired behavior.* For example, it would be quite appropriate for a child to fear losing TV privileges for having sassed a parent. But if that child is threatened that God will also punish him, the resulting fear will be excessive in relationship to the offense. The punishment should *always* fit the crime.

(3) *Pay close attention to whether your child is beginning to worry about the fear of punishment or about doing wrong.* If there is evidence of this, you are creating too much fear in your discipline (through threats or physical punishment). Children need to feel some anxiety about whether they are doing right or wrong, but this anxiety should never turn into excessive worry.

(4) *As a parent, carefully and prayerfully review the list of acceptable and unacceptable behaviors that you wish to see evidenced in your child.* Often we project our own weaknesses and demands onto our children, making our problems their problems. For example, a father may have had a problem with excessive masturbation as a child and therefore become especially vigilant in this area with his own children, for fear they will have the same problem. This is unfair! Keep your problems to yourself; don't create fear by projecting them on your children.

(5) *Having carefully and prayerfully reviewed the list of acceptable and unacceptable behaviors for your child, ask yourself how many of these are absolutely essential.* Many of the Christian parents I have met tend to make excessive demands on their children and condemn insignificant behaviors in ways that almost guarantee a rebellion during the teenage years.

Children have a keen sense of justice; they *know* what is fair and what is not. True, they will push you to the limit and squeal about being disciplined at the time, but they know when the discipline is reasonable. When it is unfair—when the punishment is out of proportion to the crime—deep resentment and anxiety can build.

I think it's a good idea to discuss discipline with your children and get their feedback. (Do this at a time when no immediate discipline is required.) Then try to weigh what they have said against your own opinion before you act.

IMPERFECT PARENTS

Before we proceed much further, however, let me remind you that it doesn't take a perfect parent to make a happy child—if it did, there would be no happy children! Failure, to some degree, is inevitable in parenting—it is a "given." My task is to help you *minimize* these failures, not eliminate them.

In fact, I have a theory that there are *two types of parents* who produce neurotic children: bad parents and perfect parents. By "perfect" parents, in this context, I really mean parents who *try too hard* to do everything right.

Both these extremes of parenting produce distortions in children. Most of us are pretty clear how and why bad parents do it, but have you ever thought about how dangerous "perfect" parenting can be? Let me suggest a few ways:

- They never make mistakes, so they never model humility and repentance.
- They never make wrong decisions, so they don't teach children how to be flexible and change what they are doing if it doesn't work.
- They never lose their temper, so they create tremendous guilt in their children when they (the children) feel angry.
- They never make mistakes, so their children have impossible standards to live up to.
- They always know what is right, so children don't get to discuss or debate the rights and wrongs of things. There is never any dialogue in the home.
- They always correct children for what they have done wrong, so children never enjoy that marvelous feeling that they've gotten away with something!
- They always remember past mistakes and hold them up for their children to see so the children will be encouraged to be perfect themselves.

If I were a child, I would pray and ask God to protect me from such "perfect" parents! I would want parents who can teach me love by showing me how hard it is to give love and how God can give us power to love those we don't like. I would want parents who can teach me how to forgive because they struggle with forgiveness daily themselves, who willingly admit their own mistakes and quickly seek to correct them. I would want parents who can teach me patience because they run out of patience themselves and know how to replenish their own resources when they run dry.

In short, I would rather be raised by parents who know they are imperfect and who can teach me how to be a better human being through the example of their own struggles than by parents who think they are always right, who believe they can never make mistakes and thus never admit their errors, and who never have to ask forgiveness. They are not "perfect" at all—they just think they are.

So if you feel inadequate as a parent—take heart and join the crowd. An open, honest environment, free of an exaggerated expectation for absolute perfection, is the best environment in which a child can grow.

OTHER CAUSAL FACTORS
IN CHILDHOOD ANXIETY

There are a number of other important causal factors in childhood anxiety in addition to the excessive use of fear by parents in training or punishing children and the failure to teach the importance of forgiveness:

(1) *A child can have unusual physiological and psychological sensitivity.* Some children are "easy" to condition to fear situations because they respond with exaggerated biological or psychological reactions. This seems to be a function of the child's basic chemical makeup or personality. Such a child needs constant reassurance and a safe, fear-free environment to avoid becoming overly anxious.

(2) *Extraordinary life circumstances for a child, such as frequent or serious illness, accidents, or losses that involve pain and discomfort, can cause anxiety.* Children who are hospitalized for severe illness over a long period of time or children who have been abducted by an estranged parent would fall into this category. Traumatic life events undermine security and have an intense negative effect on the child's adjustment process.

(3) *The experience of divorce is a special circumstance that creates much anxiety.* Because of the frequency and growing ease with which parents seek divorce these days, this subject warrants a more detailed discussion.

Divorce is a life event that many people no longer consider to be a serious problem for children; the popular wisdom is, "Kids are flexible; they'll adjust." But as I tried to show in my book *Children and Divorce,* divorce is *always* a problem for children—it has many aspects that can generate anxiety.

From a child's perspective, divorce is worse than the death of a parent; it usually involves disruption of normal routines, exposure to ongoing conflict, and continual threats to security. Boys are usually affected more deeply than girls, and the negative impact is greatest when the divorce occurs around puberty. Some of the emotional consequences of divorce include:

- Feelings of being abandoned by the departing parent;
- Loss of a stable environment, with the imposition of demands to make new adjustments;
- Embarrassment and a sense of stigma, even when friends are understanding and accepting;
- The creation or aggravation of separation anxiety;

- Insecurity regarding the future and fear of the unknown;
- Feelings of guilt (especially in younger children) and a sense that the divorce was the child's fault.

All these in themselves can be significant generators of anxiety. And the anxiety is worsened when parents, who are often preoccupied with their own conflicts during and after a divorce, either become indifferent to or detached from the child and do not provide adequate guidance for the child's adjustments.

With this in mind, divorcing parents should endeavor to provide as much stability as possible for their children. There are two basic rules:

- *Change as little of the child's world as possible.* As much as possible, keep children in the same school and the same neighborhood and encourage them to keep in touch with the same friends.
- *Change things as slowly as possible.* I believe we all adjust better to slow change than to rapid change. Adjustment takes time, and the more time allowed between adjustments that must be made, the better.

Grandparents and other family members can be very important in providing a stable environment and continuity of security when divorce occurs. Children must feel that *they belong* somewhere, and the extended family is an important resource for this.

Children should never be confronted with more change than their capacity for anxiety can tolerate; they need to master each step of change one at a time. "Timing" and rate of change are critical variables that *can* be controlled by sensitive parents, even if their own relationship is deteriorating. Set aside your personal conflicts and give priority to the well-being of your children.

PREVENTING ANXIETY
PROBLEMS IN CHILDREN

When it comes to anxiety, prevention is clearly better than cure! Once an anxiety problem has become established in a child, it is likely to have lifelong consequences.

In some cases, as the child develops wider interactions in school and increased peer-group contacts, there may be a beneficial reduction of anxiety. Teachers may be good models and a corrective influence, especially if they are able to recognize and respond positively to overly shy, anxious, and withdrawn children. Constructive interpersonal relationships and positive, successful experiences in mastering the skills of growing up can build the child's confidence and restore security.

What are some of the ways parent can prevent the development of severe anxiety in children? Here are some suggestions:

(1) *Provide a safe, secure home.* Anxiety flourishes when children don't feel safe. When parents in therapy are confronted with the realization that they are not providing safety, they invariably feel shocked. "What do you mean, there's no safety? I'll have you know that nothing can happen to my child in my home . . . ." Their shock is tied to the traditional way they think about safety—they think only in physical terms. Now, it's true that some parents don't even provide this, but in most households the problem is more with a lack of "psychological safety."

Cindy, for example, is the youngest of three children. When she turned thirteen, she had to have corrective work done on her teeth. You know the sort of stuff—braces and some minor surgery. Her two older brothers were the pets of their father, who doted on them because they were good at sports and could do fun things with him. Cindy often felt left out. Her mother was kind, but did not have the same chummy relationship with Cindy that the father had with his sons.

Ever since Cindy can remember, her two older brothers had teased her, but not in typical older-brother fashion. These boys were cruel; they competed with each other to come up with the biggest putdown or criticism. And when they did this, the father did nothing to intervene; in fact, he laughed louder than they did at their malicious antics. The mother was afraid to intervene, fearing that she would offend the father if she tried to stop the boys. It was almost as if the father saw the boys' behavior as a part of their masculinity; they had to show their dominance over the sister to prove their manhood.

To Cindy, home was far from a safe place; danger lurked in it as surely as if wild animals roamed the corridors. It wasn't until she became extremely anxious that her mother got up the courage to seek help.

Now, no family is perfect, and living in close quarters with other people inevitably causes hurts. Some hurts, in fact, are necessary for growth and maturity. But how unsafe can a home become before it starts to be harmful? How much criticism should be tolerated or mistrust endured before it goes beyond the bounds of reasonableness and becomes a source of damage?

This, of course, is a matter every family must decide for itself. Many families might well inventory their behavior patterns to see whether they are violating the rule that a child is entitled to both physical and psychological safety. The excessive use of derogatory labels is particularly effective in making a home unsafe. "You're lazy," "You're a bad boy," or "God must hate you for doing that" can turn a home into a minefield of dangerous experiences.

(2) *Provide an understanding, empathic home.* Children are highly susceptible to being traumatized. They are helpless, ignorant, inexperienced, and immature. It is natural that they will not anticipate the outcome of their actions, nor will they understand why things turn out the way they do.

Given the frequency with which traumatic events can affect a child, it is a miracle that they become normal adults at all. The reason so many do is simple: Psychological bruises can heal, and children do bounce back, because they are remarkably resilient.

But what facilitates healing? What makes the difference between one child, who experiences rejection from a friend but turns it into a learning and growth experience, and another child, who becomes devastated and demoralized? Some of the difference lies in the child's personality, but a lot of it involves whether the child lives in an understanding and empathic environment.

Understanding and empathy, especially from sensitive and caring parents, turn traumas into growth trampolines. Cold indifference or rejection turn traumas into anxiety and despondency.

How often have you heard parents say to a tearful child: "Go to your room until you get over your upset. Don't come out until you're pleasant." Many parents don't like their children to show strong negative emotions around them; the child's bad feelings upset them also. So children learn that bad feelings are taboo and should be avoided. This only makes matters worse.

When children are upset, what they really need is someone who can be understanding and empathic. They want to be heard with *real* understanding, just as we want when we are upset. Children who receive understanding instead of rejection and ridicule when they are hurting can learn to handle *any* circumstance. The understanding provided by a caring and loving parent restores security, helps the child to confront imagined threats, and sorts out "false" alarms from "real" alarms. With such a supportive environment, a child becomes almost immune to anxiety.

What does it mean to treat children with empathy? It means understanding things from their point of view, entering into their world, listening to both their *words* and the *feelings* behind the words. Empathy does *not* mean trying to change a child's feelings but simply *understanding* them.

Here is the wonder of it all: Being understood helps a child develop security from *within;* it helps a child create a safer world for him or herself.

Allow me to illustrate empathic understanding. Let's suppose that you live in Los Angeles (as I do) and that your five-year-old son, George, experienced his first earthquake when the East Whittier Fault did its thing in 1987. George was getting ready to go to school when the rumbling and shaking occurred. He became upset by the experience and wouldn't allow himself to be separated from his mother afterward. (I live close to the center of the earthquake and experienced firsthand the effect it had on both young and old. George's subsequent feelings are by no means extraordinary or extreme.)

Let's say that the first day after the quake you are quite impatient with your son. George wants to talk about how frightening it was to have the house shake and furniture fall, but you cut him off, fearing that encouraging him to talk about the experience might make his fears worse. Or perhaps you resist talking about it because of your own unconscious fears. For whatever reason—you don't want to hear about it.

The second day you become even more impatient with George. "You shouldn't go on like this," you tell him in a loud voice. "Earthquakes are no big deal. Once the shaking is over, there's nothing else that can happen. You shouldn't be afraid. You're a big boy, and others will think you're just a sissy if you go on like this!" George slinks away, ashamed, confused, and still frightened.

How many mistakes (or should I say unempathic responses) have you made? Let's count them:

- *First,* you told George not to "go on like this," implying that no one has the right to feel afraid or be upset.
- *Second,* you told him that earthquakes "are no big deal." You're trying to reduce his fear, but you are not being honest. Earthquakes *are* dangerous, and it would be better to tell him the truth.
- *Third,* you tried to use logic: "Once the shaking is over . . . ." When a person is afraid, logic only makes him or her feel guiltier.
- *Fourth,* you implied that boys "shouldn't be afraid." When boys hear this message they become confused. Boys *do* get afraid. When the expectation is that they *shouldn't* be afraid, they become more anxious because they begin to suspect there's something wrong with them.

How would empathy respond to such a situation? Here are some suggestions:

- *Always admit the truth.* Honesty *is* the best policy. To admit to George that earthquakes also frighten you would reassure him that his fear is quite normal. This may not reduce the fear, but it certainly will reduce the anxiety.
- *Listen with your heart, not with your head.* Listen to the feelings behind the words and *show* that you understand these feelings. Explore the imagined fears so that if there is any exaggeration you can draw attention to this.
- *Hold back on logic for now.* Logic is only helpful when the danger is past and can be looked at objectively.
- *Don't be judgmental.* Don't impose your own fears or condemn the child for his or her fear. Accept the feelings as legitimate, and give the child permission to be weak and to own up to the weakness.

(3) *Provide clear instruction on taboo subjects.* Many childhood anxiety problems revolve around "taboo" topics such as sex, child-bearing, and death. Anxiety thrives on ignorance. And ignorance of sexual matters, especially, can create very significant anxiety reactions in childhood. Girls seem to suffer more than boys in this area, perhaps because they are more likely to be given distorted messages by their parents.

Curiosity about oneself as a sexual being begins very early in life. Unfortunately, we tend to view sex not just as a functional capacity, but also as a major moral issue. As a consequence, the discovery of one's sexuality almost always involves some anxiety. The experience of sexuality seems always to be tainted with guilt in our culture. Because I grew up in Africa, I know this is not true in all cultures.

Premature exposure to sexual stimuli and any activity that borders on molestation will damage the child's sensitive sexual development. But avoidance of the topic of sex on the part of parents who are themselves somewhat neurotic in their own sexuality can in many cases produce as much anxiety as premature exposure.

The discovery of the differences in anatomy and function between the sexes should not be the cause of anxiety, and it will not be if parents engage in sensible and appropriate instruction in these matters. Of course, the child's exposure to information about sexual matters should not outstrip the child's capacity for understanding.

Answer your child's curiosity about sex frankly and with an amount of detail that is appropriate to the child's age. If you are anxious about this subject, try not to communicate your anxiety to your children; certainly avoid painting sex as something dirty and evil. You may think you are helping to protect your child from promiscuous sexual interests, but you may in fact be doing irreversible harm to the child's attitude toward sex.

(4) *Provide a forgiving home.* Next to excessive or inappropriate punishment, guilt must be the other major creator of severe anxiety reactions in children. To prevent anxiety, parents must guard against creating excessive guilt feelings in their children.

When working with older parents in therapy, I am often alarmed to hear how seldom their grown-up children come to visit. The fact that their children feel uncomfortable around them is a source of much sadness for these patients. When I explore the reasons for this avoidance more closely, however, I invariably discover that excessive guilt feelings are involved. The adult children don't want to be around their parents because the parents make them feel guilty. When you love someone, you normally want to be near them. But you do not want to be near someone who makes you feel guilty or who frequently criticizes you. It creates too much anxiety.

It is here that we have a most important *antidote for childhood anxiety.* Children invariably must be taught right from wrong. They have to develop healthy consciences that will guide them into maturity and a well-balanced life. Discipline, therefore, is essential for children. It is imperative, however, that *all* discipline have an element of forgiveness built into it. Whenever an act of discipline is invoked, there must be a clear message that *the misbehavior has been forgiven.*

Reflect for a moment on how important forgiveness can be to a child. Let us suppose I am a boy of seven. I have, in a moment of impulsive naughtiness, raided my piggy bank and taken out a couple of dollars to buy a magazine I wanted. Now, I have been told not to take money out of the bank without permission. My mother has said, "It's important that you learn how to save, so put odd cents and dimes in the bank and *leave them there.*"

I can't explain exactly why I took the money out. I remember reasoning, "It's mine, after all—I put it there." I didn't exactly forget what Mom said; I just sort of lost sight of it.

So now I've been discovered. As a penalty, Mom has taken all the money away, leaving me an empty plastic pig with a slot in its back and no rattle. Mom says nothing more; as far as she is concerned, she has disciplined me and her job is over. But I still feel guilty—only I don't know what the feeling is and can't explain it. I'm a little scared—I don't know what of. Perhaps she'll come back and spank me, too—who knows?

If this happens a lot, I'm likely to become an anxious kid, not knowing what to expect. I start to bite my nails. My stomach hurts a lot.

I feel like I just want to be by myself. Soon I'm beginning to imagine all sorts of terrible things happening to me, and I wonder if life is all that great!

What should Mom have done when she discovered I had raided my piggy bank? Sure, she must do what she said she would do and take away the other money I had saved. I can start again—no big deal, it's all her money anyway!

But to a young child feeling guilty for his misbehavior, *discipline isn't enough!* What I crave above all else is *freedom from my guilt feelings.* My state of guilt is resolved (I've paid the penalty for my sin by having my other savings confiscated), but now I need my feeling of guilt to go away. All it would take is for mother to give me a soft touch and assure me that all is forgiven. After all, what's the point of discipline if it doesn't restore our fellowship and love? I certainly think I would be more obedient if treated this way, than when I am left with all this guilt.

Parents frequently forget that forgiveness must be deliberately and overtly given. It's not enough to say, "Oh, he knows I've forgiven him because I don't bear grudges." Children need to hear and feel the forgiveness. Discipline—and especially punishment—must always be followed by an overt act of forgiveness.

How can we show this forgiveness? Here are two ways. First, we can *say it.* And how we say it is important. It's better to say "You are forgiven"—including God and whoever else is involved in the forgiveness—rather than "I have forgiven you."

Speaking forgiveness is as hard for some parents as speaking love. Just last week, a pastor I was seeing in therapy told me that not once in all his forty-five years had his father (also a pastor) told him he loved him. Not once! If you were to ask the father, "Do you love your son?" he would probably be insulted. But speaking love is something the father can't seem to manage. Speaking forgiveness can be even harder—but it's worth the price in terms of preventing anxiety problems in children. Besides, in time and with practice it gets easier.

The other way we can show forgiveness is to *demonstrate it.* Some people may find it easier to speak forgiveness than to demonstrate it; they can say words that are contrary to their feelings. But no kid I know is going to be conned into believing only words.

Demonstrating forgiveness demands changing your attitude, giving up your need for revenge, and putting every ounce of will behind your words. *Remind yourself that the debt has been paid, all is restored.* Now try to show through every word and deed that follows that your forgiveness is real.

Every act of forgiveness you demonstrate after you have disciplined your child is a precious gift to him or her. With these gifts, your child can build happiness and freedom from debilitating anxiety. I guarantee it!

SPECIFIC CHILDHOOD ANXIETY PROBLEMS

Since childhood anxiety always translates into specific problems, let us briefly examine some of the ways in which children manifest their anxieties.

Bed-Wetting

This has to be the most embarrassing consequence of all. If it occurs in older children, it will almost certainly undermine self-esteem.

Bed-wetting is a complex but common childhood problem. Experts believe its cause may be physical, chemical, or emotional. Physical and chemical causes are easy to understand. Muscles that control urination may be weak; the nervous system that controls the muscles may be sluggish; or the bladder may be too small to hold a night's load of urine. Infection, diabetes, low blood sugar, or kidney stones can also be factors, as can certain medications.

But what about the emotional causes? If physical causes are ruled out, then stress, fears, and especially anxiety must be considered. Just how anxiety triggers bed-wetting is not clear. Perhaps the anxiety distracts attention from the bladder, so that the child doesn't recognize when it is full. At other times it disturbs sleep, causing nightmares and triggering a "letting go."

In younger children, bed-wetting can be a deliberate attempt to control or get attention. I recall several cases in which a five-year-old child who had been potty-trained started to wet the bed following the birth of a younger brother or sister. In order to get to sleep with Mom and Dad, the youngster would deliberately urinate in his bed so that he had an excuse to transfer to the parental bed. Unfortunately, the parents were too soft to resist—and the habit, once established, took many years to break.

How should one deal with bed-wetting? If the child is younger than five, probably nothing, unless the child has reverted from being dry previously. Here are some general rules for children older than five who wet the bed:

(1) *Obtain a thorough physical examination* and take corrective medical steps where appropriate.

(2) *Avoid making your child feel guilty or ashamed.* The less other children in the family know, the better. Don't even discuss the problem with your spouse in front of the child.

(3) *Provide the beds of all children in the family (not just the bed-wetter) with the same kind of undersheet needed to avoid soaking the mattresses.* This helps "play down" the problem as just belonging to the one child.

(4) *Keep the child from drinking all liquids within two hours of bedtime.* This will help ensure that the child empties the bladder before going to bed.

(5) *Build the child's sense of control with reassurance and encourage the child to talk about his or her fears before going to bed.* Find out what is bothering the child and help him or her to express these feelings openly and without condemnation or ridicule.

(6) *If any part of the fear can be changed, change it.* For instance, if the child finds it embarrassing to be driven to school along a certain route, find another route. If particular items of clothing cause embarrassment because the child is teased, don't force them to be worn.

(7) *Reduce anxiety wherever possible, especially conflicts in the home, fighting, shouting, or other threats.* Set these aside for the sake of your child's well-being, at least for the time being.

(8) *If what the child fears cannot be changed, encourage the child to talk out his or her feelings.* Obviously, some feared circumstances—such as going to the dentist, facing a friend, or going to class with a particular teacher—cannot be avoided. In such a case, *allow the child to talk about his fear* and then offer assurance that "this too will pass." Remember this important point: Comfort comes from feeling that you have been deeply understood.

(9) *Pray with the child,* mentioning each fear specifically and entrusting them to God's care.

There are various devices on the market designed to help bed-wetters master their problem—for instance, an instrument that can detect moisture and wake the child just as he or she starts to wet the bed. Such devices can be helpful up to a point, but only if the underlying cause is clear and can be dealt with. No amount of "wake-up calls" by a monitoring instrument is going to help a child who is troubled by family conflicts or a problem at school. If the act is clearly a deliberate one, then consider professional help in understanding the real issues.

Fortunately, medication can help in some cases and can provide relief until such time as understanding and alternative relief is obtained. A tricyclic antidepressant such as imipramine, for up to three months (but no longer than six months) can reduce bed-wetting or even eliminate it in some cases. The medication is safe when used under medical supervision and does not produce any dependency.

Nightmares
Bad dreams are mostly the consequence of bad experiences and over-powering fears—once spicy foods and other causes of gastric upset have been eliminated. Children's dreams, like adult dreams, are tools for sorting out experiences, and negative feelings and experiences will naturally emerge through nightmares.

Fears are very common in children. In G. Stanley Hall's landmark study of fear (mentioned in chapter 6), the most detailed descriptions came from children. Their most common fears were of storms, snakes and other animals, darkness, strangers, fire, death, and disease. And these are still the objects that form the content of most childhood nightmares.

School Phobias
Many children find school an especially difficult and threatening experience—they are constricted in their movement by classrooms and schedules, confronted by strangers and bullies, and overwhelmed by teachers who don't understand them; and their access to home and parents is cut off. A reluctance or even a refusal to go to school is therefore quite common. An actual school phobia is rarer and much more serious.

While some have seen a refusal to go to school as being related to separation anxiety, especially forced separation from the mother, many experienced clinicians report that about 80 percent of the cases have an onset related to a change in the child's life—change that precipitates anxiety. Typical precipitating events are moving (changing school or home), a relative's death, divorce, or illness. All these cases involve loss of some sort, so depression is also a problem.

Children with school avoidance problems also become socially withdrawn. They attach themselves to the home or parents and see social contacts as threatening. Furthermore, since these children are highly anxious, they are often intensely self-conscious and easily shamed. Consequently they avoid friends for fear of being embarrassed by probing questions like "Where were you today?" "Why do you always skip school on Mondays?" or "Why do you hang on to your mommy so much?" Children can be extremely cruel because they lack tact and understanding.

Fear of school may also be related to other factors:

- Fear of a particular teacher,
- Fear of a particular child,
- Fear of a grouchy bus driver,
- Mean schoolmates,
- Fear of rejection by a friend,

- Inability to understand a teacher,
- Unrecognized hearing problem or learning disability,
- Loneliness or awareness of unpopularity.

It is important, therefore, to identify the particular cause of a school phobia and not try to treat it as a global problem. This may require some long chats with your child or consultation with a psychologist. When you know the cause you can invoke appropriate action.

Here are some guidelines for helping a child overcome a school phobia.

(1) *Before you do anything, review the child's circumstances.* Is the child under eight years of age? If so, the cause may be fear of leaving home. Is he or she over thirteen? School phobias of older children tend to be more of a rebellious reaction to pressure than a reflection of anxiety. Is there too much competition? Does the child feel like a failure? Psychotherapy may be necessary to help the child come to terms with the issues underlying rebellious school avoidance. Between ages nine and twelve years, school phobias have mixed causes. For some there may be a fear of rejection or other kids' "ganging up." And some may have a lingering separation anxiety that was not resolved when they were younger.

(2) *Explore what changes the child has been through recently.* Can these changes be slowed down or avoided? Explore ways in which the child can be kept in a regular routine. For example, if a divorce is in process, keeping routines as regular as possible will help provide a measure of assurance and security.

(3) *Try to determine if the child is depressed.* A loss of interest in normally exciting activities, avoidance of friends, desire to be alone, increased fearfulness, and a high level of lethargy or fatigue could point to an underlying depression that may need professional attention.

(4) *Since heightened anxiety is the primary cause of school phobias, look for sources of fear.* Remember to see these fears from the child's perspective and don't belittle them. For the child they may loom large as the sun, whereas to you as an adult they may seem minor or even ridiculous.

If the child's fears can be identified, treat them with respect and find ways to address them objectively. You may need to talk with a friend or to a teacher about a particular cause. Do so, however, without blaming anyone for the fear. Often, childhood fears can arise spontaneously and vanish again as mysteriously.

(5) *Don't underestimate the power of prayer to both reassure your child and to change specific fearful situations.* Praying with your child

over some fearful event and seeing God work to remove the fear or to strengthen the child to face it can be most rewarding and will reinforce the child as he or she builds faith.

Fear of the Dark

All children go through phases when they fear the dark. Darkness triggers fantasies of vulnerability and danger, to which children are particularly susceptible. Extreme cases need professional help, but try the following before you head for the therapist's office:

(1) *Provide the child with a nightlight and rearrange the room so that there are no dark corners.* Start with a bright lamp and gradually move to a very low level of light over a period of two or three weeks.

(2) *Survey the room with the child before going to bed to show that all is safe.* Examine inside closets, behind curtains, and so forth.

(3) *Provide a bell or other signaling device so that the child can call you if scared.*

(4) *Play games in the darkened room, showing the child how to use a flashlight and hide until found.* Turn darkness into an opportunity for fun.

(5) *Talk about why the child is scared just before you put her or him to bed.* Reassure the child that we all have had these fears and that they will soon pass away.

(6) *Don't encourage the child to come into your room or sleep with you, except in very rare situations when something has happened to frighten the child.* For instance, after an earthquake, severe thunderstorm, or loud bang, letting the child sleep with you may be appropriate. Most of the time, however, giving in to the child will only reinforce his or her fears and make it increasingly difficult to separate the child later. Children can be very manipulative, and you need to be on guard against this.

(7) *Once again, pray with the child and build his or her faith in God's care.* Remind the child that God watches over us in our goings and in our comings, in our waking and in our sleeping—even in the dark.

Nail-Biting

This is a particularly bothersome childhood anxiety problem and often accompanies other anxiety problems. Nail-biting occurs mainly in times of tension and anxiety, so the first consideration should be to reduce the tension, if possible. For instance, if there is a lot of conflict going on between parents, it is better not to show this conflict in front of the anxious child. Go where you can be alone if you have to fight, and save your child's teeth and nails!

Nail-biting can occur in tension situations outside of the home also, and it is here that relaxation techniques can help. Read again the section on relaxation in chapter 11 and teach your child how to produce a relaxed and calm response. Encourage relaxation practice by doing the exercise together with your child. Because anxiety and relaxation cannot coexist, the symptoms of anxiety subside when one is relaxed.

Sometimes a child's nails are too soft and this makes it easy for them to break and then be chewed on. Nail hardeners are available and can help to set up some resistance to the biting. Also available "over the counter" are awful-tasting substances that can help remind a child when he or she is biting.

There is no doubt in my mind that nail-biting begins as a symptom of intensified anxiety, although it may continue even after times of tension are past. Certain anxious personalities tend to be more prone to it than others, and during times of increased stress the problem may become worse or return after a period of absence.

THE USE OF MEDICATION

In closing this chapter on childhood anxiety problems, let me briefly address the use of medication in dealing with more severe problems.

While there is a tendency to resort to medication too quickly in our culture, there is also a tendency on the part of Christian parents to resist medication even when the problem is severe enough to warrant it. I would plead for a balance here. Don't jump to medications too readily, yet don't hesitate to use them (under a physician's guidance) if you have tried everything else without success.

As mentioned above, the tricyclic antidepressant imipramine (Tofranil) can help in controlling bed-wetting. Many studies have also shown that imipramine is very effective in helping children control the anxiety of separation. And since separation anxiety sometimes underlies school phobia, imipramine is also sometimes effective when children resist going to school. Even when these children do not actually return to school, imipramine seems to decrease their anxiety levels markedly.

Whether this means that all these disorders are a form of depression is not clear, but the medication certainly does help. The fact that adult panic disorder sufferers also get better on imipramine indicates that some biochemical factor may be common to both anxiety and depression.

Tranquilizers such as the benzodiazepines can be helpful for anticipatory anxiety, but these medications should be reserved for older children and adolescents.

How long should medication therapy be continued? Not very long. Children usually respond completely within six to eight weeks if the medication is going to help at all. The medication is continued for at least eight weeks after remission and then is gradually withdrawn.

If the medication doesn't work it should *also* be withdrawn gradually, following the directions of the child's physician. If you don't fully understand what to do, then *ask*. Assertiveness pays off here and avoids a mistake that could cause a further anxiety reaction in your child.

Parents need to be much in prayer as they seek to provide an environment that is free from the conditions that could create anxiety problems. We cannot prevent all childhood fears, nor should we even try. However, we do need wisdom to avoid mistakes that will later terrorize our children, and God has promised us this wisdom. All we have to do is ask for it (James 1:5). How else would we even dare to become parents?

EPILOGUE:
A BALANCED LIFE ——————————

As I come to the final pages of this book, I ask myself: Of all the advice I can give for overcoming anxiety, what is the most important? The answer is simply this: Live a *balanced* life.

In the final analysis, disruptive anxiety is the consequence of unbalanced living. This imbalance can occur in many areas of our lives—our priorities, our values, our commitments, or our ambitions. The anxiety that we experience when we are unbalanced should serve as a corrective force, a warning that we are about to topple over. Unfortunately, we do not always heed this warning.

I used to do some flying. Because I frequently had dreams that the pilot got sick while I was in an airplane and I had to take over, I decided to take flying lessons and learn how to fly myself. (Interestingly, the day I went solo I stopped having the dreams—sort of expensive therapy!)

One of the warning devices that a pilot comes to value very much in the cockpit is called a "stall indicator." Just before an airplane stalls (which, of course, can be disastrous if you are close to the ground), this device sounds a loud buzzer. It is a rather raucous sound, but I don't know of any pilot who resents its message!

Well, there is this healthy side to all anxiety: It serves as our "stall indicator." It tells us when we are too slow, not angled properly, or, in a host of ways, flying through life too dangerously. The person who does not heed its warning and take corrective action is in for a crash!

What are some of the ways we can tell our lives are unbalanced?

- We value the approval of people over what we know God wants us to do.
- The focus of our personhood is directed inward and not outward.
- Our life lacks discipline and we are driven by short-term rather than long-term goals.
- We neglect the spiritual dimensions of life.
- We do not give priority to family needs.
- We are too centered on material things.
- We are too anxious about failure.
- We manipulate others to meet our needs instead of being concerned about theirs.

218

- We no longer take pleasure in simple things and constantly search for excitement in new or novel activities.
- We prefer to pursue a spirituality that is void of fellowship with others.
- We are dominated by selfish pursuits.
- We place our own happiness above the happiness of those nearest and dearest to us.

How then can we become balanced? This is a topic that would need a whole book all to itself, so I will confine myself to just a few remarks.

Some psychologists would suggest that you are "well balanced" when you are adjusted to all your surroundings. There is some truth to this, but one would hardly think that a pig is well-adjusted simply because it is comfortable with a pigsty! Being balanced doesn't mean that you are adjusted to a low level of living or that you are content with life's second best.

I suggest to you that being balanced means achieving a level of maturity in your values, morals, and ambitions where you no longer tackle life as a child, but rather as a full-grown person, and you do it according to the plan that God has laid out for you.

The gospel specializes in maturity, in catching us in our fallen immaturity, and presenting us complete and full-grown, through Christ, to live a life that is full of meaning. All our Christian resources—Scripture, fellowship, and prayer—converge on the production of this maturity. Unless your faith and spiritual walk moves you to maturity, it is second best. This is the message of Colossians 1:28, where Paul writes:

Him we preach and proclaim, warning and admonishing every one and instructing every one in all wisdom, [in comprehensive insight into the ways and purposes of God], that we may present every person mature—full-grown, fully initiated, complete and perfect—in Christ, the Anointed One. (AMP)

Such maturity will produce a life that is balanced in its priorities, its values, and its ambitions. Such balance is the best protection I know for overcoming destructive anxiety.

FOR FURTHER READING

Agras, Stewart. *Panic: Facing Fears, Phobias and Anxiety.* New York: W. H. Freeman & Co., 1985.

Beck, Aaron T. and G. Emery. *Anxiety Disorders and Phobias: A Cognitive Perspective.* New York: Basic Books, 1985.

Benson, Herbert. *Beyond the Relaxation Response.* New York: Times Books, 1984.

Gettelman, Rachel. *Anxiety Disorders in Childhood.* New York: Guildford, 1986.

Gold, Mark S. *The Good News about Panic Anxiety and Phobias.* New York: Villard Books, 1989.

Wilson, Reid R. *Don't Panic: Taking Control of Anxiety Attacks.* New York: Harper & Row, 1986.

Abuse, child, 82, 95–7, 100, 105, 109–10, 205
Adrenaline blockers, 189, 192–3, 195
Agoraphobia, 12, 16, 38, 58, 69, 74, 83–92, 189
Alcohol abuse, 8, 56, 67, 73, 98, 105, 111, 135, 163, 171, 184, 194, 198
Anorexia nervosa, 116–17
Antidepressant medication, xiii, 35, 52, 68, 186–7, 189–90, 192, 195, 197, 212, 216
Antihistamines, 189, 193–4

Bed-wetting, 107, 199, 211–12, 216
Bulimia, 116–17
Burnout in childhood, 98
BuSpar (buspirone), 192, 197

Caffeine, 44, 63–6, 82, 172–3, 174, 184, 198
Childhood anxiety, 94–107, 199–217
Compulsions, 15, 33, 36, 69, 88–9, 92, 97, 108, 112–15, 189–90, 194
Concern vs. worry, 21–6
Conscience, 47–51, 209
Constructive anxiety, 12–14, 46, 53

Defense mechanisms, 108–115, 181
Definition of anxiety, 7
Denial, 23, 36, 109–12, 115, 135, 181–2, 189, 195
Depression, xiii, 15, 33, 43–4, 46, 51–5, 67–8, 84–6, 104, 123, 162, 175, 183, 186–90, 196, 213–14, 216
Destructive anxiety, 5–6, 12–13, 53–4, 121, 135, 168, 219

Divorce, 97, 101, 105, 158, 203–4, 213–14
Dreams, 148, 176–82, 213

Emotional abuse, 109, 205
Endorphins, 15
Excellence anxiety, 41–2, 97
Exercise and panic anxiety, 62–3, 72, 162
Existential anxiety, 5, 10–12, 134–7

Fear anxiety, 10–11
Fear of dark, 80–1, 107, 199, 213, 215
Fear of death (oblivion), 9, 122, 134–7
Fear-of-fear reaction to panic, 69–71, 157, 188
Forms of anxiety, 4, 9–12, 33, 36, 39–44, 46, 51, 134–5, 194
Free-floating anxiety, 12, 42–4
Food as tranquilizer, 115–16

Generalized anxiety, 11–12, 39, 43–4
Guilt, 17–19, 32–3, 46–51, 53–5, 87, 91, 112, 114, 116–17, 128, 167, 202, 204, 207–11

Hyperventilation, 33, 44, 61–2, 70, 158, 160–1, 163
Hypoglycemia, 44, 68–9, 162

Insecurity, 5, 42, 121–6, 204
Insomnia, 33, 172, 184, 191

Loneliness, 129–31, 214

Meaninglessness, 5, 11, 132–4

Nail-biting, 107, 199, 215–16
Natural (brain) tranquilizers, 9,
    14–16, 60–1, 73, 164, 196–7
Neurotic guilt, 46, 48–50, 53–4
Nightmares, 43, 101–3, 211, 213

Obsessions, 33, 54, 69, 74, 92, 104,
    112–13, 117, 176, 190, 194
Obsessive-compulsive disorder, 36,
    88, 112–13, 114, 189, 190, 194

Panic anxiety, xii, xiii, 4, 6, 11–12,
    15, 16, 32–3, 35–6, 38, 51, 56–74,
    84, 97, 98, 101, 116, 133, 151,
    156–69, 170–1, 186, 188–90, 192,
    195–6, 216
Parents, imperfect, 201–2
Perfectionism, 19, 21, 89–91, 104,
    112, 123, 201–2
Phobic anxiety, 11–12, 37, 69, 72,
    74–83, 93, 170, 192, 194
Physical abuse, 97, 100, 105
Physical causes of anxiety, 44–5, 194
Premenstrual syndrome (PMS), 64,
    67–8, 162

Rejection, 9, 25, 43, 109, 116, 122,
    126–9, 141, 206, 213–14
Relaxation, 73, 164–7, 177, 184, 216
Repression (defense mechanism),
    108, 110, 135

School phobias, 107, 199, 213–15
Self-image/self-esteem, 68, 85–91,
    98–9, 104–5, 127–8, 156–7, 200,
    211

Self-talk, 144–7, 152, 161, 168
Separation anxiety, 40, 101–3,
    121–2, 199, 203, 213–14, 216
Sex and dreams, 181–2
Sexual abuse, 82, 95–7, 100, 105,
    110
Sleep, xii, 4, 8, 35, 37, 73, 101, 104,
    127, 147–8, 169, 170–85, 187,
    211–13
Social phobias, 74, 81–3
Stress inoculation, 146
Stranger anxiety, 40–1
Symptoms of anxiety, xi–xiii, 33–4,
    42–5, 56, 61, 63–4, 66, 71, 73,
    85–6, 101, 104, 121, 156, 163,
    168–9, 188–9, 191, 215

Tranquilizers, external (medication),
    xii, 8–9, 15–16, 33, 35, 59–61, 64,
    67–8, 73, 115–16, 138, 161, 186,
    189–93, 195–98, 216
Thought redirecting, 148–51
Thought initiation, 148–50
Thought stopping, 148–50

Valium, 60, 190, 193, 196

Worry anxiety, xi–xii, xiv, 8, 10–12,
    14, 16, 19–31, 33, 38–9, 42, 44,
    91–2, 98, 100–2, 104, 114, 140,
    154, 159, 170, 172, 177, 180, 183,
    200–1
Worry as sin, 20–1, 26–7
Worry habit, 26–31, 91–2, 100–1

Xanax (alprazolam), 60, 68, 190–3,
    195–8